AS I RUN TOWARD AFRICA

Selected List of Books by Molefi Kete Asante

The Break of Dawn [Arthur L. Smith] (1964)

Rhetoric of Black Revolution [Arthur L. Smith] (1969)

Rhetoric of Revolution [Arthur L. Smith] (with Andrea Rich, 1970)

Toward Transracial Communication (1970)

How to Talk with People of Other Races, Ethnic Groups, and Cultures
    (with Deluvina Hernandez and Anne Allen, 1971)

Transracial Communication [Arthur L. Smith] (1973)

Contemporary Public Communication (with J. Frye, 1976)

Intercultural Communication: Theory into Practice (with Eileen Newmark, 1976)

Contemporary Public Communication: Applications (with Jerry K. Frye, 1977)

Epic in Search of African Kings (1978)

Handbook of Intercultural Communication
    (ed. with E. Newmark and C. Blake, 1979)

Mass Communications: Principle and Practices (with Mary B. Cassata, 1979)

Afrocentricity: The Theory of Social Change (1980)

Contemporary Black Thought (ed. with A. Sarr Vandi, 1980)

Afrocentric Idea, First Ed. (1987)

Afrocentricity (1988)

Umfundalai: Afrocentric Rites of Passage (1989)

Kemet, Afrocentricity, and Knowledge (1990)

Book of African Names (1991)

Historical and Cultural Atlas of African Americans (with Mark T. Mattson, 1991)

Thunder and Silence: The Mass Media in Africa (with Dhyana Ziegler, 1992)

Classical Africa (1993)

Malcolm X as Cultural Hero: And Other Afrocentric Essays (1993)

Classical Africa (1994)

African American History: A Journey in Liberation (1995)

Love Dance (1996)

African American Names (ed. with Renee Muntaqim, 1997)

The Afrocentric Idea, 2nd Ed. (1998)

African-American Atlas: Black History and Culture, An Illustrated Reference,
    2nd Ed. (with Mark T. Mattson, 1999)

African American Book of Names and Their Meanings
    (with Renee Muntaqim, 1999)

Scream of Blood: Desettlerism in Southern Africa (1999)

Egyptian Philosophers: Ancient African Voices from Imhotep to Akhenaten (2000)

African American History, 2nd Ed. (2001)

100 Greatest African Americans: A Biographical Encyclopedia (2002)

Culture and Customs of Egypt (2002)

Scattered to the Wind (a African metaphorical saga) (2002)

Egypt, Greece, and the American Academy (ed. with Ama Mazama, 2002)

Afrocentricity: The Theory of Social Change, 2nd Ed. (2003)

Erasing Racism: The Survival of the American Nation (2003)

The Painful Demise of Eurocentrism (2005)

Encyclopedia of Black Studies (ed. with Ama Mazama, 2005)

Handbook of Black Studies (ed. with Maulana Karenga, 2005)

Race, Rhetoric, and Identity: The Architecture of the Soul (2005)

Cheikh Anta Diop: An Intellectual Portrait (2007)

History of Africa: The Quest for Eternal Harmony (2007)

Spear Masters: An Introduction to African Religion (with Emeka Nwadiora, 2007)

Encyclopedia of African Religion (ed. with Ama Mazama, 2008)

The Global Intercultural Communication Reader
(ed. with Yoshitaka Miike and Jing Yin, 2008)

An Afrocentric Manifesto: Toward an African Renaissance (2007)

Maulana Karenga: An Intellectual Portrait (2009)

Erasing Racism, 2nd Ed. (2009

Afrocentric Infusion for Urban Schools (with Ama Mazama, 2010)

Rooming in the Master's House: Power and Privilege in the Rise of Black Conservatism
(with Ronald E. Hall, 2010)

Speaking My Mother's Tongue: Introduction to African American Language (2010)

The African American People: A Global History (2011)

The Barack Obama Handbook (ed. with Ama Mazama, 2011)

The Global Intercultural Communication Reader, 2nd Edition
(ed. with Yoshitaka Miike and Jing Yin, 2011)

Resolve: Communication and Conflict Management (with Julie Morgan, 2012)

AS I RUN TOWARD AFRICA

Molefi Kete Asante

Paradigm Publishers
Boulder • London

Copyright © 2011 Paradigm Publishers

Published in the United States by Paradigm Publishers, 2845 Wilderness Place, Boulder, CO 80301 USA.

Paradigm Publishers is the trade name of Birkenkamp & Company, LLC, Dean Birkenkamp, President and Publisher.

Library of Congress Cataloging-in-Publication Data

Asante, Molefi K., 1942–
  As I run toward Africa / Molefi Kete Asante.
    p. cm.
  Includes index.
  ISBN 978-1-61205-075-1 (hardcover : alk. paper) — ISBN 978-1-61205-076-8 (pbk. : alk. paper)
  1. Asante, Molefi K., 1942– 2. Asante, Molefi K., 1942– —Childhood and youth. 3. African American scholars—Biography. 4. African Americans—Georgia—Dooly County—Social conditions—20th century. 5. African Americans—History—Study and teaching. 6. Afrocentrism. 7. Africa—Civilization—Study and teaching. 8. Dooly County (Ga.)—Biography. I. Title.
  E185.97.A78A3 2011
  305.896′0730758895—dc23

                                                        2011022143

Printed and bound in the United States of America on acid-free paper that meets the standards of the American National Standard for Permanence of Paper for Printed Library Materials.

Designed and Typeset by Straight Creek Bookmakers.

15 14 13 12 11   1 2 3 4 5

To the memory of the Great Mother, Frances Chapman Rackley of Dooly County, Georgia, whose life gave birth to a large family of Smiths, Turners, Simpsons, Holmeses, and Spiveys, all Africans with European names who have forgotten neither her nor her deeds.

CONTENTS

CHAPTER 1

GEORGIA SWAMP LESSONS

I CAME OF AGE DURING A PERIOD of social unrest, when demonstrations against racial segregation abounded and protests were beginning to rise against the unrelenting political oppression of the American South's black population. In my youth Black Studies was neither an idea for universities nor a destination for black students. The colors of my youth were red with the violence of physical abuse and black with the people who surrounded me in the coastal plains of South Georgia. Cruel history teachers who were often hidden behind hooded masks wrote the lessons I learned.

I am a child of the South, born during the Second Great European International War and reared in the heated environment of the turbulent age of social and political transformation. The revolutionary thinkers and actors of the 1960s who sought to create the discipline of Black Studies largely came from similar backgrounds or were inspired by the lay historians like J. A. Rogers, John Henrik Clarke, Yosef ben-Jochannon, Edward Robinson, and numerous others who were linked to that same America.

My story begins in a small-town family, a Georgia family, with its feet firmly planted in the realities of wars, both civil and uncivil, and reactions to racism. My own path from Georgia has led me to run toward Africa, both psychologically and physically, while retaining a strong and uncompromising attachment to my own experiences in the heroic struggles of African Americans.

I was born neither Molefi Kete Asante nor Nana Okru Asante Peasah; these are names I would later legally and traditionally acquire. I should have been given an African name at birth, and had my birth not come as it did after the history of black enslavement and racial segregation in America, I might have well started with an African name rather than an English one. Most African people in America have the names of slave owners: Washington, Williams, Lincoln, Gordon, Hunter, West, Connerly, Jeffries, Hilliard, Gates, Thomas, Sowell, Faison, Johnson, Jackson, Jefferson, and Smith are not African names; they are the names of our European oppressors. I hated these names. They meant nothing to my history but oppression, shame, domination, defeat, and depression.

"What's your name, boy?" the man dressed in blue overalls asked. I was ten years old and didn't like my birth name. "I am LeRoy, Larry LeRoy Smith," I muttered. I tried to change my name by fiat, but it did not stick. No one ever called me LeRoy or Larry. Now I am happy that I was neither Larry nor LeRoy. I did not like those given names, but I disliked my surname most of all.

Carrying the surnames of those who enslaved your ancestors is a constant reminder of a lack of self-determination, a badge of conquest. I resented the emblem from the earliest moments I can remember—and told my parents so. I told them that I wanted a different name, a new name, a name that fitted me. They seemed to concur but did not have the foggiest idea of what they could do to get rid of those slave names. Neither of my parents completed high school or knew a black lawyer; they were victims who could not advance beyond what they knew. In their most reflective moments they always admitted, after some discussion, that they knew these English, Scottish, Irish, Dutch, and German names did not go with black people. It would take others like me to rebel and make the difference they wished they could have made.

These strange names for African people were indeed "slave names," and wearing them without question was tantamount to accepting the enslavement and all of its violations of our Africanity—all of those traditions, motifs, habits, proverbs, artifacts, and nuances that make Africans different from Asians or Europeans. The baggage became heavier each time we were called by names that were not ours. Our own African ancestors' names were unheard in some families for generations. I do not know how long our family went without any African names, though it might be said that we used nicknames to try to overcome our lack of authenticity. So I was "Buddy."

Having an English name and not looking like an English person would plague me most of my early life, and it caused me to change my name. Even before I knew Africa in an authentic, historical sense, I would variously be LeRoy, Larry, and DuWayne—all names I naively believed were closer to Africa because few whites had those names. These names were not African, but African Americans certainly used them as alternative names during the 1940s and 1950s.

Yet even the names that I used for a week or a month did not satisfy me, and I would eventually have to abandon all relationship to English names. I knew that a correspondence between one's name and one's historical reality made it easier to maintain sanity. I desperately wanted to be sane, to be normal. And being normal meant having a name that made sense to me. Neither Arthur nor Smith made sense to me in the context of my African cultural legacies. Yes, it was true that I was born in America, but I felt no identification as an Englishman.

Mature people give themselves names from their history and culture; others are like pets that are given names by humans. A dog does not know that it is called "Rover"; as far as we know, it has no capacity to name itself. African Americans can name themselves.

I recalled that the Nation of Islam dealt with the issue of mismatched names by issuing its members the surname "X," which stood for "unknown." Of course, they have since allowed individuals to choose Islamic names, but this seems to be a re-enslavement of the African person. Why choose an Arabic name instead of an English one and think you have arrived at freedom? This was to become one of the biggest points of contention between myself and others who denied themselves and others the self-determination called for by Pan-Africanists. I never understood why Muhammad Ali and Kareem Abdul-Jabbar would leave English names for Arabic ones. There was a lack of historical consciousness somewhere in their decisions, but alas, for me, I had to run toward Africa itself.

Back then most African Americans never even considered the abnormality of having a European name—that was the norm—and yet it is like a Chinese person having a Jewish name or an Arab having a Swedish name. After many years it might seem normal, but it still would not match the history of your people.

Naming is a religious experience because it grants us access to the mysteries of creation. I knew this when I was very young, though I was ten before I first called myself anything other than the name my mother gave me or my earliest nickname. As I child I thought somehow that saying the word would make the reality: if you could say who you were, just call out the name, you could be that person. It would prove much more complicated than I knew.

"Buddy!" Whenever my mother called me by this name, I would run to her, answering, "Yes Ma'am." It was the diminutive of my father's Bud and my uncle Alfred's DeBuddy. I never knew who generated the nicknames, but I suspected my grandfather Moses was the source. My mother seemed to take to Buddy rather easily and called me by that name more than my father did, who preferred the name I was given at birth.

Almost everyone on our street had a nickname, and it was almost expected that you would have one—as a sign of affection, a badge of how much people really paid attention to you. One of my brothers, Paul Calvin, was almost always called Red. I am not sure he felt he needed any other name. Another brother, the second oldest son, was given the name Eddie (who became Esakenti) but was called Sonny. On Oliver Street we had Dimp, Backyard Dog, Goose, and Turtle. We all accepted our nicknames and lived with them in perfect harmony—it seemed.

The naming phenomenon would sit at the door of all discourses in philosophy, black studies, and history for many years; it fueled cultural debates deep into the 1980s and 1990s and would still not be settled in the twentieth century, as attempts to relocate ourselves historically and culturally would occupy African Americans even more after the election of Barack Obama, a president with an authentic African name.

<hr>

I trekked behind my uncle DeBuddy with my fishing pole, step almost for step, as we came in sight of the slowly moving water in the cypress swamp. In our family I was the male closest to my father's youngest brother in age, so he took me under his wing. He was the first one to take me to the Okefenokee to show me the swamps with the ancient pregnant cypresses standing knee-deep in the water like platoons of John the Baptists ready to cry aloud—but they were silent. They were like sentinels over the mysteries of the watery maze, ready to initiate anyone who dared to enter this holy watery shrine to the alligators.

I learned to always stand back, waiting for a signal from my uncle to indicate when to go forward and when to step to the side, when to stop and fish, and when to move on. There was always respect, with nothing pretentious; everything was as the elders had dictated in their ordinary lives. I lived by the words of the adults. But I was not alone; we were quiet children then, listening and learning, waiting to speak when we had something to say and moving only when we were instructed to move. It was this ethic that often protected an entire population from wanton death. Watching was an act of survival. One never wanted to be out of line with this behavior because you would be severely corrected with, "Did I ask you to say something?" Of course, we learned to be keen observers, and this skill remained with me throughout my young adult life.

"Man, when we landed at Omaha Beach in October 1944, you were just two years old, but you were my brother's son, my nephew, and I felt that we were fighting for you," my uncle said to me. "Yeah, ol' Patton couldn't move his army into Germany without the fighting Black Panthers." He kept talking until he reached the bank of the large creek.

Uncle DeBuddy, a muscular man with the physical appearance of a world-class athlete, had managed to return to Valdosta after being a tank driver in the 761st Tank Battalion that fought its way from France through Germany and into Austria in search of Hitler. He was confident and strong; some would call him cocky, like some superior boxer or football player, because he knew that he had been a part of something great. He drove a tank through the Siegfried Line and helped get General Patton's 4th Armored Division to Austria. Nothing in his clear, dark eyes spoke of the horrors he had seen when we sat at the water's edge, holding our fishing rods.

DeBuddy, the most handsome of my grandfather's sons, was proudly blue-black in complexion with the whitest teeth in a family of men with the whitest teeth. He always had a smile on his face, like he was eternally happy about meeting you, and yet there was something mysterious about him—not like the mystery that surrounded his father or his grandfather, but a priestly mystery related to his good looks. There was also a little conceit in him, the kind that comes with knowing that you look good and that others know it too. And to see him standing in our little house on Oliver Street, talking with my father or mother, was to see an African god commanding attention and casting his charismatic spell over the entire house from his kitchen pulpit.

He mesmerized me with his war stories. It seemed so incredible that my uncle had been to Europe, fought against Hitler's armies, and returned to Valdosta. I respected him as I respected my parents, and I honored him as I honored them. As it was in the South among African people, my uncle was a second father to me.

Sitting with Uncle DeBuddy, I was in the presence of a history teacher, and I learned very early about perspective and agency—what you can see and what you can do—concepts that would later return to me as a mature adult. There was more to our discussion that day in the Okefenokee than roots or my birth. There was also something of blood and water as well as something literary and historical, though my uncle would not have called it that, and at the time I would not either. Today, upon reflection, I see more clearly how he opened me up to my journey toward Africa.

"I remember when you were born, boy, thirteen years ago," Uncle DeBuddy said, with his baritone voice so low that I had to cock my head to one side to hear him. His broad, white smile registering light in his coal-black face, making his stories even more organic, natural, and effective. He was not the first of my grandfather Moses's children to reach adulthood. My Aunt Jessie Mae, my father Arthur, and my uncle Moses Jr. were all older than uncle DeBuddy. However, he would be the first to die; yet his shadow, elongated to cover my early years, seems to have stretched over me like a protective blanket filled with comfortable memories and a guardian spirit.

DeBuddy, a war hero, who brought me so much myth, history, and mystery, gave me the multicolored dream of possibility when I was young. Not that the dream itself would have been any different had someone else given it to me, but as it stood, it was a dream richly drawn from the soil of one black family deep in the American South.

While we got ready to wade back toward the car, DeBuddy continued his stories. His rich, dark-chocolate complexion glowed in the Georgia sunlight as we walked through the muddy water, our boots up to our thighs. I kept thinking I saw alligators behind every fat-trunked cypress until he told me that what I was seeing were old rotten logs.

Sploshing through pond after pond along the swamp's outer rim, with lilies scattered in every direction, we were two-for-the-world sportsmen, and we seemed to be a million miles away from America when I asked him reverently, "How did you feel—a black man fighting for America?"

"Fighting for you, boy," he said, ending the question, I thought.

Treading more gently over the same terrain I asked, "Do they still have segregation in the army, being black and all that?" I guess I added the "all that" to include anything that I may have missed in my question.

"Not really." His answer shocked me.

"What do you mean? Not really?"

"I mean the black soldiers preferred to fight alongside black soldiers; they trusted them. Didn't trust no southern whites to look out for no black. Most of us fought in black companies."

"But that's segregation."

"The world's segregated, always will be. You just have to be better than anybody else and can't take no offense to your person. Then you'll always be free. Yeah, it was the time of segregation. The army was segregated. Truman would later try to integrate it, but for me and my company, we were happy to be with other black soldiers. The whites were too prejudiced." Uncle DeBuddy stopped the trek back to the car just long enough to throw his line into the water one last time, and a large catfish wrestled with his fishing hook, creating a minor typhoon in the lily pond until he finally lifted it out of the water while I stood back, admiring his luck.

I often wonder whether my uncle was teaching me to love myself as a black person in a racist society or just expressing the conditions as he saw them. Either way, I admired him. My family would have a profound impact on my thinking, my ambition, and my commitment to African culture. It would not always be easy or comfortable, but enough influences would be there to give me the guidance that I needed.

"Work harder? Is that what you're talking about when you say 'be better than anyone else'?" I asked sheepishly.

"Just do what you do best, and do what you can do, and you'll almost always outdo everybody else. Hell, I don't know what you call it except doing the best you can."

"You have to work together with all types of people, don't you?"

"Oh yes, I'm not against working together with others—you should. You must do that, but you've got to find the leader that's in you! If you don't, you won't be working with others; you'll be working for them."

"Everyone can't be a leader, can they?" I asked, because I had heard somewhere that not everybody who wants to be a leader can be one.

"That's a lie. Everyone's got it in them. It just has to be found," he said.

Puzzled and worried that I had stepped into a twisting perceptual machine much too advanced for my rather straightforward logic, I ventured, "You can't really mean everyone can lead. Can you be serious, Uncle?"

"Naw, I didn't say leadership ability. Don't get me wrong. I'm not going to say everyone has leadership ability, but I know that everyone has a leader in them. I saw people in the army who had no leadership ability, if you mean skills for knowing how to inspire others, but they found the leader in themselves. When you assert yourself, that's your leader asserting. When you're not afraid, that's your leader being unafraid. When you take a risk, that's your leader taking a risk. A black person who's found his leader don't take no mess." I knew he wanted to say "shit," but in deference to my youth he didn't. It was like that in those days.

As we sloshed back through the swamp, disturbing huge bullfrogs that croaked and then dove into the water, we finally came to the pine-scented clearing where we had left the car. When we got in, my uncle reached into the glove compartment of his red and black Ford and gave me a bag of pork cracklings that tasted very good after we had spent hours in the middle of the swamp.

As we drove toward home he mused aloud about the brave soldiers who had fought in Europe. "Those boys fought alongside the French and stayed in their trenches without giving up a foot of territory," he said, and I was supposed to know what he was talking about. He didn't share much about the 761st Tank Battalion; I had to learn about it for myself. It was not in the history books used in class, but I learned that the "Black Panthers"—the 761st, the 24th Infantry, the 99th Squadron of the Tuskegee Flyers, and the 92nd Division of the 183rd Combat Engineers—fought with extraordinary valor and bravery.

The 761st and the 183rd Combat Engineers, made up entirely of black soldiers, had been responsible for freeing Jews from Nazi death camps at Dachau and Buchenwald. My Uncle DeBuddy didn't like to talk about this too much. He would just say, "I was a tank driver." His battalion won 391 awards for 183 days of combat, the longest period any military unit ever served under constant enemy fire without relief. The 761st knocked out 331 German machine-gun nests and captured a German radio station.

There was enough action, fear, and adrenaline to make heroes of black soldiers in the Pacific and Europe. Dorie Miller of Waco, Texas, was the first hero of the Pearl Harbor attack, shooting down three—some say five—Japanese airplanes, and yet he had to suffer the humiliation of being ushered through the back doors when he toured America to tell his story. No wonder my uncle did not want to talk. He would leave it to me to speak the unsanctioned word.

He was not my only uncle; Moses Jr. was older, but Uncle DeBuddy was the one who often stood in place of my father. Like my father, he was a narrator of pursuits, and I would return often to his words. When Uncle DeBuddy and Aunt Bernice's children, Lillian, Valencia, Cynthia, and Alfred Jr., were small, my uncle, who had poured his soul into fighting for his country, would often take me with him on trips to the woods, showing me how to tell which plants were poisonous and which were not, how to listen for the rattle of rattlesnakes, and how to bait a fishing hook. My Uncle Moses Jr.'s son, Dwight, who was about my age, lived in Nashville, Georgia, and we only got a chance to play together when his parents came to Valdosta. Uncle DeBuddy's children lived across town from us. My first cousins were too young to be dragged along, and Uncle DeBuddy enjoyed telling me about life and nature. Ancestors must have whispered secrets to him, because he seemed to know so much about history, war, and automobiles.

On another hazy morning, when the dank humidity hugged us like a lost relative not wanting to let go, we sat under the Spanish moss draping close to the river's grassy bank, and my father's youngest brother told me what he knew about life.

Uncle DeBuddy had been here many times; he felt comfortable walking along the paths or sitting on the old, damp stump of a tree that became a plinth for our lunch boxes and jackets. I will always remember everything he told me there. His words are etched in my mind like hieroglyphics on the walls of old African temples. I remember his strong voice, deep, low, and melodious, like that of a good blues baritone, saying the words that would stay with me for a lifetime. He had recounted the time I was born so often. It was not my mother or my father but my uncle DeBuddy who told me of my birth.

He said that it was as if my mother, Lillie Belle Wilkson Smith, were at the hub of the universe, and the sparks of shooting stars flying across the midnight August sky way down in the South Georgia plains near the rivers and streams feeding the Okefenokee Swamp were forerunners, not of the rolling thunder to come later the next morning, but of my mother's screams as she gave birth to me. That Friday morning, by the time the midwife buried the umbilical cord in the backyard to make the ancestors' journey easier, I had been bathed and put to my mother's breast. Uncle DeBuddy could have been a preacher, so eloquent was he with his words, but alas, he was just my uncle who had returned from fighting in Europe with a different sense of himself than when he left. He was a free man in his mind, and he told me everything he could to make me a free man as well.

"Yeah, you were a big baby. We all thought you would be much bigger when you grew up, but look at you—you're shorter than your younger brother Eddie," Uncle DeBuddy said, teasingly. It was true, of course.

"How you know all that?" I asked. "You weren't there."

"Your daddy told me—after all, he's my big brother. Your mother was pregnant when I left for the army in April 1942. But your daddy knows what happened."

"He wasn't there either," I ventured, never really knowing.

"You were there, but you didn't see it," Uncle DeBuddy said, and laughed.

The story of my mother's birthing me would be told so many times in my presence that it would seem like I was not only present but also conscious of my presence. I was a baby who could not wait to come out, pushing to come into the world, to open my ears to the blues, Spirituals, and jazz of Georgia. It seemed that the motto of my life was set from those first moments. I resisted confinement, any type of confinement—mental, physical, spiritual, or social. I would always seek to break the barriers that stood between the world and me.

I did not know how much of this story was fiction or fact, but I relished my uncle's telling of it. His cadence, alternately slow and fast; his voice, low and rising; and his expression, serious and humorous, were parts of his special gift of drama. I felt he relished telling it as well. Sometimes he would add stuff, I believe, just to juice the story: "And when we had stopped praising your arrival, I told your daddy that you had a funny-shaped head and that they should shape it so it wouldn't look like a peanut." He laughed heartily. They must not have shaped my head well, because when I was in elementary school, I got in several fights because someone called me "Peanut Head."

Everyone was happy to see me, as my uncle DeBuddy told it, because I was the first acknowledged grandson of Moses and Willie Maud. There were rumors of an older brother, rumors that later, much later both my father and mother would verify, but I have never been able to trace this brother. I have always felt comfortable with calling others "brother" because, as my father would later say, it might be true. Although the Smith family would not acknowledge this brother when I was growing up, once I was grown he was mentioned often, particularly in my parents' verbal spats as their marriage deteriorated, but he was never introduced in our family.

My parents and grandparents were the healthy roots from which I grew, and without the nurturing of cousins and near-cousins, those who claimed the family and whom the family accepted, I would have been a broken twig of some lonesome family tree. As it turned out, the roots of my family ran deep and wide into the sandy loam of South Georgia and back into the red clay of Nigeria—indeed, as I would later discover, to the banks of the Nile River in Sudan. Nevertheless, every male in the family seemed to be a traveler, an adventurer, and full of wanderlust. I was not to escape this passion for movement, the motif of travel, this obsession with coming and going. In time it became both a hedge against rage in one location and a bet for happiness somewhere else.

☙

In his own time, each male in our family would have stories to tell of standing up and defending himself or someone else during a moment of crisis. Each would recite mantras of movement, leaving and returning, something our enslaved ancestors for 246 years could not do as freely. We would all learn to give respect and accept no disrespect; this seems to have been the legacy of my great-grandfather, Plenty Smith. In his nineties, as Plenty leaned his tall body on his sturdy oak cane toward his corn fields and peanut patches, his children's children and their children—me included—leaned toward Africa. We saw this not only in the spiritual possessions in the church, where Plenty was the key influence, but also in the ordinary behaviors of the family members who lassoed their children with anklets of rabbit feet and bathed them in oils to ward off evil.

I was one of the children who ran toward the Africa that I did not know from any reading. I only knew the myths, mysteries, and mores of my family, which was steeped in traditions that were still tied to Africa, although I would never be able to persuade some in my family that they were truly Africans. It did not take much for my great-grandmother Hattie Shine Smith to "rare back" in her rocking chair and recite the stories she had heard from her grandmother about Africa. Even though those stories seemed so fantastic at the time, with haints, magical people, healing medicines, and lots of rivers and streams, they were the glue that helped me to build a usable past.

Years later, when I created the first doctoral program in Black Studies at Temple University and inspired the Afrocentric movement with the publication of the books *Afrocentricity, The Afrocentric Idea,* and *Kemet, Afrocentricity and Knowledge,* I would recall my family's early trips to Dooly County, my great-grandmother's and great-grandfather's stories, and discussions around the fireplace at night that gave me the historical and psychological warrants I needed to come closer to a discovery of my identity. The Smith Family home, deep in the heart of Dooly County and presided over by Plenty and Hattie, gave one a sense of robust belonging. I liked it there; I liked the darkness at night and the brilliant sun of the day sparkling through the thickets down by the creek that ran through great-granddaddy's land.

It was always in August that the children of Plenty's clan gathered to hear stories, to play in the big yard, and to wrestle each other on the hard, packed dirt outside the smokehouse to the delight of our elders. Our joy, as children, was to hear a new thunder clap, to see a red butterfly, to be amused by the novel, this time at the old Smith house. Then, in the hot and humid evening, sitting on the front porch, we would hear the stories.

The stories were told as far back as Plenty: how he ran off the white night raiders who came to take the farm he inherited from his mother and how he shot a couple of men who threatened his wife. Indeed, we grew up hearing that my great-grandfather Plenty had killed a man over a woman, but he was never charged or arrested because it was all in self-defense. The story of my own father, Arthur, was less dramatic but still awesome in its challenges, as I would hear over and over again. He became "the man of the house" to help his family out of the Depression crisis when he was only a young teenager and his father, Moses, had gone to find work in the North.

The Depression was a foreboding valley of despair in the South. The profound havoc it wreaked on the North was compounded in the South's small towns. If you lived on a large farm, perhaps there was some cushion, but if, as in the case of my family, you had migrated from the farm to the town, your condition was as dire as dirt. People went from pillar to post looking for work. The Smith family felt the full brunt of the Great Depression, and the search for food became a permanent condition.

My father became a traveling man early in his life, but before he left Georgia he scavenged for berries, blackberries, gooseberries, and wild strawberries along the tracks of the Georgia-Florida Railroad. He learned to hunt for rabbits and squirrels, to seek out turtles, and to shoot sparrows and robins with BB guns and shotguns. He also dug herbs and vegetables from the red clay soil that was often a source of calcium for pregnant women. When he felt comfortable that his mother and siblings could live without him for a few weeks, he traveled to bigger towns to find work, like Macon and Jacksonville, hitchhiking on trucks and hoboing on trains to get there. He always returned with a few dollars. It would be much later, when he had a family, that he got a job on the railroad and then learned watch making and shoe repairing.

Living in the city—if one could call Valdosta a city at that time—my father did not have to farm as his grandfather and relatives had farmed in Dooly County. Neither my father and his siblings nor their father, Moses, farmed. In some senses they left behind the farms of Dooly County, first farmed by Plenty Smith's mother, Frances, for the tough life of the city. My grandfather Moses's nephew, J. T. Spivey, would take over the family farming lands when Moses left for Valdosta with his young bride, Willie Maud Anderson.

Everyone was depressed because of the Great Depression. Rich white men committed suicide and poor black men became hobos on the mighty black trains that tore through the southern forests at night like quick jaguars in an African savannah. My father thought of leaving for good every time he heard the long mournful whistle of the train, but he couldn't leave the family during those early hard days. He was barely ten years old when the Depression took hold of the land, but his memory of the events were so precise that he could enthrall his children with stories of great deprivation. If there were times when I did not speak, they were the times when my father spoke his evocative memories into the air. We all listened.

My paternal grandfather, Moses Smith, a tall man at six feet five inches, left for work in Ohio as the Depression deepened. However, he had a farming background and knowledge of plant roots and flowers— an herbalist, our family would call him, and others referred to him as a root man. He lived with his ear attuned to the voices of other root men—doctors of herbs and hoodoo practitioners. I don't remember if he ever got to the next level, where he would be called a root doctor, but he practiced what he knew anyway. When Willie Maud, my grandmother, sent his children to find him, as she often thought he was lost, they would invariably find him near the Withlacoochee River or in the swamps on the edge of town, digging for medicinal roots. He was a good river man.

"Nature has an answer for everything; every sickness can be cured by what's already in nature," Moses taught his children. His grandchildren were more in tune with Western medicine and sought out doctors with the pills and vaccinations for their health, but he would have no part of it. "Makes you sicker than you are already," he would always say. "People just don't give nature time to do what it can do. If you got something wrong, then something out there in nature can deal with it." He loved to spout off different versions of his natural theory. He would become variously a dream interpreter, an herb user, an active hoodoo man, an ancestor-believer, an itinerant preacher, and an elder in the Christian tradition. I believe it was his African eclecticism asserting an acceptance of all ways to divinity.

Jessie Mae, Arthur, Moses Jr., Alfred, and Georgia, the five of his ten children who were born alive, understood the African traditions out of which their father had sprung. In general, they too believed in the power of roots, although my aunt Georgia was always skeptical. If anyone was rational, she was more so, unconvinced by emotion, signs, speculations, and hearsays.

Aunt Georgia, the princess of the Smith family, once told me, "Pop believed in all that root stuff, but it didn't keep nobody from dying." Holding her elegant head high, she gave the impression that Granddaddy was more a dabbler in mysteries than a successful healer. She said, "He would be reading his dream book, mixing roots, and collecting plants, but he would always want to give somebody something, make you feel like he was helping you."

Georgia was everybody's favorite. I remember her as a "gal into dem books all de time," as Aunt Vanessa, with her stout self, would say, moving around, placing golden fried chicken and just-right chitterlings on the dinner table while Georgia smiled a self-conscious weak smile. "She what y'all should be. She doin' the right thing," Aunt Vanessa continued. Yes, the whole family loved and appreciated Georgia. "She never give nobody no trouble," the old folk always said. I wanted so much to be like her.

Later, Georgia would be the first to give me a new suit of clothes; the first to take me to Florida, just over the state line to my stepgrandmother's people's place; and the first to give me a book that I could call my own. There was always something special about her spirit—indomitable, elegant, and caring. I faintly remember someone saying that she was "stuck up," but her own life was a demonstration of personal discipline and moral commitments to family. I never knew her to fear anything or anyone. She was truly the princess of our family.

My paternal grandmother, Willie Maud Anderson, a rich chocolate-complexioned woman with a small nose and a round face, had come from a much less mystic, animatistic background than my grandfather, but even she, as I remember, recognized the spiritual song in Moses's voice. Sometimes, when asked where granddaddy was, she would say, "He back in dem woods talkin' to trees and huntin' plants." She must have believed in him too, because when he left on his trips to the North, she never knew when he would return, yet she remained steadfast in her love for him.

Willie Maud scooted around the house on Gaynor Street, cooking, canning fruits and vegetables from her garden, and talking. She was no gossiper though, claiming that gossiping was the work of the devil: "It is a shame that some people got nothing mo' to do than talk about other people." She would stretch her small frame up to attention, put her hands akimbo, and instruct us in good living, saying, "Some people are looking to see what can't be seen, and some others are going where they can't go, but if you follow your own destination, you get farther than you can dream."

She would defend Moses in front of anyone. He could have been anything he wanted to be if it was not for segregation. She said so. "The white folks won't let black people go to college at Valdosta State, won't let black people learn engineering, won't let black folk study law or medicine. Your granddaddy Moses is a smart man," she told me when I lived with them. I learned to respect the wisdom that he had, to learn as much as I could from him, and to show him no disrespect. She was thought to be the driving force behind Moses, and this was true. She was reinforced concrete—matter-of-fact and determined. Nothing escaped her attention, and she showed an immense capacity for protecting her family. She would sit in her oak rocking chair, knitting sweaters and socks, and talking survival. Her lessons were free to her grandchildren: "Get up early in the morning, take care of your business, and keep your head up all the time. You come from good people."

Moses never tired of seeking for what he called the truth. One day, when I asked him if he ever found what he was looking for, he replied, "Ain't never found what I was looking for, but I know evil is never defeated—it always exists somewhere out yonder. I just have to keep looking to beat it." As a child I was fascinated by this lean muscular man who always seemed to be wearing worn shoes like a man who had traveled by foot for many miles, but his speech was fresh, brisk, like he had just awakened to a different time. I think that was the energy he bequeathed to all of his descendants.

Grandmother heard him and said, "Now that don't make no sense, because everyone knows about evil in this world, but you better keep looking, cause ain't nothing out yonder to deal with evil but human beings."

"You ain't saying nothing mo' than I'm sayin'," he shouted.

Long into his seventies and into his early eighties, he became increasingly like a old television set that could only receive the public broadcasting station's signal, because he had no interest other than discovering what it meant for a black man to be alive in Georgia.

I do not know when Moses Sr. proclaimed himself or was proclaimed a preacher, but by the time I was six I knew he was capable of reducing the arguments of most of his peers to rhetorical ashes with his fiery tongue and scattered knowledge of scriptures. My family was one of strong men: Moses was in line from Plenty, and my father inherited his attitudes and styles from Moses—and they all used the Bible as their main text.

Moses would say, "Jesus is the Christ and the son of God. How do we know he is the Christ?"—always making a statement and raising a question in the same breath. He would answer his own question: "Because the Bible says so." If someone objected, and that person would have to be naïve indeed, he would say, "John 3:16 says, 'He is the son of God'."

When I was twelve, I thought that Granddaddy Moses knew more than anyone I had ever met, perhaps with the exception of my father, Arthur. But Arthur, Moses's son, never thought he knew as much as Moses, or if he did, he never showed it to his children or his father. Whenever Granddaddy came around, Daddy held back on what he knew and what he would say, listening, thinking, and probably only agreeing half of the time. But he taught us by example to revere the knowledge of the elders, and so he became a master teacher.

In this quickness to cite Biblical verses, Granddaddy Moses was like so many roving black preachers in southern Georgia. Moses took his name seriously and would claim that to "lead God's people," he might have to go through the lonesome wilderness of condemnation by some who did not understand his version of religion.

I honored my grandfather, greeting him when he entered the room and offering him my chair if there were no other, and I enjoyed his endless forays into religion and root mysteries. Sitting around the cramped living room in the little tan-colored house that had been my first school, I listened to the old heads before I went to school. My grandmother was ill during my earliest years, and she passed away when I was about six years old. Mose, as the neighbors called Moses, carried on with the teachings from experience, dream books, almanacs, and the Bible. He also kept traveling, mostly as an itinerant preacher in places like Waycross, Tifton, Adel, and Quitman.

Once, when I was in his house, he said to me, "How does God work? God works in mysterious ways his wonders to perform," and when he said it, he stretched himself almost to the heavens and walked out the back door to tend the gourds growing on the vines in his yard. He was the perfect picture of a sage, standing there at the broken-down fence, checking the huge green gourds that came to visit his yard every summer.

"Everything God made has a purpose. My old man, your great-granddaddy, spent his life trying to find out the purpose of herbs and plants. That's where I got it from. Look at these gourds—you can use them for many things, and some things you could use them for, we don't even know yet," he said. His thoughts and words seemed to make him sad momentarily.

He was always working to stay independent when segregation and racism in the South made it difficult for blacks to survive without whites. Periodically he worked for some big lumber company but often he was a loner, eking out a living for his family through his own talents: building houses, teaching, preaching, and tinkering with machines. He did not like farm work and had left Plenty's farms in Dooly County years earlier. "Best thing for a black man to do in Georgia is to work for himself," he repeated over and over again to his grandchildren.

Years later, when my grandparents were dead, my father would say, "Neither Moses nor Willie Maud begged, and we have no beggars here." Arthur Smith took self-determination very seriously. Most of the Smith men derived this die-hard attitude from Moses. They would rather suffer than ask for anything from anybody. This was the worst type of pride, however, as during times of great distress, the attitude often caused unnecessary hardships when other family members could have assisted.

However, years later I would see how this had to be the attitude of those seeking to create any academic program in African American Studies. We could not be beggars for intellectual ideas either. Later, my mother, Lillie, would say that I "took after" my paternal grandfather. Moses was her father-in-law and the only father she knew. He showered her with his quotations from the Bible and his knowledge of roots.

My mother never knew the Big Red man, Alfred Wilkens, her own natural father, who impregnated two sisters, Cora and Ruby Day. He had met my mother's mother, Cora, and her sister Ruby when he had come to Georgia from Florida as a "season" worker, which was when a person followed the harvesting of various crops. My mother Lillie, never remembered seeing him. She did, however, hear that in 1927, when she was only ten years old, that he was killed by a live electric wire in Oviedo, Florida, at the age of thirty-five. Ruby Day was the mother of my mother's only sister, Vanilla. Because Cora Day was adopted, she and Ruby were not blood-related, but they grew closer as the mothers of Alfred Wilkens's children, Lillie and Vanilla. But Alfred's early death deprived him of any genuine relationship with his children or grandchildren along with any shrine of remembrance in the family. Was he really a true Muskogee or was he a Roma, a Gypsy? The maternal side of my family was muddled from the beginning, and much later it would take mitochondrial DNA to clarify a part of the story.

Soon after my mother was born, her mother left her with Mary Day, Cora's godmother, and did not return until my mother was ten years old. Mary Day had raised Cora and then Lillie, her adopted daughter's child, because even when Cora returned, my mother refused to leave Mary Day.

I think my mother always missed her real mother; longing intensely for Cora Day, she never wanted to let her own children go. Tears would well up in her eyes when we asked her about her mother. "I saw my mother once when I was very young," she would repeat often, "and I never saw my father." We knew then that we had invaded an unforgiving terrain. We retreated and left the ground undisturbed, but our voices must have rung loudly in my mother's ears. To her, Mary Day was her mother because the old lady had raised both Cora and my mother, Cora's child out of wedlock. Growing up, the only pictures I ever saw of my mother's family were of Cora Day, my mother's mother, and my mother's father's mother, Grandma Wilkens. My maternal grandfather remained unknown and invisible, so the only grandfather I knew was Moses Smith, though the more I knew about him, the prouder I was to be identified with him.

These were the roots from which I sprang.

CHAPTER 2

ORIENTATIONS

I WAS BORN ARTHUR L. SMITH JR., named after my father's own slave name, in Valdosta, a town in south Georgia with pleasant weather and a history of violent race relations. Apprehension, danger, and violence existed at every turn, and African Americans knew what lurked in the swamps of hatred that entangled the Georgia of my childhood, especially in our small town, the "Azalea Capital of the World," that sat on the edge of the Okefenokee Swamp. In this sandy, often muddy town, the only thing that blacks and whites shared were the mosquitoes. Here there were no bridges to human relations—only walls to separate and alienate one from the other. The region was soft, verdant, and full of wildflowers and wild gooseberries and blackberries, but it is the thorns that I remembered most.

Valdosta considered itself a city of flowers—but this was branding more than it was an expression of the population's horticultural skills. It is true that many people had azaleas and roses growing in their gardens and a few had potted begonias on their porches, but more simply, the town lay on the edges of one of the great wild swamps in America, and wishing for beautiful things like parks of bougainvilleas and sculptured gardens with perennials of all colors bloomed in the human imagination. Black people were the gardeners, as we had been since the founding of the city, and when I was growing up, we often regarded the gardening jobs at the big antebellum houses as a throwback to the days of slavery. Nonetheless, the whites referred to Valdosta in their literature as the "City of Azaleas."

What Valdosta had instead, along with the scrappy beauty of an inadequately manicured landscape, was the whites' racial hatred of black people and a history of terrible sins against many defenseless, poor African Americans. There were no floral bouquets to make life easy for us; Valdosta was a place stressed to the maximum by a history laden with animosity and hatred. Living on the edge of the great swamp was like living at the ends of hell.

As a young boy I would get up each morning, look to the right down Oliver Street, and wonder what was past the end of the street—past the Baldwins' house, past the trestle if you took the railroad, past the bridge if you slipped under the brush and followed the crooked canal behind our house. What was way down there, to the west? If I looked from our house to the left and the east, I thought of the Okefenokee Swamp.

Somehow the swamp shadowed our every meaningful thought and intimate conversation, and I thought about it often. I do not mean that it was a constant thought, just that it was present there, in the sweet aroma of the humid air, as the muck in the swamps burned, and in the flooded back roads full of alligators that created havoc for the farm families going to their subsistence fields or some still-used white plantation.

For the black people who lived in southern Georgia and northern Florida, the swamp was a metaphor that meant death, life, capture, freedom, grief, joy, and, above all, secrets. One could get lost in the swamps sooner than one could in the woods, and there were always stories of someone being attacked by alligators or being lost in the silence of the waters covering a vast portion of the South Georgia woods. I was, in many ways, a child of these humid, snake-infested swamps, and yet I did not travel into them more than three times in my life.

My birth, seventy-nine years after the Emancipation Proclamation, on August 14, 1942, gave my mother, Lillie, her fourth child after Juanita, Lucille, and April—all children of men other than my father. I was my father's second child and, therefore, the second grandchild of Moses and Willie Maud. A brother whose name I never knew—because my father never kept up with him or his mother and I only heard about him in passing whispers when I was young—was to be the shadow in a thousand conversations. I think I came close to finding him at Florida A&M in the 1970s, but I lost track after a few years. So I was the first child for Arthur Lee Smith, twenty-four, and Lillie Belle Wilkens, twenty-six.

My mother's real last name would not be revealed until after her death. Throughout my youth we thought her name had been "Wilkson" because that is what she told us. But my mother was the mistress of allusion and illusion. She mastered the device of feigning better than anyone I had ever known, with a sense of demonstrating, much like the ancient Africans did, that what you see is not what is really there. We later discovered after talking with my aunt Vanilla that Lillie's father's last name was Wilkens. There would be much more to this story to come.

My mother came to Valdosta, a metropolis to her young mind, from the countryside of Naylor, Georgia. She was born near the sweltering oak and pine forests bordering the swamplands and had grown up in the clear, fresh rural air of South Georgia. Mary and Jack Day, who raised her, lived in a log cabin and had a small pond on their land, in which the children fished and swam. My mother spent her childhood working in the fields, hoeing cotton, cropping tobacco, and picking berries and peas. On the weekend she and the rest of Mary Day's "house full of children," including grandchildren from Mary and Jack's five natural children, sang and danced for family and visitors until late on Saturday nights. They went to church occasionally, but they were not regular church-going folk.

Lillie found her voice in the easy breezes of the southern wind; she cleared her mind and opened her heart to the sacred elements of nature. There, Lillie heard the sounds of her twinness, maybe African and Indian—that is, Nubian and Muskogee—and listened to the saints of her ancestral past. She knew about voodoo and hoodoo and could count the times the closest neighbors had been "fixed" by some itinerant priest of the African religious traditions: "Dat ole man had been lyin' to his wife 'bout his girlfriend, sayin' he ain't had one, when everybody know he did."

"What happened to him?" April asked.

"Well, ol' preacher man, dressed in a white suit, came to his house when he wasn't home and told his wife to sprinkle some sweet basil, wild tobacco, sage, and green callaloo on the floor in the bedroom. If the man got sick within a day, dat mean he was guilty. If he bought her a new dress, he wasn't guilty."

I was eager to hear the end of the story. April must have felt my impatience, so she said to my mother, "Well, was he guilty or not?"

"Guilty as sin. He got sick, couldn't get out of the bed for a month, but when he got better, he didn't talk to dat girlfriend anymore."

Mary Day, Lillie's god-grandmother, taught her everything she knew about keeping a house and a man as well as the art of capturing crawfish down in the muddy Withlacoochee River. I must have been six or seven years old when Mother took me down to the river to catch crawfish. I didn't much like the business of handling them, although I enjoyed eating them. The flesh was sweet.

A lot of love came with a whole bundle of my mother's teachings about how people survived by living off of the land. These teachings came in shadows, in haints, back in the groves of pecan trees swaying in the night breeze, in the aromatic essences of farm life, in the distant reaches of the inner spirit that brought about joy in daily life, and in the wonderment of full moons in the firmament of warm Georgia nights. I would love to sit on the back porch and look up at the stars as Mother gave us her stories.

My mother told me that old men, with oversized overalls and thick brown shoes, came and talked, as well as old women, in calico, telling stories that the children in Mary Day's house carried in their bosoms forever. Whenever the children found the occasions, they would speak those words.

Sitting at the edge of the bank, Mary Day, herself an exceptional storyteller, told seven-year-old Lillie, my mother, the story of the turtle. In it, a large muddy turtle, bigger than a rabbit, came out of the water, looked around, and saw three or four people sitting on the river bank with their long fishing sticks lazily lying on some rocks near them. The turtle watched the humans and waited to see if they would react to it, and when they did not, turned and slid back into the water and grasped all of the fishing lines and pulled the poles into the water. But what did the story mean? I asked. I am sure, knowing her spirit, that my mother must have asked the same question of Mary Day. The answer was the same as it had been years before: you better watch your fishing poles!

My mother loved Mary Day, but she also loved the knowledge and wisdom that came with the priests of words, the priests of herbs, the priests of divination, and the priests of fixes. And so, when the sun set in the pine forest, Lillie would visit the neighbors' houses and listen to the stories of High John de Conqueror, the Fixing Man, and the Power Woman. She soon began to imitate what she knew of them from the tales. My mother said she learned to whistle like the Power Woman and mix herbs as well as the Fixing Man, and she could fly like High John de Conqueror.

When she was nine years old, my mother could tell the fake doctors from the good herbalists. "The good ones don't have to ask you for nothin, dey know that if you get better you gon gie dem somethin," she would say. Lillie knew how to listen to the ancestors' voices and how to sing the songs of the wind. How much was African and how much was Muskogee, she did not know—and it did not matter. Her soul desired only to find the peace that had to come from knowing what life was all about. She thought she knew, and every day the questions that plagued her were the ones that Mary Day could not answer. "Where did the Big Red Man really come from?" "Were the black folk and the red folk working in the same cotton fields before the Big Red Man met Cora?" If Mary Day knew the answers, she never shared them with Lillie. But how beautifully African it was that Mary Day agreed to keep her when her own mother had abandoned her. Lillie found her voice in Mary Day's house and never let it go away.

Mary Day became my mother's mother. She looked like one of the pine trees that stood at the back of the farm—tall and straight, bending neither to the left nor to the right when she stood and delivered her bits of wisdom. My mother, I was told, intrigued Mary Day because, even when she was very young, mother had found her voice. She was reflective, almost shy, and yet she would speak when something interested her, and what interested her most was the nature of the spirit world. But she could not read and did not come to her spiritual interest through literacy. In fact, she would be well over twenty before she could read her own name.

My mother had a mystical quality, ethereal and surreal, and her friends and peers spoke of her in lyrical terms: "Lillie is like a flitting bird; Lillie is a river," or, "Your mother Lillie is like a whiff of heat." The language was always distant, hard to grasp, out of the ordinary. She flourished in the presence of others, just lit up like a light bulb, my step-grandmother Corrine thought when she met my mother in Valdosta.

And so it was that old, wise, snuff-dipping women, their walnutty faces bearing the evidence of too many nights awake, praised Lillie's manners, saying, "She done been here b'fore." Young boys eyed her, their senses full of desire, and admired the grace in her walk, her talk, and her comings and goings. They said, "She gone make somebody a mighty fine woman."

Lillie held her head high when she walked—not arrogant, but confident, firm, definite. There was no ego or self-centeredness in her, but there was determination. There was a rhythm to her feet touching the earth in time like they had ears attuned to the full majestic music of those buried underneath. So she stepped easily, lightly, treating the earth as sacred, holy ground. And she had been blessed with abundant love and attention. Neither the old women nor the men could love her as much as her sister, Vanilla, or her brother June Wilkens did. My mother's children never met her brother, although we knew Aunt Vanilla. Uncle June and Aunt Vanilla shared the same mother and father but only shared their father with my mother Lillie. Neither June nor Vanilla saw Lillie often, but they knew each other. While they were not born to the same mothers, the father they shared allowed them to claim a family relationship.

The children who lived with Mary Day played under the massive and bewildering oaks and tall spiny Georgia pines near the canebrakes away from the white people. They fished in the rivers and ponds, watching carefully where they stepped so as not to be trapped in one of the dangerous sinkholes that often swallowed animals and people in quicksand. They tended the cows, planted and harvested corn, raised beans and cucumbers as well as a patch of watermelons and peanuts for enjoyment. If this was not bliss, it was bliss's first cousin.

Lillie did her work as cheerfully and as gracefully as she lived her life, without complaint, without excuse—happily. Vanilla, just a year younger than Lillie, watched her and wished that she could have a similar gift of happiness in all things. They said that Vanilla was sweet, like watermelon juice, the drink she loved so much, but she loved her sister more than anything. But though everyone loved her and admired her for her soul and rhythm, Lillie was not at peace with herself. She was restless.

Sometimes she wanted to fly away to Africa. She did not know much about it, and it seemed so distant, almost like another planet. She would one day tell her children that "Africa is like a fairy land, a fantasy, but it must be real, because there are so many Africans here."

The tall, thin pine trees seemed to whisper to her to run away, to go to Africa, though the thought frightened her. She heard the gently rustling voices as real voices. Perhaps it was her mind working on her after hearing the old men and old women who gathered at Mary Day's house, talking about African powers. They said there were seven powers that gave human beings considerable insight into the meaning of the world, and some of them even said they had acquired the magical powers or that the magical powers had acquired them. These were the hoodoo expressions of the Yoruba religion.

It was only after I started traveling with my grandfather that I learned that Shango, Oshun, Ogun, Eshu, Yemaja, Obatala, and Oya were the powers spoken of by so many black people in the South. Each Yoruba deity was seen as controlling a certain aspect of human life. Years later, in Milwaukee, when Matahochi, the African American *babalawo*, threw the cowry shells for me, it turned out that Obatala was my head, my *orisha*, my spiritual power. Although I had not taken time to explore it when I was in my twenties, I knew that it something that would keep returning to me year after year until I submitted to the powers of Obatala.

Lillie only knew Africa as a mysterious entity, somewhere in the sentiments of real spiritual people, not so much a place as a state of mind. In the quiet evenings when Mary Day, nearly seventy years old, would sleep, Lillie looked out the window of the weather-worn house they called home and toward the oak trees with the Spanish moss draping them in sadness. Those old moss-wreathed trees had seen more terror and witnessed more brutality than trees anywhere else in the world; the lynching trees in the South were the bearers of so much history. But what she saw out of the window was nothing but woods, thick and abundant, as well as bushes that covered the river, but she reflected on the meaning of the Spanish moss, so scary and so ever present in the Deep South.

Lillie learned early how to manage history's burden. She would go down to the Withlacoochee River and watch its muddy bosom, brown with rich earth, move past the old diving trestle where the children like to play, and she would count the ripples on its surface. It was not idle activity but rather studied concentration that took her away from the farm's mundane duties. What she saw around her were the markings of age. The women washed and hoed, cooked and sewed, but grew old quickly. And even more quickly did the men grow old, with their bent backs protruding from their bodies as signatures of hard labor. So my mother moved to Valdosta, erstwhile vale of beauty, where she met my father and experienced the hardship laid down by segregation.

As tranquil as our world was in Valdosta, it was racially segregated by the white ruling class—perhaps the reason for its relative outward tranquility as far as we children could see. We lived separately from whites, as my mother and father and their ancestors had. We were born at home or in black wards of hospitals. Not even the afterbirths were treated the same way. By law, white and black blood had to be separated at all costs and in every situation. We got our fast food at separate, abnormal, untrustworthy "hand-through windows," like the Chinese fast food stores in many urban areas today. We drank out of separate water fountains. We went to separate "Black Only" toilets. We went to school separately. We attended separate churches, and I never saw inside a white church or visited a white home. We died and were buried separately. We lived in the poorest, most dilapidated section of the city, our schools used secondhand books with too many white children's names in them to count, and our cemetery was different from that of the whites because it did not receive the municipal support the white side received. The segregated dead rested in peace like the seductive separation of the living dead.

So Valdosta was outwardly the beautiful Azalea City, but this façade concealed the real Valdosta. Somehow the whites managed to say the name meant "Vale of Beauty," but in reality it was something else for Africans. It was a valley of desperation. In 1836, during the period of the US government's Indian Removal Act, residents of what is now Lowndes County took part in a massacre of Muskogee Indians and Africans who had been walking with their families through the county to join the Seminoles in Florida. A company of militia under the leadership of four white toughs, Henry Blair, Enoch Hall, Levi Knight, and Hamilton Sharpe, fought the battle of Brushy Creek, which was in reality no battle at all but instead a slaughter; twenty-two Indians and two Africans were reported killed by the militia as they tried to defend themselves from the whites. The white militia had surprised the Indians and Africans at their camp overlooking the Withlacoochee River at about daybreak on July 10, 1836. Needless to say, the migrating party was severely disrupted, and Lowndes County got the reputation of being dangerous for Indians and Africans.

This reputation was well earned. A little under one hundred years later, in 1918, a pregnant woman, Mary Turner, was lynched for defending the honor of her husband who had been wrongly killed by a group of white men. A white woman overheard her saying that she would seek revenge for his murder—whereupon a group of whites kidnapped the pregnant woman and lynched her; cutting open her womb and taking the fetus out, they stomped it to death. The lynching of Mary Turner, her husband, and her unborn child showed that there was an element of insane hatred and irrational action buried in the whites' hearts in Valdosta. No whites came to the defense of the Turner family, and no blacks dared raise their voices. It was into this environment that my grandmother, Willie Maud Anderson Smith, gave birth to my father, Arthur.

The violence against us was attributed to many things. It may have been based on the inferior status that whites had assigned to us. It could have been the envy that whites felt for our way of life: easygoing, forgiving, hospitable, rhythmic, loving, and affectionate. But the violence against us was most insidious when it robbed us of our resources and possibilities and kept us without shoes, clothes, employment, houses, schoolbooks, and information because it was a violence that denied us opportunity for economic advancement. Furthermore, our memories bled from the wounds inflicted upon us by violent Ku Klux Klan–types who harassed, abused, arrested, assaulted, humiliated, and killed black people with no fear of being brought to trial.

We lived in a maze of rumors and memories about brutalities and killings of African Americans. In our house we were put to bed by the fires of the hearth, bundled up together to keep at bay whatever climatic or social terror waited for us. We learned at an early age how to recognize racism, colorism, and anti-Africanism. This is probably why I became a keen observer of the doctrine of white supremacy at a very early age.

I am sure that those who have never experienced an oppressive atmosphere filled with fear, trepidation, restrictions, rampant violations of personal space, and death threats for the smallest infractions cannot understand the hell in which blacks lived in South Georgia in the 1950s. I also know that the people of Mississippi, Alabama, South Carolina, and Louisiana knew the same hell. We also felt the same will to overcome the condition of our political, social, and economic impotence. If need be, we would fight violence with violence to achieve our ends, but along came a preacher of nonviolence, Martin Luther King Jr., himself born in Georgia with some understanding of the plight we suffered.

Valdosta in the late 1940s and early 1950s was the typical southern American city. There were no beautiful nuances of relationships between the blacks and whites; there was only black and white, good and evil, right and wrong. The city held no great potential for African Americans, but if we ventured out of our community, we learned the dangers of being successful in the American South. Most black people felt that living in Valdosta was a dead end—after all, you could not be what you wanted to be or what you may have dreamed you wanted to be. You could only exist in a netherworld of unknown human ghosts, living amid the most venal system known to the world at the time. You could only escape or make your way in the interstices, small as they were and dangerous, where whites chose not to be. We had our teachers, our preachers, and our undertakers; they were our elite, and they were restricted to serving us because this era of racial segregation was something like the apartheid system of South Africa.

People who did not experience it often said that it was better than apartheid, but by the time I was twelve I knew it was immoral and unethical. I did not know about apartheid, but I was a victim of racial segregation in the middle of the most consciously white nation in the world. I did not see anything godly or better in abusive and second-class segregation; I only experienced a stunting of my ambitions, a ceiling to my desires, a limiting of my possibilities. The regime of hatred dictated what we studied, appreciated, and worshipped as well as how we interpreted our oppression. An enveloping racism that smothered every potential for blooming flowers among our people always constrained us. It would be a long time before I felt safe when I ventured among whites.

My parents, Lillie and Arthur, had twelve natural children together in addition to me. My father also assumed the fatherhood of Juanita, Lucille, and April, my older half-sisters. And so I began my journey toward the voice I would have in the future, ever more surrounded it seemed when I was young by the regularity of the annual dawning chant of a new baby.

Each newborn brought a pristine purity into the little house on Oliver Street. The smell, the noise, the music, the gathering of the midwives and friends, and the hurrying back and forth as my mother ended her labor came so regularly that I began to expect them, to look for them each year. "Momma, when the new baby's coming?" I would ask.

"You want another li'l sister or brother, huh?"

"Yes ma'am."

"Well, soon we'll have another little baby in the house," she would say.

My father's family stretched back to the eighteenth century in Georgia, and further in Africa, through his great-grandmother's line; beyond Florida, my mother's family was uncertain—all we ever heard was that her paternal grandmother was a Gypsy woman—that is, Roma. This had no special meaning for us as children except that the Gypsy people or Roma we saw in Georgia seemed always to be moving somewhere. It would be a long time before the scholar Ian Hancock, a leading Roma authority, would take me by the ear and lead me toward a better understanding of my childhood memories. From him I learned of the relationship between the Roma and nature, the Roma and fate, and the Roma and movement. From what I learned from Ian Hancock, I don't think I ever saw any Roma influence in my mother's religious or natural beliefs. All I knew is that Lillie Belle Wilkens was a proud, hardworking, gregarious, expressive, and stubborn person. She could take care of herself and her children. She would always say, "If somebody hit you, knock the stew outta dem and dey won't hit you again."

The Roma held a particular relationship with Africans in South Georgia; we knew them and they knew us, and their freedom reminded us of so many things that were possible. My father would later use this Roma connection as an insult when he wanted to explain a particular behavior or attitude of my mother's. "After all, she's a Gypsy, you know," he would say when my mother was late coming home from visiting friends and relatives or when she asked him for money to travel to Sarasota or Leesburg, Florida, to visit her sister or brother. You could say he had absorbed the anti-Roma sentiment of the southern whites without questioning the basis for the beliefs. If anything, to him my mother was the prototype of the Roma. Yet science would say that through Cora, my maternal ancestry was Sudanese, most likely Nubian, through Lillie's mitochondrial DNA. Years later I would raise the question of science and history: "How did my mother's mothers get from Sudan to Georgia?"

Then there was always the story about her Muskogee Indian background, though the way it was put then was that she was "part Creek." Perhaps she was part Creek—that is, both Muskogee and Roma—but we know she was African too. She claimed the Muskogee part more readily than the Roma part. Sometimes the Roma story and the Creek story converged, as in the time when my uncle Moses Jr. said that my mother's paternal grandmother was "a Gypsy-Indian-looking woman."

We heard from my paternal grandfather that my mother, through Big Red Alfred Wilkens, was the sixth-generation descendant of a Muskogee man who had escaped to Florida with the Seminoles after the big defeat of 1813–14, when the Muskogee nation lost its fifty or sixty towns in Georgia and Alabama to the US Army.

My mother could only tell part of the story; her half-sister, Vanilla, would tell the rest. The Muskogee gave twenty-three million acres of land to the United States, and I remember thinking after hearing my mother's history when I was ten that all that land in southern Georgia and Alabama might have been partly ours had the Muskogee not sided with the British in the War of 1812 and thus been punished by the United States.

Most of the Muskogee people of Georgia were relocated to Oklahoma. The runaways that escaped to Florida lived among the Seminoles and Africans. General Andrew Jackson had wiped out the towns of Tallusahatchee and Talladega and slaughtered eight hundred Creeks at

Tohopeka in Alabama. The Muskogee of southern Georgia were forced into northern Florida and then deeper into the center of the state. Big Red Wilkens was probably from that branch of the Muskogee who merged into the Seminole. The only thing belonging to Big Red, other than his genes, that my mother ever had was a photograph of his mother.

With a background similar to 65 percent of the African American families, according to Lerone Bennett, author of *Before the Mayflower,* no one in our family clung to the "Indian" past. We did not know anything about it except the physical appearances of some family members and the stories passed down from generation to generation. But that did not make us understand anything about being Indian, and certainly we were not Indian like we were African.

There was no need to claim a heritage in which we had never really participated. At various times we were Africans, blacks, Negroes, and Afro-Americans, and we were very proud of this fact. None of our family was ever even "colored," which carried with it a certain pretension to whiteness or, at least, a distance from blackness. No one knew of any organized communities of Native Americans, and anyway, in the Georgia of that period, nothing mattered legally except the fact that we had more than one drop of African blood. And then again, so many Africans explained that the features of certain members of the family looked "Indian" in order to claim Indian backgrounds so as to hide, out of embarrassment, some white background—most likely, the light complexions among some African Americans were more attributable to slave masters than to neighborly Indians.

Quite frankly, I am who I am because of both the speaking and silent voices that surrounded me. Some of my family members were loquacious—actually, most of them were—but it was the silence in some of them that produced in me a contrast that taught me reflection. My character is a result of the conditioning of those early years. I wanted to find my own voice, and I had nothing to go on but the people who talked or did not talk.

When the discussion turned to our relationship to the First Nations, the Native American people, my fourth brother William Charles would slip out of the discussion, scooting to get outside the house and far away from the rest of us. Charles sought neither to escape embarrassment nor to claim any Native American background, but he just did things that made people remark, "He's like an Indian." I always wondered why his actions could not have been "like an African's" because that was the culture we knew—in religion, colors, aesthetics, ancestors, cuisines, and music. Most of us just thought the boy liked running around outside, digging in the woods, and gathering herbs; it would only occur to me as I got older that his behavior was his connection to Granddaddy and Great-granddaddy. He was a child and later a man of few words.

"Buddy, you and Sonny want to go catch some coons?" he would ask initially before he got the idea that neither Esakenti nor I were interested.

"It's too cold outside to be tramping through the woods," I invariably said during the winter.

"That's the best time; we can walk farther," he replied, and before I could count to ten, he was up and out. If he really had his mind set on going hunting or trapping, nothing could keep him home.

The day when Big Bob got stabbed right in front of the little red grocery store on Oak Street, Li'l Nolan, who lived next door to us, and I went to the very spot to see the dried blood on the ground. We were both shocked by what we saw because it was the first time that we had ever seen real dried blood from a dead man.

Big Bob had owed Sweet Willie one dollar and refused to pay him when he got his pay from the tobacco warehouse. When Sweet Willie asked him for his money, Big Bob complained that he was going to pay him, but he wanted to pay him in his own time. Well, the end of the story was that Sweet Willie took out his switchblade knife and stabbed Big Bob, who died on the spot.

"Looks like a lot of blood came outta him," Li'l Nolan said.

"Yeah, I ain't never seen no blood caked up like this," I responded.

When we got back to Oliver Street, Mrs. Koontz, Li'l Nolan's grandmother, sternly rebuked us for going around to the very spot where Big Bob was killed. "Y'all don't have no business 'round dere," she told us.

We were silent, but we were not unaware of the dangers that lurked in our community when anger went unchecked. Everybody knew—at least all the young men knew—that the switchblade was king. Most people did not have handguns; they had knives, and the best knife to have was a switchblade. It was thin, shiny, and quick. Some people had shotguns for hunting, and once in a while there were shootings in Valdosta involving shotguns. But nothing like a shotgun or pistol was ever pulled on a person on our street as far as I could remember.

Under lock and key my dad kept his own shotgun, which most of my siblings and I never touched. It was sacred, as if he were keeping it for some special time when he would have to defend his family. But I never remember him shooting it. That was one thing about my dad: he'd talk, argue, joke, banter, talk some more, but he would never threaten nobody. And nobody ever threatened him. It seemed that there was an unspoken understanding between him and his friends that he was serious—he would hurt you if you tried to hurt him. This was his tradition. It had come down from Plenty and had been told so many times in the family that it became a mantra for everyone: "Don't mess wid'm; he one of dem Smiths."

William Charles was one of the Smiths, but he was not a fighter; he was a woodsman, a hunter, a person of the forest, a lover of peace, and he often took Daddy's gun hunting along the Withlacoochee River. He was a gun man, not that he would point a gun at a person but in the sense that he loved hunting animals with guns. The only knife I ever saw him with was a Swiss Army knife that had a can opener on it. He was always tinkering with animal traps, cleaning Daddy's gun, and singing mournful tunes.

William Charles was my brother, but he always seemed eccentric to me; he was a stray shock of light in an otherwise cloudy sky. I think he heard voices. They spoke to him and then they were gone, though it was not the first time, nor would it be the last, that someone in my family had heard voices.

Some of the voices Charles heard must have told him to go to the woods. He would get up on Saturday mornings when we were little and go to the woods, to his own particular stand of pines about half a mile from our house, and bring back turtles, frogs, rabbits, and possums. Nothing natural was strange to him; all the beauty of the universe was contained in each little rodent or small piece of a plant. In the simple act of going to the woods, he was purging himself of so many of the evil spirits that had come to crowd his mind.

I also thought of Charles as the one who would clear the path for the rest of us. He was curious and inquisitive, with the hunter's insight into human nature. There was something Ogunic about him. Ogun is the Yoruba orisha, or spirit, that can cut through a forest of trees—or lies or confusion—to reach a proper space of peace. Charles was Ogun in our family; he had the ability to slip away into the night in search of his prey. A consummate mechanic, whenever he had time he would work on his bicycle and later his motorcycle; he could fashion any tool he needed out of scrap iron. In another time he would have been a blacksmith.

Charles was the only one of us who really loved dogs. I once had a dog, Spot, when I stayed with my grandparents, and he was the only dog I ever loved, but I did not love my dog the way that Charles loved his dog. Dogs are valuable if you are a pathfinder, and Charles was a pathfinder. I think that he found in dogs a kind of companionship that he could never find in his relationships with family and friends. He was a loner of sorts.

However, although his dog was a companion, he was never allowed inside the house. In that regard, Charles was like the rest of the family. Dogs should be outside or under the house, but not in the house, and certainly not in the bedrooms or kitchen. This was an African thing: animals belong outside, and humans, inside. Of course, we had a few relatives who wanted their dogs close to them—there is always an exception to any rule.

Charles's dog was a hunting dog, a basset hound, used mostly for chasing rabbits. Dogs are carnivorous mammals, and one approach to feeding them was to allow them to go to the woods. Charles's dog literally had to earn its own meat; I never remember him "looking after" the dog. Food for dogs was plentiful in the numerous rabbits, squirrels, and other game that populated South Georgia. In Valdosta any dog could go to the canal and find fresh running water or drink from puddles from recent rains; the place was moist, wet, and swampy. Charles's dog did not lack for water or food.

One summer Charles bought a new Harley-Davidson with the money he had saved from construction work. It added to his air of freedom, hitting the back roads, particularly the lonely stretches of Highway 41, a road that our father had worked on in his youth but had not been replaced by Interstate 75. Riding high and fast—and probably drunk—one evening he struck a blind man, and after a short while, the man died of his injuries. It was ruled an accident, yet Charles was broken, cut into like he had been sawed into pieces by a lumber saw. He walked around with his head hanging low and his shoulders drooped, and he took to drinking even more whiskey. He died soon afterward, depressed, dejected, having drunk too much whiskey at an early age.

All of the boys in our family had some passion. The girls—and eventually there were ten of them—had interests too, but I do not remember any passions in anyone other than April. She was clearly the artist: a musician, a dancer, and a choreographer. She won all the dance contests held during her teen years and perfected her talents with performances in New York. Vera, Brenda, Carolyn, Willie Mae, Sandra, and Shirley found men at much too early an age; Linda found religion. My two older sisters, Juanita and Lucille, had families before I was out of high school. Their passions were their families.

Now the boys had distinct interests. While I was interested in philosophy, Esakenti, who was named Eddie at birth and called Sonny as an adolescent, moved toward commerce, and Ozzie Lee held an interest in human relations of the social sort. Ralph loved sports, particularly boxing, until he got knocked out, and Paul was passionate about carpentry, building things, and then religion. Charles was the naturalist, the carrier of our nature-loving heritage in an active way. But I don't think he ever considered it that way; neither did I, as his brother—I just thought he was weird. Because we did not consciously live according to a Native American ancestry, we were Africans living in America with an urgent sense of our own cultural heritage. But we were not always eager to share this African culture because Valdosta was still light-years away from any sense of black consciousness, although the sparks existed in our house.

"Colored people ain't got nothing to do with Africa," said one of the local preachers of our church. "We are colored people," he said emphatically, almost as if African Americans were white people who were painted brown. It was as if whites were "real people" and we were just a shade different. My father said that the preacher was either crazy or did not have any clue about the lives we lived. I loved my father for his sense of pride in African culture, although he had limited knowledge of it except as it was practiced in his own family.

It annoyed him that he couldn't get Lillie interested in the things that mattered to him. He was often alone in his thoughts, a gladiator facing impossible odds without his closest ally. My sister April tells me that there was another side, not simply our father's. Indeed, my brother Esakenti confirms her statements, but I only know what I know from the periodic visits that I made home during the summer or religious holidays.

My daddy enjoyed talking to me about honor and integrity. If Arthur's head did not wear a crown, it was only because his head, always held high, was crown enough. He loved heavyweight boxer Joe Louis because he had beat Max Schmeling when the Germans thought they were the superior race. He loved Jesse Owens for winning four medals at the 1936 Berlin Olympics while Hitler viewed it from the stands. You could not tell my father that black men could not do anything anybody else could do. He would say that defeat was possible, but it did not mean that a person had to be destroyed. Arthur had seen many black men and women who had been defeated, but he knew in his heart that racism played a role.

"I've been in the North and I've been in the South, and I ain't never seen a white man that could do something a black man couldn't do. In fact, if you asked me, nine times out of ten, he could do it better than the white man." He would state a position and wait for a rebuttal, but most often there was no rebuttal to his positions. He was the head of the house, although he was a paraplegic by the time he was forty, having injured his spine lifting sacks of peanuts, and suffered through an unsuccessful spinal surgery after being rushed to Grady Hospital in Atlanta, almost 250 miles north of Valdosta. He lived until the age of seventy-four, dying almost a year after my mother.

However, my father's illness sent us from being part of the upper poor down to the lower poor class. Most of the time he had been a good provider, but his illness forced him to rely on watch making, a craft he taught himself, or shoe repair, which he also taught himself. He believed that a person should never be idle. If we had ambitions because of his two "good" jobs at the Georgia Southern and the Langdale Mill, now our ambitions were splattered against the reality of his inability to work. He too questioned what would happen to my mother and his children. As resourceful as my mother was in taking in washing and ironing, the children still ended up having to work in the fields.

One time, the white grocer from the store around the corner came to our house to get some information about a problem with his radio. He soon got into an argument with my father. "Smitty, you can't find Negroes who know how to work anymore."

"I don't know what you are talking about, Mr. Dasher. You found me," my father retorted. Dasher Store was a fixture in our neighborhood and served only a black clientele, but Mr. Dasher insisted, "Black people ain't got no experience in doing things right."

My father reminded him that he had come to him looking for information on his radio. If he believed whites were more capable, then he should go to the white shops downtown. He added, "Most of what white people know in the South, they learned from someone black." The man did not respond. He just took his radio and left; he was in a hurry, he said.

My father was always a man to speak his mind. I remember when I realized I had to return to the South to see him. It was when he told me on the phone, "I can't hold the pen anymore." That was one of the most frightening things I had ever heard him utter because he wrote something every day, a tradition that he started after finding himself confined to his bedroom. It was in his blood, as it had been in Moses's and in Plenty's, to speak his mind and to have his say. If he could not speak it vocally to an audience, he would write sermons and poems and songs. And he did so until the day he could not hold the pen. A few days later, he was dead at seventy-four.

My mother was a different story. She was a storyteller, an opinionated woman with a good sense of the dramatic. I believe that my sense of drama comes from her. My father authored over one hundred songs and many poetic essays, but my mother was the dramatist. She wrote nothing—in fact, she could hardly spell her own name. But she could talk and talk. Few people could out-talk her. She was willing to tell you the story on everybody, and she often commented on her children's and her relatives' appearances as well as their clothes, behavior, and potential. She was talkative, and conversation about other people was her forte. This was how she set the record that would be believed by everyone else. She delivered her lines with numerous facial expressions, showing disgust, anger, joy, intrigue, suspicion, and irony. There was persistent contorted drama around her conversations.

My father, the oldest son of the oldest son of the oldest son, met my mother in Valdosta, Georgia, the metropolis for southern Georgia, where she had come to live with her three previous children, all born in Naylor. She was attempting to leave behind the life of the rural South, and Valdosta, the City of Azaleas, was a world away from Naylor. Valdosta had department stores, banks, theaters—although blacks had to sit in the balcony—and the black areas of downtown, South Patterson and South Ashley Streets.

My father's estimation of Lillie Wilkens, as he told us, was written in our memories. "She was a fine 'oman," my father would often say. "Every man in town wanted Lillie, but I got her." His pride showed on his large bronzed face. In effect, he was her fourth man, as she had already had three children by three different men when my father met her.

They were married in Valdosta, and soon thereafter I was born. Those who came after me were Vera, Esakenti, Shirley, Paul, Carolyn, Ozzie Lee, William Charles, Willie Mae, Ralph, Arbrenda, Sandra, and Linda. We were never all home at the same time, and I best knew the older group of siblings, and yet we were bonded by community, by common love. There were no social solitaires among us when it came to family, although some of us sought solitude more than others. Our family was about what we went through together; it was about the stories of what our grandparents went through, and this gave us a past. We experienced births and deaths—a few deaths, in those early years—but our common refusal to go under economically gave the family a sense of resistance to disaster. I never once thought of not working to do my share of bringing in dollars to the family; it was expected, and I never questioned it.

When I was about four years old, my mother and father seemed very happy—a state that would eventually disappear with time. My parents lived together until most of the children were in high school, but then my mother left—fed up, it seemed, with the inconsistency of my father's commitment to her; he was plagued with the same insidious wanderlust that had attacked his father, and in many ways he bequeathed it to my brothers and me.

"One of dese days, God's goin' to make you stop carrying on lak you do," Mama would shout at Daddy sometimes.

"Well, God's already took care of me by bringing you to me," Daddy would retort.

"You oughtta be shame of yourself, talking like that."

"We both have faults; it ain't all my fault."

My daddy was restless; this was an undeniable fact. He was driven by the desire to see more, to know what was around the corner, to discover what was outside of Valdosta. Never one to dwell on what was, my father always wanted to believe that there was something more to life than what he knew. This was the crux of his inconsistency, and perhaps he should not have married when he did. He had to follow his father Moses to Ohio to look for work. He had to follow his urge to see more and to do more. All of my mother's talking failed to convince him that they could make it without him taking the night train to the North, and he was gone. He would always return, but he could never be kept from leaving.

You could suspect that not being able to travel, to attend college, to explore the arts and sciences, or even to finish high school because he had to work during the Great Depression to support his family had made my father long for something beyond Valdosta. Nevertheless, when I was born, he believed that he had made a good choice of a wife, and as a child, like most children, I believed that my mother was the best woman for him. Only later did I come to realize that although their two spirits had united, their time with each other was only for the purpose of creating the reality of our lives; it seems that the longer they remained together, the more they could not stand the reality they created for themselves.

Once, when I was five years of age, my father was home—and that was something because he had often been away, and several times remained away for three years: one time in Ohio, working on the railroad, and another time in prison for desertion. The sensual passion between Arthur and Lillie was visible, palpable, and concrete. They laughed together and sang Spirituals and imitated the Five Blind Boys singing group that was famous during the Second World War. They were playful, dancing, joking, and teasing one another in a gentle manner. The future seemed so much like everlasting sunshine. We basked in the resplendent light of this familial sun.

I still find my father's pride, given his situation in Georgia, awesome. He was so convinced that Africans were the equals of any white man that he refused to stop respecting the religious practices of African people even once he became a Christian. Our house was frequently painted with the telltale green or blue streaks around the old maroon paint. When the house was green, it still retained the symbolic colors but with white added as a border. The green and blue paint considered superstition by some and a way to keep away evil spirits by others was customary among blacks in southern Georgia. I drank as much of the raw Gullah culture as I could get, never too drunk with the narratives to desire more.

Fortunately for me, the rural counties of South Georgia were home to some of the most persistent African beliefs. Much like the Florida of Zora Neale Hurston's time, the South Georgia of my early years was filled with ghosts. Some black people believed that the ghosts of Confederate soldiers killed during the Civil War lurked in the swampy lands of South Georgia. You had to protect yourself and your family from all evil spirits, and painting the house a certain color to ward off evil was in the deepest tract of our minds, though we knew it was something that the white people would not do to their houses. They were different; we were Africans.

Under our house, in the soft sand of the South Georgia plains, we looked for dirt daubers that often burrowed themselves into the earth and made veves of our special African signatures, much like the religious symbols of voodoo. We did not know, as children, what we were doing; we were only doing what came naturally—or at least to us it seemed quite natural. Some of the symbols looked like snakes, others were like fish, and some were like men riding horses. Our parents simply passed on to us the things they did under the tall houses.

Inside our house heaps of secondhand clothes were piled in a large cardboard box. They were mostly multicolored, and when they were not, we mixed them when we got dressed to affect a multicolored style. Pink and black, red and green, purple and yellow—these were colors that one would never see in the white community. Ours were not dull colors; they spoke about our spirits, our personalities, and our aspirations. I am certain that some whites considered us as "country" or "exotic" when they saw us decked out in our bright colors on Patterson and Ashley, the two main shopping streets. Adding texture to the colors would make the look even better, and if you were going to a party, it would be necessary to have a combination of fabrics: nylon and gabardine, wool and cotton, rayon and velvet. Leather would put you in another class all by yourself—no one in my family seemed to get to that level.

Nothing reminds me more of the importance of leather than when Mr. Koontz came down from Newark, New Jersey, to visit his children, who lived with their grandmother next door to us. He stepped out of his big white Cadillac with New Jersey license plates, and we all thought he had come from heaven. We had no understanding of "Up North" except for knowing it was better than where we were. Mr. Koontz was a short, square man who looked like he could have been a sparring partner for Ezzard Charles. When he waved at us and walked up those loose wooden steps into his mother's house, decked out in a black leather coat and dark blue suede shoes, we thought he was the richest man in the world. Of course, all we knew about Mr. Koontz was what we saw of him when he came to Valdosta. None of us had ever traveled to Newark. Maybe he was rich, or maybe not, but he sure looked rich to us.

Valdosta was the epicenter of the African American community in South Georgia, and in some senses it was an African town—in community, conversation, drama, and activity. Almost nothing was missing, except you couldn't ignore the reality of being in America. Droves of people would enter Valdosta on the weekend from outlying towns, some coming from as far away as Waycross, Tifton, Fitzgerald, and Thomasville. Quitman people saw Valdosta as their capital; Atlanta was in a distant galaxy. We sort of looked down on the country folk who came to town on the weekends to spend their farm wages. We thought we had more material possessions than most of them, but they often seemed happier. The city would be bustling with country girls in fanciful red, green, and yellow dresses as well as young men in equally colorful pants, suits, and shirts. The musical speech was loud, rhythmic, boisterous, and warm with the cadence of remembrances.

I once went downtown with my sister April on the weekend. I had never seen such beautiful people with their hearty laughter, jokes, back slapping, and general good nature. As I look back on that Saturday, I believe that I was seeing the release of the pent-up emotions of a people who had worked hard on the farms during the week and now felt the joy of associating with others who had come through the same experience.

Valdosta was turned into an African village on those weekends. Let me be precise: the African American business area, a short two blocks on the south end of Ashley Street, *was* an African village. Into the few stores and bars that constituted our village was packed the entire social spectrum of the black community. We did not care that preachers preached against going down to Ashley; we went anyway—and often found them down there too. They had to go down there if they wanted to find the sinners, they would explain. We just saw it as a scene of endless summertime happiness.

The special priest wore multicolored shirts, bright trousers, and jackets. He was no fool, no clown; he was no laughing matter. He was the remaining connection between us and them, between black and white, between good and evil; he was an albino named Brother Stanley. I never knew if that was his first name or just the name by which we called him, but he performed his priestly duties along the same African block where the people gathered. He could foretell the future, mend relationships, and tell who was the enemy of the community. He was to be feared because he held in his own hands or in his mouth, by the words he spoke, acceptance and rejection.

The street was bustling with life on these weekends. Here one could see friends and family, trade stories of white guile, meet girls and boys from other school districts, play billiards, buy cheap wine, eat barbecue, and stroll the block. It should be clear that all the people of Valdosta did not see themselves as Africans. However, enough people had connections to the spiritual world, the unseen kingdom of spirits, to be exact, to know that we must have been carried across the "mighty great bosom" of the ocean to this place for a reason. They knew they were Africans.

If others did not know, they heard enough of the blues to take them to the deepest parts of their pathos, creating an ethos that was nothing other than African. So much humming, scatting, and rhythm making went on that Ashley Street could become a veritable club on Saturdays, with the music of the singers, musicians, and hamboners merging with the chatter and laughter of women and men free to spend money and search for lovers. We were the poor, the lost children of Jesus, the suffering masses of the world, the forgotten of the orishas of Africa, who always knew who we were.

Almost everyone in our neighborhood traced their origins to either Savannah or Charleston, the biggest centers of retained African culture in America. My family's Dooly County roots were closely connected because it is believed, though never proven, that the white Rackleys and the Smiths, for whom my people were named, came to Dooly County from Savannah, bringing enslaved Africans to work on the region's cotton and peanut farms. We identified with the Geechee culture straightaway.

The Geechees maintained more of our real African origins than other people did, and although we didn't know where my mother's mother was from, we thought she looked like she had the same roots. I would later receive the results of the mitochondrial DNA and Y chromosome tests that would say our father's line was Yoruban and our mother's mitochondrial line was Nubian. Because my mother's father was the Big Red Man, we did not know what her ethnic paternity would have been. She claimed it was Muskogee or Creek, so we claimed it as well.

Our house in Valdosta was a bizarre faded maroon until it was painted lime green with white highlights. It stood—it did not sit—on eight three-foot high brick legs. Two other houses of the same ghastly ilk, perched on their pillars, flanked our house, giving our house unneeded central attention; the three were all World War I houses that had been built for the early twentieth-century black poor.

The house stood pedestrianly, almost drabbily but with a rose bush, on Oliver Street, which was named after some long-dead Civil War veteran of the South. It stood near the outer fringes of the city, less than a mile from the woods. In effect, to paraphrase an oft-quoted description of the earth, our house was a poor family's insignificant structure on an extremely poor unpaved street of houses near the outer limits in the most depressed part of the Azalea City, itself a struggling center of cotton, logging, and tobacco.

The old house on Oliver Street was a mythical meeting place of goblins, spirits, goons, and souls. Feasts of conversation about the most trivial and mundane subjects took place with regularity. There were also occasional fights between siblings that created distance, anxiety, and sometimes long-lasting feuds. I learned that siblings could sometimes be more severe with each other than strangers. For several years my brother Ralph and I did not speak, but once we understood our problems with each other, we started to speak, and since that time we have never stopped talking. In fact, it was our father's death that released us both from competition and misunderstandings that dad had inadvertently caused between us.

An argument between my sisters Willie Mae, whom we called Bebe, and Shirley would turn into a shoving match, quickly transforming the whole house, like some giant arena, into an ancient battleground of gladiators—pushing, cursing, and signifying—until April or I stepped in to stop the melee between sisters over a misplaced hairbrush, probably waiting on the settee to have a bundle of clothing removed so it could be discovered.

I believe that in times like these we learned respect for each other. The lesson was not always obvious, but our family was large. There is something to be said about a large family in regards to sovereignty, individualism, autonomy, and the collective interests of the family.

Children in such a big family know full well how not to step on someone else's toes unless you actually wanted to step on someone's toes. From the time we woke up in the morning until the time we went to bed at night, we were aware of the presence of other people.

My mother was the key teacher of valuing sharing and community. If I had a quarrel with my sister, my mother would step in. "She's your sister," she always said, indicating that there ought to be a special relationship between blood kin. I could always get her to talk about her immediate family. When she scolded me, I would listen and then say, "Well tell us about how you met daddy?" She would smile, bring us to the kitchen, and, while she worked, talk.

She told us how it was when she saw Arthur Lee Smith for the second time. She saw him standing on the porch of the little house in his denim overalls. There he was, his eloquent physique speaking the emotions she knew—love, desire, need. Tall, buoyant, and dusky black like the inside of night, he pranced up and down the stark wooden porch, which, she recounted, was empty except for a small grotesque purplish serving tray holding an empty Coca Cola bottle.

He had seen her walking toward the house from nearly a mile away, and her slight frame dancing in the dusk had fascinated him. Through the pinkish haze draped over the road, she appeared like a little girl. As she drew nearer to his house, he called out, "Sweet thing, how are you?"

"Who you talkin' to?" she asked, being coy.

"Who else do I see, besides you?" he said, pursuing.

And they met and met again. And soon they married, and soon I was born, a Leo child, in the summer of their love. And they threw dust into the air from feeling the enormous task of raising children, and whole nations emerged in their heads and they tasted the succulent pleasures of parenthood—for my mother, a fourth time. And when they finally counted us, we were sixteen children. Our house was full—I mean, full—of people and noise and music and argument and, of course, laughter.

Not one of Lillie and Arthur's children was quiet, weak, or nonargumentative; we were loud, dynamic, intense, emotional, and passionate in our conversation and beliefs. Although we did not fight physically, we did not hold back our thoughts and ideas from each other. We would tell you about yourself in ways that I would later learn was just like the way the North Philly people could tell you.

Shirley, my fifth sister, had a special way of making her points direct, sharp, and powerful. She loved to akimbo and shake her finger and snap her neck to alert you about yourself. Her words hurt because you knew she knew what she was talking about. My brother Ralph and my sisters Sandra and Carolyn had reading challenges, but they were nonetheless willing to debate or argue with anyone on any subject. You can just imagine the type of rhetorical heat in such a household. We lived close, loved each other, and fought for each other, but we were always willing to confront each other.

The part of the South in which we lived was a place of great misery. The land was full of haints, and no place in the South had as many as South Georgia. I later learned that other people, mainly northerners, referred to them as "ghosts." Well, I didn't know anything about ghosts, and I cannot recall any grown people showing me one either. But haints—there were many in the coastal plains, and I saw some myself when I was about nine years old.

They only came out at night, usually if you were alone. Your chances of seeing haints were better on a dirt road with large drainage trenches on both edges and drooping oak trees costumed in dangling Spanish moss about fifty feet on either side of the road. If someone in your family had recently died, it was even more likely that you would see a haint. Summer evenings just before or after a rainstorm were sure to bring them out.

Bro Boy and Sammy, the two King brothers who lived down the street from us, spotted "Doc" Holiday's haint, and the haint of old man Thomas, a black man lynched in 1951, frequented the moss-draped swamps at the black end of Gordon Street past the cemetery. It was said that his haint sought to avenge his lynching by snatching the minds of little white children and drowning them in the Swanee River, right where it entered the Okefenokee Swamp. When the little white boys tried to swing on the vines like we did, they often fell to the earth. Whenever one of them fell, we knew that his mind had been snatched. We all believed it, and because none of the little black boys ever fell, as far as I know, we figured that old man Thomas's haint wanted only little white minds. However, we didn't swing on those vines after sunset. No one wanted to give the haint any undue opportunities.

The most seasoned haint of them all was the one who lived in the cornfields near the serpentine Withlacoochee River. Someone told us that it was the haint of a woman. I only saw it once—or something I thought was a haint—when a few of my friends, my brother, and I went swimming in the river at about five o'clock one afternoon. But I can't say that it was a woman's, as I don't know if haints have gender. A shiny, spherical mass, about the size of a full-grown man, appeared, cruising through the cornfield. I could see it clearly and told my brother and the others, but they couldn't see it. I watched it eagerly as it went to the end of the row of corn, turned around, and came back. It must have been a good fifty yards away, but it was too close.

I was so let down that they couldn't see it. Nevertheless, because I was the oldest, they followed my lead, and we got out of the water and went home. I sometimes wonder if it was a stray mist of a cloud, a fog fragment. On other occasions others, bigger than me, had seen the cornfield haint, and I was just a corroborator.

When I told my grandmother—my mother didn't believe my stories—she said it could have been the cornfield haint. After all, she had witnessed many haints herself, splashed across the red glowing horizon after an exceptionally hot day or in the afternoon during the warm rains on a partly sunny day. She told me some people were born with special veils over their eyes that allowed them to see things others didn't, so she told me not to worry when my friends refused to believe what I actually had seen.

It is said that I had a caul over my face when I was born. Some people even told my parents that the birthmark over my eye, which we always called blueberries, was a result of the amniotic membrane that found its way over my head at birth. This caul was to bring me good luck, the old people had said. Although I have always carried my family's understandings with me, I have always known as well that my good fortune has been as much a matter of good choices as good luck. If you do not overeat but instead exercise and get your rest, you will probably not be exposed to as many dangers as those who do overeat, refuse to exercise, and never get enough rest.

"Count you blessings, boy. Count you blessings," my grandmother said. "Just count your blessings that you have the special gift to see."

"Yes, ma'am," I said, trying to count my blessings, but I also thought it just could have been some vague movement of trees, stalks of corn, or shadows.

A few summers later, when I was eleven, I got my first job as a shoe-shine boy at a white barbershop. I just took my wooden shoe box and went inside the shop and asked the owner if I could set up and shine shoes. He said, "Yes, boy, you can set up right over there by the window. You just give me ten cents on every quarter you make." The informality of the decision held no message for me at that young age. Barbershops had always been readily accessible to black boys and men who wanted a job in the Old South. Shining white people's shoes was a guaranteed position; after all, it was nonthreatening and subservient. So I was not surprised that I got the job; other than working in the fields, it was probably the only job that I could have gotten at the time.

I set up where the owner had indicated. He was a middle-aged man who told me that he was a Langdale; I did not know what difference his family made, but I had every reason to expect that I would make a little bit of money from the job. My first customer, a young white man in his twenties with black shoes, sat in the chair near the window, and I took out my polish, my rag, and the toothbrush I was going to use for trimming the soles. He didn't look more than ten years older than me, although I may have misjudged his age.

I asked him to put his foot on my box so I could shine his shoes. He placed his right foot on the box and I began to shine, first brushing all of the dust and dirt as I had seen my father do when he shined his own shoes. Then I spread the polish over the shoe thoroughly, as this was my first customer and I wanted to make a good impression.

As I was bent over polishing the second shoe, I suddenly felt something wet on my head. The customer had spit on me. What venom had possessed him, I do not know. What unbearable urge to punish me, to embarrass me, to assault my senses, to humiliate me in the presence of other white men, what rage must have been in his heart for him to stoop to one of the lowest human actions against a young child.

I did not hesitate; it was almost as if his spitting and my leaving were the same movement. I placed my rag, shoe brush, edging toothbrush, and polish back into the box, and to the laughter of the white patrons of the barbershop, led by the man who spat on me, I walked out of the shop and home.

My father comforted me and told me that it was alright that I did not have the job. He never got over his own anger at the whites for the way they treated young children. "God'll punish them," he assured me. I was very proud when he told me that, as a child of my age, I demonstrated great presence and courage to walk out of the job because of the white man's evil. This was the first time that I realized I was always trying to please my father.

I remember asking my father if he had ever seen a good white person. "Well, I think … well, no, son, I figure I haven't."

"Not one?" I insisted.

"I guess I know some who won't call us niggers, but that don't make them good." Arthur Smith had learned very early to make a distinction between whites who were liberal progressives and those who harbored an obscene and irrational hatred. The Langdale family was one of the white families that hired black workers in their mills and factories. They did not have a reputation for being rabid racists, although Valdosta had quite a lot of them too. When I told him that the man who owned the barbershop said he was a Langdale, my father was relieved that it was the customer and not the Langdale man who had spat on me. Yet I felt that the owner had done nothing to chastise the man; acquiescing in the bad done to others is almost as bad as doing the evil yourself.

These pale people who ran Valdosta—immune to human feelings, passionless, mean, and quick to attack us with their barbed tongues, their fists, and their guns—were intent on punishing little black children, ensuring our continued abhorrence of their evil ways. And for our parents, this hatred was a redemptive feeling. Even if we as children did not see too many white people, we knew them from our parents' psychic and economic wounds, and we knew that one day we would rise up and confront racism. We would be Shakas of resistance, Sundiatas of rebellion, and Harriets of revolution. It was written in the very way we consciously held our heads high when the old folks told us stories about the whites.

We walked the sensuous dirt and sand roads of our neighborhoods, either south side or west side, until we got to the paved roads of their side, and then we walked faster because we were in the land of the Viking beasts who preyed on black people; you did not want to be caught on the white side of town too late in the evening.

Harassment was the first order of a chance encounter with whites; fights were the second; and the third order of the encounter was a meeting with the police. For black people in Valdosta, that was a no-go. You would end up in Big Twelve, as the jailhouse was called because it was built in 1912. Thus, the whites always had the advantage because they had the police on their side. If one of the whites harassed us and we whipped him up, we would find ourselves in a lot more trouble than we expected. So when they harassed us, we could ignore them or just turn around and walk to the police station to report the incident—of course, the police would do nothing.

The heroic presence of our black ghosts in Valdosta, coming again and again with the precision of the azaleas on the manicured campus of Valdosta State University, sustained me through my childhood. In a sense, my ghosts reduced the absurd hatred of blacks by whites to a commonplace notion that made it possible for me to consider all whites forever incapable of appreciating blacks as people. The vile racism of Georgia during the segregation era was palpable. In South Georgia there were no whites that I ever met or heard of who were active against the racist system.

It was in Big Johnny's barbershop that I first heard arguments that white people were devils. The Honorable Elijah Muhammad's rhetoric had reached South Georgia in the form of a short, stout, goateed man named Benny Goodman. He was convinced: "If they aren't devils, then how come they do so much evil? The devil is responsible for evil, right? Well, who do you see that is causing so much evil in the world?

"I know you love the white man; you don't want to accuse him of being the devil, but his actions suggest that he is the only devil you will ever see in your life. Have you ever seen a devil look like a black man? Have you ever seen a black man treat people like dirt because of the color of their skins? Naw, you haven't, because if you had, you would have told me. What does the devil like? I'll answer for you: he likes devilment, evil, that's why he is the devil. Are you sure you don't know the devil?" He could get wound up like a clock, unleashing a torrent of questions that no one in the barbershop could answer. I was enthralled; he seemed so passionate.

Years later I discovered that Benny was one of the first people in our town to really read and study the words of the Honorable Elijah Muhammad of the Nation of Islam. It gave him authority, presence, and knowledge that the rest of us didn't have or didn't care to have. We respected him because he was a black man who had information that did not come from the white man. He was a spark of freshness. Unfortunately, Benny fell on hard times years later because of an addiction to alcohol, and he never really reached the potential that we had all predicted for him. His passion, however, had a permanent effect on me. Nobody believed anything as strongly as Benny Goodman did.

I was a child of fourteen when I first went to Big Johnny's for a haircut; before that time, when I was in Valdosta, my mother or my sister cut my hair. When I was big enough to sit in the leather barber chair in Big Johnny's, I had reached a plateau from which I could hear everything that was being discussed in the community: women, politics, religion, racism, and history. I first learned about Joe Louis, Harriet Tubman, and W. E. B. Du Bois from Big Johnny discussions.

When you left Big Johnny's, you had definitely been to school. Although the information was often incomplete or inaccurate, you would have enough snippets of truth to feel that you had learned something. This talk of Booker T. Washington and W. E. B. Du Bois was hot talk. I loved Du Bois and didn't much care for Washington.

I wanted to care for Booker T. Washington because Brother Keeble of the Nashville Christian Institute saw himself as a Washingtonian. But Du Bois was the man. I would have given my pocketknife, an heirloom from my great-grandfather Plenty Smith, to have W. E. B. Du Bois smile favorably upon something I did. To me, there was no greater living human being. The range of his intellect and the sensitivity of his soul, according to my father, made him a giant. In fact, the old men in the barbershop said that Du Bois was more brilliant than Einstein—at least, he knew more about more things.

Only later did I even find out who Einstein was, but I never forgot the stirring arguments made for Du Bois. He was denied his rightful role in America, yet he fought, wrote, and achieved. Du Bois was a poet, scientist, novelist, historian, sociologist, linguist, and social activist, people like Benny Goodman would say.

Late at night, in our little house, long after my hair was closely cropped, I would follow up on these discussions with my father. It seemed so spiritual, so holy—the candlelight flickering and the bronze figure of my father almost whispering through the amber haze, like some ancient Egyptian teller of the mysteries, telling me what he knew about our history.

When he finished, I would always pray and do my libations to the ancestors, or what I thought at the time were libations. Later I discovered that just throwing your hands over your head and saying, "Protect me, Great African souls who crossed the river with us," was not really a libation but instead a kind of prayer I had heard from someone somewhere at sometime or another. Libations always involved sharing of drinks with the ancestors by pouring the liquid on the ground, as the old men did down at the pylon of the canal where they sat and sipped their whiskey. My Christian faith would not have allowed the pouring of libations.

Between my father's admonitions and cultural inclinations, and the words of my uncles, grandfather, and the barbershop debaters, I learned strength from black men; I learned to challenge, compete, and seek to win by giving my best argument and performance. I was able to learn a lot about "speaking up" during the summertime in Valdosta.

I had to be essentially ambidextrous to live in a country and a city where racism was as permanent as the color of my skin. I had to learn to know when to speak and when not to speak. It was about propriety. And the old folks would straighten us out if they thought we needed it.

I wanted to be a writer. But I knew that I had the potential to be a victim and a predator, a proponent and an opponent, depending on the specifics of my writing. I knew, however, that I would write as a passion to tell the truth about what I saw and experienced as well as to exorcise the demons of anger and hatred that dwelt in my consciousness. But I would first have to box my own hatred and defeat in my own heart.

Being ambidextrous was itself one reason for my anger with society; I managed to contain my rage, but barely. I questioned every conceivable sacred book, all the sages, and my grandparents. I wanted to know what the Bhagavad Gita said about hatred, so I read deeply in it and discovered that I could not deprive myself of all physical desires. Indeed, I did not want to deprive myself. I looked into the Koran and discovered that Allah was a god of vengeance and knew that I did not feel such hatred as to want to murder my enemies. Was some form of Christianity still angling to get me to let the white racists off the hook? But the Christianity I knew was wrapped up with the racists, and they saw it as their shield. I was utterly alone. Only at this point could I interrogate the African ways of knowledge.

Does Eshu give me more paths than I can choose? Do I have to stay at the crossroads forever? Of course, in the Yoruba construction of the universe, Eshu as Elegba makes all things possible, even the negotiation of the many crossroads. I made it past the teenage years protected by the abosom and orishas of Africa. Nothing was greater for me than the understanding that, as a child, I could possess the same spirit as our heroes. Everything had force, energy—even the inanimate things in our yard, like the giant tub used to make soap and the ax used to cut wood. The animate things like the magnolia tree and the walnut tree were witnesses to a lot of history.

I could not be conquered by the destitution of soul that I often saw in Valdosta when white children rode by us on school buses while we walked to our classes. Little had changed in Valdosta since the Civil War era; many things were still the same during my childhood. I grew up in the midst of actual racial segregation, so I became a child of the Civil Rights era. Like other descendants of Plenty Smith, I can say that my soul was never broken, the petals were never pulled from the flower, and I had enough family reserve and resolve to beat back the attempted coups against my spirit.

Valdosta taught me that when I walk into a room full of white people, they change and I change, and we rarely speak the same language. And the language I speak—the metaphors of pathos, the tropes of fear, the figures of power, and the icons of my own African sensibilities—is not the same as that of whites. They have their own fears, passions, figures, and icons. There is almost no amount of writing that I can now do that speaks adequately to my own experiences and the fragility of my memory in a time of bitterness.

Years later this would be the experience of my son, who entered a literary contest but wondered aloud if his use of African terms, words, and concepts would keep him out of the running for the top prizes. He vowed to maintain his own convictions, principles, and commitment to the terms that captured his experiences, even if he lost the competition. He lost that particular competition, coming in second. Like my father had done with me, I consoled my son and told him I was proud of him for knowing that conviction, commitment, and integrity are ultimately more important for character than any mental acrobatics you could go through just to make people comfortable. I knew that the challenges he faced were not the same for everyone, but they were vivid in his fertile mind, and I wanted to make reasonable sense out of his predicament.

In the summer after the spitting incident at the white barbershop, I went through a period of intense hatred of Valdosta's white people. It was a proper emotion, historically correct and psychologically therapeutic at the time. There is something pure about hating evil. I hated the arrogance that paraded its privilege in the face of our people. I hated the lack of power that we had. Every time I walked down sandy Oliver Street where we lived and then found myself on paved white Patterson or Stanley or Ashley streets, I hated the whites of Valdosta and their smug, racist ways. They had devised the system of Valdosta's hell, as well as Waycross's, Thomasville's, and Quitman's—the places I knew then. Whites held a stupid belief that we were inferior to them and could be spit on at will, laughed at, and dismissed. They had listened too long to their own music; soon they would hear another melody. I itched to be a player in the giant symphony being arranged against segregation.

Whenever I saw the huge pseudo-Greek antebellum mansions, I hated them. If I had known that they were really copies of the temples at Abydos, Waset, Abu Simbel, Kom Ombo, Edfu, Esna, and other places in Africa, I would have had a different reaction, but then the whites in Georgia and throughout the South who copied those styles would not have used them if they had known that the Greek buildings were only copies of African temples that existed thousands of years before the Parthenon!

Spanish moss and oak trees stirred up in me a tornado of hatred. It took many years for me to overcome the image of the oaks draped in mourning, in the most solemn gray capes of Spanish moss, for some hung black person.

I could not stand to walk past the Confederate monument standing on the lawn in the city courtyard. Even as a child I understood that it had something to do with white hatred for black people. Its very presence in the heart of the city of my birth, this city of flowers, was an insult to our existence. Standing so proudly, with his face pointed upward and his gun slung martially, the white boy in stone and concrete was a sign to me of the tremendous disregard white people had for our black feelings. When I passed the Confederate statue on the far side of the wide street, I shook the fingers of my hatred in the face of white insensitivity with a smirk on my own face. And I felt good, hating.

In the evenings I would mow the huge lawns of the white middle class, who I thought were rich—and they were, as far as we were concerned—for $1.50. In my mind, I was like High John de Conqueror, so I flew away to the tallest pine tree to shit hatred on their heads for making me sweat with a push mower for three hours for the dollar-fifty. Slavery was alive and well in Georgia.

One time, when I walked with Sonny Boy to Willie Boy's house and we saw white children swimming in a new municipal pool that was not open to us because we were black, I hated them for the incestuous tribalism of their bigotry. However, I never had the courage to throw dog shit into the pool at night, like my friends did. Maybe it was the church, perhaps the teaching of my parents, or just plain fear of what would happen to me if the police caught me, but I didn't do it.

My anger took other forms. My soul fired the engine of my will to resist degradation, my mind was a constant source of willpower, and I vowed to escape the deprivation of oppression and secure for myself and my community, within my limits, respect and admiration. I would create organizations, brotherhoods, unions, collectives of people who would have consciousness. Together, we would challenge every form of discrimination.

It was a childish dream, not because it was impossible or immature, but because the history of my people was replete with willful individuals before me. I later found that I had merely trod in the same path as every other sensitive and articulate black person in the South; our genius was secure, but white respect and admiration had to await a change of racist hearts. And yet years later I discovered that among us had always been a wealth of respect for our heroines and heroes. Then I knew why my father put before me the names and deeds of Charles Drew, Ernest Just, Mary McLeod Bethune, Paul Laurence Dunbar, W. E. B. Du Bois, Joe Louis, Madam C. J. Walker, Harriet Tubman, and Marcus Garvey. He gave me what he had, which included what he had been given and what he had learned.

The Christian church interrupted my season of hatred, and I have never known whether to forgive the church or curse it for stifling my hatred, thus keeping me from purging myself.

On this particular day, I went to my church on West Street to hear a famous black preacher, Luke Miller. My parents wanted me to hear him because he was one of the best orators in the land. Black people loved orators and still do.

Brother Miller was a short, dark vanilla–complexioned man with a close-cropped haircut. When he started preaching, he came down hard on hatred and anger. I sat in the pews, listening, my young ears hearing this famous preacher say, "You can't hate anybody, not even the devil. You've got to hate his deeds, but not him."

After church services, I thought about that for a long time. Hate the deeds but not the person? How could one do that? What was the mechanism of separation? And was not hatred a rational response to evil? And didn't white people operate on the basis of hating people, not deeds? Didn't they hate us, apart from any deed we had ever done against them, because we were black and different? I hated them intensely because they were the reason for their deeds. Deeds could not exist apart from people; white people built segregated facilities, white people created racist laws, and white people practiced racism against small children such as myself.

And it was a white man who had spit on my head at the barbershop: a dastardly, self-conscious, deliberately abusive act against a child. No, I never knew any black person in Valdosta to so disregard a child as to take out feelings of inferiority on him. Behind the deed had been this man with blue eyes, dirty rust hair, and a proud grin because he had "spit on a little nigger." White people did things like that, not black people, so I hated them.

But as a young person, I wanted to go to heaven, the heaven of Jesus, Peter, and Paul. I wanted to walk the golden streets in my own white slippers. I wanted to see the seraphim and cherubim for myself. I wanted my own pearly wings so I could fly over God's heaven, singing, "How Great Thou Art" to the music of Gabriel's horn. Blow on your horn, Gabriel blow!

And so I knew my hatred was unchristian, but I liked it anyway. It felt good; I relished its carnality, its evil. It made me feel good to hate the evildoers. Indeed, it was a thorn in my religious side and an obstacle on the road to heaven. I was restrained in my actions because of my conflict with religion. This was probably the first time I understood the influence of the church on black people's actions. It dulled the censor, created inaction, and made the people passive, even in the face of the most abusive and hateful acts.

Years later, when I had renounced the traditional church, I could again hate the racists, oppressors, and bigots of this world with total abandon and once again find my sanity in working against all

forms of discrimination. The church doctrine taught by little way-
ward preachers who proclaimed the white man's verdict—"Seek ye
first the kingdom of God ... and all these things will be added unto
you"—had tied hands that were now loosed to seek justice, freedom,
liberty, and equality. Hatred of evil and injustice is not only a logical reaction but also an ethical one for a person seeking to right the
wrongs in the world.

I did not grow bitter with hatred because I found in my character
signs of power that allowed me to use despising evil to introduce myself
as an instrument against all forms of racism. My young life became
the instrument that I would wield against racism. Nothing could keep
me away from the knowledge and the skill necessary to combat white
racial domination, abuse, and injustice. That was my vow.

At one point in my youth I began to think of dying for the cause
of freedom. It was a constant thought in my mind, particularly after
the Montgomery Bus Boycott began. So many black people were ex-
hibiting acts of courage; so many young people, children my own age,
were on the frontlines of demonstrations against racial injustices that
their actions had a positive impact on me. I wanted to join any and all
movements against racism. I made friends with young people who
came to report on their activities. Joining the college students at Fisk
and Tennessee State universities, I marched on the White Castle hamburger stores. I went to the mass meetings in the black community to
learn about nonviolent demonstrations. I was committed to be free or
die trying to make a difference. My cause was social, racial, economic,
and cultural justice.

Of course, I knew that blacks could be unjust, abusive, and evil, just
like Charles Fuller would later discover in *A Soldier's Play*, but all of
my early life was spent in the South. To know what that means is to
understand something of the nature of my development as a person. It
was as if the entire hatred of the white world was concentrated in the
little corner of the earth Valdosta occupied. But I knew it was also the
same in Tupelo, Huntsville, Denton, or Pensacola. Everywhere we were
victims of the vilest forms of human interaction and forced subservience based on the fact that we were black.

I despised the haters and hated them for their insanity. The hatred
was my only path to a life of action against all crimes, intellectual or

physical, against other human beings. In fact, this gave me the right to announce my own humanity because I saw in the actions of the racists something unsettling about some humans. And everywhere I looked, it was the same: white people creating havoc and chaos in the lives of black people.

When the Civil Rights Movement started, I was galvanized to action for social justice. Marching first under the leadership of Diane Nash, James Bevel, and older students against racial discrimination in downtown Nashville and then later participating in rallies and demonstrations with various groups, I was certain that we could take down segregation. I became one of those awakened, angry, determined, not-scared-of-anyone black youths of the 1960s.

When I was born, Red Ryder, Joe Palooka, and Captain Marvel were the heroes of the average young southerner, black or white. They remained so until I was ten and probably some years after, but for me they constituted the pantheon of minor gods, all white, that demanded we kneel at the altar of a white world. A southern rebel, but not of the confederate variety, I refused to buy into the worship and set about making my own comic books. They were crude but good. No one bought them; they were not for sale. I needed at that early age to create black heroes and heroines, so I made up stories and elaborated on stories I had heard. Dorie Miller became my hero. He was the black cook on the naval vessel who shot down five Japanese planes during the attack on Pearl Harbor. Jesse Owens and Joe Louis took their places in our pantheon of I-told-you-so gods.

As much as I try to forget those times, they creep back into my memory, into my brain, when I am walking alone down some very modern Market Street, North Michigan Avenue, or Wilshire Boulevard. I can see the figures I created to usher me through childhood in America. Willie James, Dolan, Bro Boy, Sammy, and Eddie—soon to be Esakenti—with whom I shared my dreams and my actualities of comic book characters often did not believe that I was for real. "Man, you can buy a *Batman* comic for ten cents," Bro Boy would complain.

"I'll even let you borrow the *Lone Ranger*," Sammy would say.

"You're funny," Dolan would say, meaning the same as "weird" means today.

"I don't ever see any funny books with us in them," Dolan would continue. I would splatter my feelings on their nylon shirts, the tone of my voice carrying the breath of life in their faces. They would laugh and shake their long, pointed black heads to the earth in agreement, and we would run off to the Magnolia School grounds to play touch football or to skate on the new pavement they had put around the old two-story building.

And no matter what time I returned to the old wooden shotgun house on stilts with the amber lights burning, always in the back of my mind was my great-grandmother, Hattie, as black as carbon and sturdier than an iroko tree, although she was only five feet three inches tall and not an ounce over 120 pounds. You could tell by the muscle tone in her ebony hands her life had been "no crystal stair." Hattie Shine Smith was a working woman—had been all of her life. And we all knew her name and her strength.

Hattie held sway over the great annual family festival. The big day came every August—the second Sunday in August to be exact—when all of the Smiths, Simpsons, Horneses, Shines, Spiveys, and Turners gathered at the Mount Olive Baptist Church in Dooly County to renew their relationships. I loved to eat the homemade vanilla ice cream and then go wash my hands in the briny waters of the small creek running below the church building.

My great-grandmother, with eyes of fire, would come looking for me and Eddie to take us back to the church to hear the preacher deliver his anniversary sermon. "Why you think you come here?" she would ask us, rolling down our pant legs and putting our shoes back on. It always seemed better to wash your hands in the creek while standing in the water.

"To worship the Lord and sing his praises." We uttered the words our grandfather taught us—words our great-grandmother had prob ably taught Granddaddy Moses when he was a child in those country woods, running to the creek just like we did.

"Well, you ain't doing so much worship down in the creek," she would chastise. "Now get on back up there on that hill and sing his praises." We walked back, but our hearts were still in the sandy creek.

My great-grandmother would enter the church building just a step behind us, to the approving nods of the other old women. She plopped us down right on the front row. I never liked the front row because of the preacher's saliva spray, which would shower me whenever he made a particularly strong point. But looking back, trying to get my great-grandmother's eye so she would move us was to no avail. Eddie always suffered the stings of spit in silence; after all, he was two years younger than my seven and didn't seem to mind the holy wetness.

Moses, my grandfather, would always be pleased when we drove back to Valdosta. "You chilluns see how many cousins you have up there in Dooly County?"

"Yes, Granddaddy," we said in unison.

"You see how many chilluns come out to the church?'

"Yes, Granddaddy."

"I am happy that your parents let you come with me. Next year, maybe your daddy and your mama will ride up there with us. There ain't nothin' like knowing your family."

"Yes, Granddaddy."

I don't recall my paternal grandmother, Willie Maud, Moses's wife, ever making the annual August pilgrimage with us. She had been ill for several years, and pain wrecked and racked her body.

In some distant time, almost at the edge of my memory, as a young child, I saw my grandmother die. I knew even then that she was not playing, as Eddie and Vera and I had often played at dying in the veritably American game of cowboys and Indians. We groaned and twisted and contorted and hollered in our dying, but my grandmother, mother of my father, daughter of the Andersons, a worthwhile milling family, died magnificently.

There was no uneven effort in her transition—it seemed so smooth to my young eyes. The cackling of the hens outside her bedroom window eased her moments and signaled the time had come for a great soul to pass over. She was a Bible reading Christian, a saint of a woman—she had to be, I heard the old folks say, to put up with Moses all those years.

In the winter of her time the summer sun of Georgia sat boldly on the earth, offering up rays of comfort to the exhausted, watch-weary family. I entered her room, and there she lay, pure black as the serpentine of Zimbabwe, anchored to her bed, her white cotton death gown wet with perspiration, a handkerchief chalk white in her once-strong hand. Full of her affliction, but with deep, marbled eyes focused solely on me, she reached inside herself and gave me her strength before she landed on the distant reefs of her journey.

She died as she had lived: nobly.

Never had she been another woman's servant; never had she allowed herself to be considered less than the authentic royal-blooded queen that she was. Willie Maud had stood by the side of Moses, a name that had conjured up so much in Plenty's and Hattie's minds when they called their firstborn by it, and she strengthened him where he was weak. She told him he was a leader when he doubted it himself. She encouraged his spiritual quest when others spoke about it with subtle derision. Willie Maud was Moses's determination and definition, and when she died, he was without a compass for a while.

The first funeral I attended was hers; my grandmother's cold, made-up, black body lay exposed to the view of those who had known her vitality and leadership in Valdosta. She did not look like herself, not even herself as I had watched her die. In the process of embalming they had taken the fluid from her corpse and filled her with formaldehyde, and she lay in that church sanctuary, white, dull, ghostlike.

From that day forward I knew how the ghosts came. I could not sleep for weeks. Every time I closed my eyes I saw the sleeping corpse of my grandmother, and for days I had to sleep with the lights on for fear that her spirit's presence would invade my thoughts. I do not know, even now, why I had such a difficult time accepting my grandmother's death except that it was the first time I actually knew someone who had died.

For a long time as a child I lived the life of an anointed heir without really knowing it. No one ever told me that I was an heir, and certainly we did not have any money to speak of in the family; however, I was always doted upon, used as an example to other children, given oppor-tunities to sit with adults—although I was not allowed to speak—and told that the family expected me to do well. So to say "heir" is prob-ably misleading, as it was more that I was the firstborn male, and all the adults and my older sisters wanted me to succeed, thrusting upon me their own desires for achievement. They demanded a lot, and they required an awakened consciousness on my part from the time I was five or six.

I did not want to disappoint them, and I learned to listen to old people without speaking unless I was directly spoken to. In the over-stuffed chairs in the various living rooms of Valdosta's frame houses, I often sat with my ears wide open and my mouth shut as adults spoke about everything going on in their world. I was an accepted fixture; my grandfather Moses would carry me with him, and my mother would have me by her side when she went to visit friends or relatives. I never went with my father when he went out; however, I visited him at the railroad station and at the shoe repair store where he worked. My sisters and brothers, especially Esakenti, tell of the times he would take them with him to visit friends. Perhaps I had a different view of my father because I was away at school while they were moving around with him. To me, he was a saint—often misunderstood and in trouble with the law—but a saint nonetheless.

My mind was very active when I was a child. I created environments other than the poverty I knew, and I was always ready to travel; in that regard I was very much like my mother. I read and wrote poetry, or verse, as we would call it as a child of eight. Later, I traveled a lot in my mind. On the wings of the giant hawks that flew over my great-granddaddy's farm in Dooly County, I traveled to Chicago, Detroit, and maybe Cleveland. Didn't think I could make it to New York on the hawk. Didn't even try because Chicago and Detroit, which we pronounced "Dee-troit," were the biggest cities in the whole wide world anyway, and all the black people in Georgia headed for Chicago or Detroit if they could get out. Sometimes they would head for New York, but on the way to New York, they always landed in Philadelphia.

I remember hearing my daddy talk about the great black people who lived in the North, like Joe Louis, Ezzard Charles, Sammy Davis Jr., Nat King Cole, Billie Holiday, Sonny Liston, Jackie Robinson, Roy Campanella, Adam Clayton Powell Jr., Ossie Davis, and Ruby Dee. We had some great people in Valdosta too, like Mr. Pompey, the funeral home directors, the Scotts, the Harringtons, the Jameses, the school-teachers and principals, the Lomaxes, and our preacher. They may not have known the cold wind of the North, but they knew what it was like to be in Valdosta during the winter.

We called the north wind "the hawk," and when it was especially cold in Georgia, we called the wind "Mr. Hawkins." Many times during the winter I imagined the frigid wind starting up in some northern city and then descending on the South with a vengeance. I often traveled back to those origins in my mind.

Of course, I also considered the trains. We knew the trains better than we knew cars in those days. My consciousness of railroads came early; I understand the lyricism in them that Houston Baker writes about in his many books. Daddy had a good job at the railroad station; it was one of the best jobs that he had during my childhood. I think we loved his position more than he did because he got to work around the huge locomotives. It was like someone working at the airport in today's society.

I loved the railroads and listening to the stories about them told in Valdosta. The Silver Meteor, which ran through Savannah, not Valdosta, was the most famous train in our conversations. The talk was that it was so fast that when you heard it coming, it had already passed. It ran from New York to Miami, hugging the coastal areas of the state, a long way from the swamps of south-central Georgia.

Nevertheless, we had enough railroads in our town, such as the Georgia Southern, the Georgia-Florida, and the Southern railway lines. Neighborhoods were defined by where they were located in relationship to the railroad tracks. Though everyone made jokes about the African American communities being on the wrong side of the tracks, in Valdosta blacks lived on both sides of the tracks, which ran east to west. We lived on the west side of Ashley Street, which ran north to south. Ashley Street was the dividing line between the all-white east side and the mostly black west side. All the blacks on the west side lived close to the railroad running through that quarter of the city; you could hear the whistle of the train from anyplace on the west side.

To get from our house to my grandparents' house on Gaynor Street, also on the west side, I had to cross the Georgia Florida and Southern railway tracks. Hoboes would often wave at me from inside an empty boxcar, and I waved back, wondering what sense of belonging they possessed. They always seemed to be happy, contented, even comfortable rocking along in the squeaky boxcars. I thought to myself that they would be in Detroit before I could finish my education.

The train was legendary in the black community. Its cachet was its power, the strength of its roar for a powerless people, and perhaps its ability to escape the confining environment for somewhere else. My father once spoke of his childhood friend who took the train out of Georgia during the Great Depression. "I was working in turpentine when dat ol' boy, Junior, belonging to Robert Faison, hopped a train to the North. Dat ol' boy told me one day dat he was not goin' to be working in no turpentine all his life. Next thing you know, he done up and gone up North. Took the train." What my father never told us was how he got to Dayton, Ohio. We knew he went when he was a young man, just like his father Moses had gone—to work. He may have hopped a train just like Junior Faison, his neighbor, but he never said it.

Well, I was not about to catch a train nowhere out of the Azalea City. I had to finish my education, according to my Aunt Georgia. She was the diamond in our family because she had gone to college and hadn't lost her common sense—my grandmother often said it was possible for people to be "too educated." I often saw some of those people who looked like they had lost their minds. They did not speak to you in the mornings when they passed you on the streets, and they often walked with their heads in the air as if to say they were better than other people.

"That girl was nothing but an educated fool," my grandmother Willie Maud would say. "Nothing but a key in a minor universe yielding air," she would add somewhat mystically. Like all of the Smiths, Grandmother could talk you down or talk you up. She didn't have any regard for the little stout lady with curly hair who lived on Gordon Street. "Her mama done worked till her hands bled out there in them cotton fields to put that girl through one of them colleges. She come back and don't want to speak to her mama because she is uneducated. Now, that's an educated fool for you." She would drink her coffee and shake her elegant head, which was situated upon a beautifully erect neck like that of a Masai woman. She probably said a lot of these things for Georgia, my aunt.

Before me, Aunt Georgia was the one to whom everybody looked to do good for the family. She was like all the other people on her father's side of the family: dark, beautiful, strong willed, and intelligent—very intelligent. I particularly thought my aunt's education was great because she got to drive around in her car, moving all the time. If education could bring you independence, then it could not be wrong.

My aunt Georgia was one of the best promoters of education in our city; she demonstrated that a black woman could achieve great things. People liked her because she was personable—greeting everybody, assisting those who could not write with letters to their friends and family, and working every day as an insurance salesperson to be an example for the young people in our community.

I knew that an insurance saleslady was respectable, like the black postman, because "she did not work in no white people's kitchen or laundry," as my mother would say. Whenever I visited Aunt Georgia, I squeezed her hand and looked into her beautiful shiny black eyes, and she would know that I loved her. My aunt, intellectual and willful, was a special force on me. She and my father were truly brother and sister in their outlook. Both cerebral, left-brain people, they did not have too much time for small talk or child's play. In my father's case, he claimed that it was because he had to take care of his family at an early age.

My aunt was protected by her three older brothers, and each one of them believed that she had the personality and ability to be a school teacher. That was about the highest ambition that an educated black could have in Georgia in the 1930s and 1940s. My dad and his brothers were ambitious, but the ceiling was low.

I liked the family I grew up in; they were earthy, ordinary, talkative, expressive, volatile, poetic, musical, and somewhat standoffish. We were a big family, so I do not remember many friends outside of the family.

I thought the old people in my family understood everything. They could reason from the Bible, and when they did not find their arguments in the Bible, they reasoned from nature, from the birds and the bees, from anything and everything—they "could just philosofy," to use an Ebonics word for talking abstractly.

We were poor, and many other poor children laughed at us because our clothes, though always clean, had the look of obstinate poverty, the kind that was not going away, which most often means the look of the lack of choice. My mother washed the clothes daily with lye soap in a large black pot set over hot coals in the backyard at first and then, later, with her Maytag washer. It did not seem to matter to the other children that most of them were poor too. They may have had more choice in clothes than we did.

When I was thirteen, I had to go to school in Valdosta for a while because my tuition had not been paid to the Nashville Christian Institute, and the school would not let me return. One day, we had just gone out to the playground for recess. It was late October, the sun was beautiful, the air fresh, and I was feeling like the world had just been born when a group of boys stared me up and down and then startled me by starting to laugh at me. "What you laughing at?" I asked, with the characteristic final preposition.

"What you think?"

"For real now, what are you laughing at?" I asked impatiently of the three young men by the time we had walked to Mr. Dasher's corner store. I never was afraid to ask what was wrong or where something was or what time it was. Their laughter hurt my pride. I neither played laughing at the poor nor accepted it. "What are you laughing at?"

"We were just thinking, how high is the flood?" they said, and laughed like Visigoths, holding their mouths and stomachs. It wasn't funny to me, not when my mother had done her best to dress us in warm clothes for the winter. So, remembering my uncle's admonition about bullies: "Always give the biggest one a thrashing; the others will leave you alone." I walked over to the big guy and hit him with a solid punch to the stomach. No one ever said anything about the length of my pants again. I was not tough, just fearless, though not foolhardy. I knew that that guy was a bully. Although I had my share of fights, I did not go around starting them and certainly would never have started a fight with three other guys.

Sundays always had a color to them in those days. It had very little to do with my youth. Every Sunday in Valdosta a festival of enormous proportions took place, like I would later see in Oshogbo, Trinidad, Nassau, New Orleans, Salvador, Buonaventura, or Tafo, all around the great traditional durbars of African people. Children would be gaily dressed; the old women would wear their best clothes with the brightest yellows, greens, reds, purples, and blues; and the old men would wear their suspenders and hats.

A pervasive happiness brightened the sky, and somehow we were all participants in the majestic simplicity of color, of multicolors. Music was in the air, and had it not been Sunday, a great gathering of the masses would have brought out the best secular dances in the city. As it was, most of the dancing went on inside the churches, as the holy ones "got religion" or merely wanted to show off their new Sunday clothes.

Years later I attended an Adae ceremony in Kumasi, Ghana, led by Asantehene Opoku Ware II, the reigning paramount king of Asante. I sat in the front row, drank schnapps from his glass and passed it on, chanted in Twi, and poured libations. Suddenly, déjà vu hit me, and I was sitting in church in South Georgia. The city was not clear; the sense of place became elusive as I tried to grasp it, to hold onto it, so real I felt it, sitting there watching the laughter, the tears, the joys, and the wailing of the Adae participants while participating myself.

Sundays seemed to possess more possibility than other days. They were pregnant with silence, and what you made of that quiet time depended on your own courage. We would wake up with hope on our side, and at night when the day's feasts—literally feasts of food for the body and the spirit—were over, we would sink peacefully into deep slumber, often to awake on Monday mornings in a confused stupor.

Our musicians would sing about Monday blues and blue Mondays, and employers would wonder what had happened on the weekend to make Monday such a slow day, but we knew that while Friday and Saturday nights might have been spent in the Blue Moon Club or the Midnight Bar, Sunday was spent in praising the Christian god and other unknown spirits as well as African orishas who hovered over us, constantly guiding our poor feet toward some unseen light.

We endured the pain of seeing each other dressed in finer shoes, sometimes Florsheims and occasionally Church's, shiny gabardine suits and dresses, and bright ribbons. We endured the pain of watching brother so-and-so and sister so-and-so arrive in a new car. We endured the pain of old sister Massey, when her wig got caught in the rosebush outside the church building, robbing her of her crown before the Sunday School class. We endured the endless recitals of difficult names like Zacharias, Haggai, Malachi, Leviticus. We endured the echoes of holiness in the various pronunciations and sounds of Jerusalem. Most of all, we endured each other, struggling, bent but not broken, hopeful beyond hope. An oral people, on Sundays we became a book people.

The massive black Bible that lay open on the podium in our church competed with the wide-open smile of an artist's rendering of a Swedish Jesus, a sort of Björn Borg–type. Our eyes were riveted between the two objects. The book was more imposing than the Jesus; it contained all of the rules, threats, fears, hopes, heavens, and hells that we had come to believe.

Each of us saved our pennies so we could contribute to the Bible fund in order to have our own little versions of the massive black book that remained opened on the podium. If you saved enough money, you could buy yourself a little Bible with a silk page marker and red writing when Jesus spoke. I was always curious why they had Jesus speaking in red rather than black.

"Brother Jackson," I said to our preacher. "Why don't they have Jesus speaking in black and everybody else in red? They don't want Jesus to speak like the devil, do they?"

"No son, they don't, he won't. It makes no difference what color they print his words in, no difference at all," he said piously.

"Well, if it makes no difference, then I don't see why they got Jesus using red, the color of hell," my eleven years insisted.

"It is the word of Jesus that matters, my son. Do what his words say, and don't mind the color." It didn't convince me, but I knew even then when you had to leave something alone.

The church had entered the consciousness of African Americans and stolen the most rational parts of our souls. I gained some of my spirituality from denying the religiosity of the church. We were stretched on a scaffold of sin and punishment—poor, miserably happy creatures with nothing but ourselves and the mysterious unknown for support. Dreadfully real is how I have come to see those Sunday morning experiences that marked my induction into the confraternity of those blacks and whites whom Lillian Smith claimed in *Killers of the Dream* liked the old mouth-filling names, the strange adventures that the Israelites had, and the indignant invectives the prophets so eloquently hurled at the weak in flesh and spirit.

Our community crucified itself on a cross of fear. That big Bible and white Jesus made real by the law, a reflection of the sociopolitical will of the whites, came to represent one wrapped package of control and abuse. Already in the mid-1950s, when I was entering high school, I could see that the black community was taking itself off of the cross and would neither hang up nor lie down and die. The Montgomery Bus Boycott, inaugurated by Martin Luther King Jr., the attorney Fred Gray, Fred Shuttleworth, and others in Alabama, electrified the black community. We had been terrified by laws that promised quick retribution for lack of submission, laws that aped the domination of the Bible and worked magic against us for years. The Montgomery experience showed us that we could defy unjust laws. King insisted and others preached that to break a law successfully, you had to be willing to pay that law's penalty. This was his respect for the legal position. It was not Law that he was against but rather unjust laws. His was a position couched in terms of the reality of our Sunday mornings.

King kept ajar a door for rebellion, but others insisted that it should be thrown wide open. Yet the eloquence of Martin Luther King Jr., created by a dramatic style and passionate flair, mobilized a whole people and threw a light of truth on the ruthless actions and festering sins of southern whites against blacks. He was the deliverer come again in the flaming flesh of a black man fed up with brutality and persecution based on race.

I was young but unmistakably touched and called by the ancestors to participate alongside my age-group of Kwame Ture, John Lewis, Marion Berry, and H. Rap Brown. And the two or three times I saw King, I felt like I was in the presence of a deity because his courage and his unusually slow, cadenced eloquence stunned me. So simple, so focused, and so awesome in his commitment to truth and righteousness, he transformed every space he occupied. Of course it was the coming together—the confluence of the time, the person, and the expectations—that made King larger than life. One could say he was born to lead only because we know he led. But for a young man of my age at the time, he was the one: chosen, anointed, and called forth from the many years of struggle in the black community for justice. He was not appointed; he did not stand for election.

I feel now that King was to the South what Malcolm X later became to the North. Though I grew to appreciate the special contributions of both men—their brilliance, their dazzling (though of course different) styles, their oratory, their strength of will and love for their people—I knew after Montgomery that King had experienced the southern Sunday morning syndrome, and he understood that the rhetoric of revolt for the black southerner had to be first a rhetoric of religion.

To another degree, in another context, Malcolm X, in line with the urban, northern world of Paul Robeson, taught that the rhetoric could not be merely an extension of the Christian doctrine but instead an alternative. Robeson inveighed against Dixiecrats and crackers in the 1940s, and Malcolm X, a student of Elijah Muhammad of the Nation of Islam, took the baton and ran his lap of the race to freedom.

I would know all of this by the time I was in college, but I still did not feel that we were acting from the standpoint of our own sense of self. We were responding like victims and acting in resistance to whites instead of out of our own needs. I had learned from living on Oliver Street in Valdosta that sometimes the wisdom of the elders is best simply because they had done things so many times that they understood the possibilities from experience.

So our mothers were our sustenance, but our guardians were our great-aunts, grandmothers, and numerous women like Miss Sister, who worked miracles of child rearing while knitting sweaters or planting their favorite flower gardens. And we were sometimes like so many weeds, causing mischief and misery in the garden of flowers.

One time, my neighbor Willie James slipped up behind Miss Sister's house one night and banged on the wooden shutters that were her windows, scaring the living daylights out of us children who were sitting around a big wood fire in the fireplace. I almost leaped headlong into the fireplace, saved when Esakenti, my younger brother with quick reflexes, pulled me away from danger.

Willie James was apprehended and Miss Sister put quite a whipping on him that night. She beat him with a cane, and his arms and legs were bruised. He lived with his grandmother, Mrs. Koontz, who whipped him again when he got home. He would have been whipped a third time, but his father, who had been visiting Valdosta, had to leave for Newark, New Jersey, before Willie James came back from school the next day. I always believed he delayed returning home until his father left.

This was the protocol of growing up on Oliver Street in Valdosta, Georgia: manners and morality were taught, understood, and maintained. But sometimes the lessons were hard, and we did not like what was taught. My mother was a disciplinarian and believed children should speak when they were spoken to and always respect old people. Lillie Smith did not tolerate children sassing adults, and we always knew when she meant business.

She was born in an ignorant era when black people in Georgia were not encouraged to get an education. In fact, most of the whites we met in the cotton fields were illiterates right along with the blacks. My mother was uneducated, but she recognized in her children the sparks that made them "quick." I was quick, my brother Eddie was quick, and my sister April was quick. She did not speak of the rest of the children as quick. As quick as I was, I could not get my mother to understand all that I wanted. My mother, never understanding me, would tell other people, "Buddy's a good child, quick, but he's different. All the time talkin' 'bout we from Africa."

I took what my mother said to mean that I was responsible, dependable, and proud. Had she asked me to stay home from school and "follow the seasons," which means doing migrant labor, I would have protested but followed her instruction, so imbued was I with the biblical idea that if children obeyed their parents, their days would be long upon the earth. For my mother my blackness had more to do with color than politics. Nowadays, when someone says something about me and blackness, it is almost always an ideological statement. But my mother was into color. The doctrine of white supremacy had played a trick on her mind, and she was only able to see the value of whiteness in many things.

The Bible played a big role in our family, though neither my mother nor my father went to church on a regular basis. Through most of my youth, they were backsliders. But they sent us to church—I think it was the only time that they could have sex. But the Bible, a tattered old book whose pages had turned brown, lying open to Psalm 23 on the closed Singer sewing machine in the living room day after day, was a testimony that our family was a God-fearing family. There was no drinking, no cussing, no smoking, and no gambling allowed in our house. It was as if the Bible would strike us down dead if we transgressed. We were an obedient household in those days; it was only after our youth had passed that the "devil" got into some of us.

Years later I would reacquaint myself with my brothers whom I had left in Valdosta. On a visit home one summer I encountered my third brother, Ozzie Lee, and we had a remarkable engagement about life and values. Because I had been away for such a long period of time, I was about twenty-eight and Ozzie not yet twenty when I really got to know him. "A child born who brings back the ancestors," the old midwife told my mother when she saw Ozzie's wide-open eyes, full of brightness, meaning he had access to knowledge others did not have. This would prove to be an accurate assessment of Ozzie Lee.

When I announced that I was heading back to Buffalo where I was working at the time, Ozzie asked if he could hitch a ride with me to Savannah. I agreed and was introduced to his world, one from which I am never detached but a world from which I have always distanced myself.

Leaving Valdosta, I would now escape the arguments over religion with my father—why didn't I go to church and what was becoming of me and my faith and didn't I know I had a gift to preach and could have been a better orator than Martin Luther King Jr.—and about why I was wasting my time writing all of these worthless books when people didn't read and when I would settle down in one place. I could usually extend the visit a bit by visiting other relatives and friends, driving out to the old Withlacoochee River to watch its petroleum-black waters flow over the white sandy bottom like it did when I was a child, or touring the housing developments in this historic town. So I gave my farewells, hugged, kissed, promised to bring my daughter, Eka, down to see them all soon, tested the arm strength of my younger men-brothers, William Charles and Ralph, and found that I was getting older.

I put my luggage in the car and turned the ignition. "Which way you going out of here?" Ozzie Lee yelled from the whitewashed porch, where he stood next to Paul, who remained, as usual, silent, watching, Masai-like, about the whole thing.

"Waycross and Savannah," I said.

"Liberty County. That's through Liberty County."

"Yeah, I think."

"I'm going with you as far as Liberty, maybe to Savannah," Ozzie said, running into the house and grabbing a paper sack and a tie. Soon he was back outside and into the car, waving to Paul, William Charles, and Ralph. "See you in two weeks," he said.

In Liberty County, Georgia, one of Ozzie's later places of work and activity, there were those who swore by people born with "the ancestors' eyes" in them. The blue or green paint that one can still see daubed on the houses in that country, whether owned by blacks or whites, attests to the strength of the spiritual powers. This was Ozzie's heaven, not far from Ibo Landing, where one of the great concentrations of enslaved Africans lived in the eighteenth century.

Ozzie was a realist. He had never given any thought to anything except action. He was shorter than me, stronger in the shoulders, and pecan-complexioned with a round face; he could have been a Yoruba or Ibo from Nigeria, but nothing mattered to him but doing his business. Ozzie Lee didn't really give much thought to identity or politics; he considered himself working in the real world.

My brother's skin was smooth; I later learned he rubbed it with vitamin E oil—something to do with sex appeal and stamina. He would use all of his skills to attract women and eventually would claim eighteen children. It was not simply the number of children that would trouble me when I learned about this but the fact that he was in no position to assist the children with education. His several wives and mistresses struggled to raise his children alone. There was always something a little odd about the way he thought, and I learned a lot about the conditions of the world through him. The Janus quality to our lives is rather pronounced, yet I recognize that we share the same gene pool and, but for different decisions, this could have been me.

The realism in his approach to life always shattered the artificiality that surrounded us, even in our poverty as children growing up in want. "You have to take what you need," he would say when he was seventeen. Now, at twenty-six, he was a seasoned realist, a philosopher of realism, a student of existence, an existentialist, a preacher, a healer, a medical practitioner steeped in the traditions of black and white southerners, a counselor, an attorney for the needy, a breadwinner, a trader in the things other people wanted, a natural-born talker, a convincer, a con artist.

As I drove, he said, "Everybody's got some kind of confidence game. All it means is getting over on what you have. Look, you write books, that's a con. The people who teach, they're conning. It's all about giving people something they want and letting them pay you for it."

"You're not a con artist, are you?" I had heard from my mother that he once sold her a wig for fifty dollars and a few hours later asked her to return it because it was not his and then sold it to my sister Vera. When Esikenti and I heard about it, we had a little indaba with him and promised him the Promised Land if he ever pulled that again within the family.

"Why you gon' ask me that question after I just got through telling you about life? So when you get a PhD, you don't listen to your people. I told you, man, everybody's conning. You conning."

When we got to Liberty, I stopped the car to see the little slave museum. The place was old and looked like it had been a church. Ozzie Lee got out and looked the building up and down. It had a zinc or tin roof with four windows in front and some old slave cooking utensils outside on the grounds. If it had had a large cross, it would have been right in keeping—there always seemed to be so much religion in the most conservative of regions. Liberty is also the most superstitious of Georgia's counties. I was told that one could see the haints of long-dead Africans hovering over the swamps to the south of the town, those who suffered at the hands of white plantation owners. "They have a lot to ask forgiveness for," Ozzie said, as we climbed the steps to enter.

Inside were the relics of Georgia's colonial and slave past. We saw the slave collars, slave chains, utensils, and photographs of proud white revolutionaries and humble black faithfuls. It didn't take long to exhaust the museum, and we jumped back in the Matador and took off down the pine canyon of a highway.

"Ozzie, tell me, are you happy with what you are doing?" I thought my question would bring out the dissonance that he had to have had in his praise of confidencing.

"Of course," he said, his chin thrust high. "Me! Happy? I'm ecstatic!"

"How come?" It felt good to use the vernacular rather than saying, "Why?"

"You remember when Mama first moved to Sanford, Florida, when I was fourteen? Well, to go to Sanford you have to change in Jacksonville.

Bus stations ain't nothing but dens for petty thieves of all colors, languages, and nationalities," Ozzie Lee said.

"What happened to you in Jacksonville?" I wanted to know. Perhaps I could get a real appreciation for why my brother, whom I believed was extraordinarily clever, had spent so much of his time as a hustler.

"It's a long story." After a long silence, he said, "A dude swaggered up to me at the bus station as I was waiting for my bus to Sanford and sat down next to me and asked me if I could read. I told him I could. Then he said that he had been given an address; he pulled out a crinkly piece of paper and asked if I could read it and help him to find the address. I told him I had to catch my bus. He showed me a big roll of money and said he'd give me twenty-five dollars to help him find the address."

"All right, what happened next?" I asked, eager.

"It was the Murphy game," he said.

"You mean where you give them your money?"

"Yeah, like that."

"Well, how did you give it up?"

"I went with the dude, and right outside the bus station, another dude joined us, who I didn't know was working with the first one. The second one told me that the first dude was loaded with money and had offered him twenty-five dollars, too, to help find the place, but he thought since the dude had so much money, he ought to give us more.

"When we found the address, the two older dudes asked me how much money I had, so I told them I only had fifteen dollars, which was true. They suggested that the first dude exchange his big wad with me until after he came out of the house, in the event it was a set-up and someone wanted to rob him. So I stood outside as they entered the house. I waited for twenty minutes; they'd said it would take five minutes. I had to catch my bus to Sanford. I went up and knocked on the door, and no one answered. An old man across the street yelled to me to go on where I was going, because I was the third one they'd got that day. I looked at the big wad of money and it was only three dollars—the rest was paper."

"That's heavy." I shook my head in disbelief.

"No, it was profound. I learned a lesson." Ozzie spoke matter-of-factly, looking straight ahead.

"What?"

"There are takers and the taken. I did not like being took, so I had to learn to take. It was as simple as that. When I got on the bus to Sanford, I was a different person," he amused himself at my shock.

We entered the ancient American city of Savannah. It was beautiful—manicured gracefully with bougainvillea overflowing from many of the homes. The aroma of blooming flowers filled the air like a gentle perfume. I drove directly into the heart of the city and found the bus station.

I got out of the car as Ozzie Lee was gathering his baggage. We embraced, and I looked him in the eyes—they were light like Mama's—and said, "You must take care of yourself. Be careful." That is all I could say. He had so thoroughly revealed his life to me that I felt incapable of giving him any direction.

"Thanks. You take care of yourself too. Remember, I love you, brother," he said, and he disappeared into the flow of people inside the station.

My brother, Ozzie, not yet grown, had left me with a serious lesson about human nature. I cared for my brother, but I cared for the family more and wished that he would avoid destructive habits and lifestyles. I also recognize that this was more a selfish wish than anything else. I had lost one sibling at the time through unnatural causes. My brother William Charles had accidentally killed a man with his motorcycle. It never left his mind, although the law said it was an accident. William Charles took to drinking vodka like a Russian and rum like a Dominican; alcohol killed him at an early age. I did not want to lose another brother needlessly at so young an age. There was a connection between us that everyone recognized; some people even mistaking one for the other until he gained too much weight.

I found myself reflecting on our childhood as I drove off toward Interstate 95. Ozzie Lee had always been special. He was the one who questioned authority. He was the rebel. He was the one who received the most severe punishment from my parents. The rest of us knew that you didn't talk when adults talked and that you didn't talk back to your parents when they were chastising you. You didn't look your father in the eyes. You came home when they asked you to come home. Ozzie Lee never seemed to get it, and we feared for him. He was like Stagolee, the mythical character in the African community in America who was able to achieve victory over all kinds of obstacles because of sheer determination.

"Ozzie Lee, you better listen to Mama, else you gon' be in trouble," Vera would plead. If anyone was the nurturer when we were young, it was my sister Vera. In her efforts to prevent absolute chaos, she was an icon of unconditional love and sensitivity to the rest of us. Vera sometimes butted into people's business more than she should have, but I respected her feminine essence that had a way of soothing bad feelings. It was like she could tell when Mama or Daddy was seeing red. You don't bother with nobody that's seeing red.

Some people insist on seeking harmony, and Vera was that kind of person. Things could be better between human beings, she insisted. She knew Ozzie Lee was headed toward trouble when he refused to follow instructions. Her role was to intercept, to intercede, to mediate if necessary, even to deflect the most intense parental anger. She did this by talking to Mama or Daddy and telling them that Ozzie did not mean it, that he did not hear, or that he was joking. Her aim was always to protect her brothers and sisters from what she knew was the potential for family chaos. We all saluted her spirit and called her name for harmony during times of stress. "Vera would be ashamed of us talking to each other like that," someone would say.

I recall that when I was twelve, my Aunt Georgia, the first in our family to go to college, gave me a special birthday gift: a book of Charles Dickens's stories. I was proud and grateful, as it was the first real book I had ever gotten from anyone, and Dickens had inspired me at an early age. I do not know why she thought to give me a Dickens book, but I could certainly identify with the poverty, struggle, and challenges of the youth in Dickens's works. It would be later when I would learn that he was a rabid racist. For example, he wrote in *Household Words* in 1853 that "I have not the least belief in the Noble Savage, I call him a savage, and I call a savage a something highly desirable to be civilized off the face of the earth" (June 11, 1853, 7:337). Furthermore: "I wish I were Commander in Chief in India," I discovered he had told Angela Burdett Coutts in 1857, when writing about the so-called Indian Mutiny:

"I should do my utmost to exterminate the Race upon whom the stain of the late cruelties rested ... and raze it off the face of the Earth" (*Pilgrim Letters*, 8:459). Another fallen white hero entered my intellectual world.

But there was something more to Dickens's gift. It was the boldness with which the book entered our house and sat on the shelf in my makeshift bookcase, made out of slabs of wood over concrete blocks. I paraded that little book as if it were the king of all books. It was not because the book was by Dickens that I honored it so much but rather because it was a gift from Aunt Georgia. Also, there were few things that I remember as being my own, and the book was the first real item that was given not to all the children but to me. The intoxication of ownership starts at an early age and rarely leaves a person.

During this time my father worked for the Georgia Southern Railroad. In a way, working on the railroad was like traveling himself. There was happiness in his eyes when he got up every morning before dawn to walk or ride his bicycle to his job. It was a manual job—checking and clearing the tracks, inspecting the engines that came into the station, and carrying heavy loads of rocks to rebuild track foundations.

I enjoyed seeing the huge locomotives enter and leave the station. In some ways the huge trains were muscular reminders of the ease with which I could one day leave Valdosta. Of course, this was long before I had any real idea of what it meant to be away from Valdosta; I had more interest in movement, transformation, and seeing other places.

To the family's disappointment, my father was laid off when the Georgia Southern Company ran into financial problems. He then worked for the Langdale Mill, a peanut warehouse where one-third of Valdosta's employed black males worked at that time. The city was known for lumber, turpentine, tobacco, cotton, and peanuts, and securing a job in one of those industries was considered highly desirable for black men.

My father regularly went to work at the mill early in the morning, before the sun rose. He counted himself lucky that he had found two good jobs, at the railroad and the mill. My father was never known to work in the cotton or tobacco fields. He was a hard worker—steady, dependable, and intelligent—but he fashioned himself a factory man rather than a farmer.

Because he had had to quit school to help his father support the family during the Great Depression, my father only had a sixth-grade education. He never sounded resentful, but I believe he often wondered what would have happened to his mother and three siblings had he not worked while his father was away in Ohio. Nevertheless, he read everything he could get his hands on, studying law, radio repair, shoe-making, French, watch making, and religion at home. He talked about Charles Houston and Thurgood Marshall like he was fighting alongside them in the NAACP's challenge to racism.

There was nothing tragic in my father's character; he was filled with optimism. This is why the accident that crippled him weighed so heavily on his family, and yet he did not wallow in despondency. The crack of his vertebrae, softened by the many heavy loads of wood, metals, meats, and grain he had borne as a teenager, tore through his nerves and wounded him deeply, and he fell to the floor in the Lang-dale Peanut Mill.

When they had called him to work at the mill, he went eagerly, hoping to better his family. He had not worked there for many weeks before he hurt his back lifting large sacks of peanut stock. They rushed him to the hospital in Valdosta, but the medical services there were inadequate to deal with a spinal injury, so he was soon transported nearly two hundred miles to Augusta, Georgia. After staying in Augusta for medical services, he was transferred to Grady Hospital in Atlanta, where they operated on him to correct a vertebra hernia. The operation did not work, and my father was sent home, never to heal properly and never to walk elegantly again.

When he came back to Valdosta, we all waited outside, watching him come into the house on crutches. He dragged one leg and then the other. Because he was a man of great dignity, he struggled to walk as straight as he could, but the pain and weakness were too great. He soon used a walker, then a wheelchair. During the last stage of his illness he was paralyzed from the waist down.

When his illness had confined him to his bed, afflicted, he would greet me every time he saw me with the statement: "One day, I am going to get up outta this bed and fly away to Africa with you." We would both smile, and I would wrap my arms around his neck. I think he wanted me to believe that he was still a strong man, and although I did not believe that he would ever walk again, I knew he remained the strongest man that I had ever known.

Arthur Lee Smith was a proud man who believed deeply in his own ability to fight for his family and defend the nobility of his race against those who would deny our right to exist, our right to be employed, and our right to be liberated from racist laws. He was the leader of his house, and despite the poverty that always surrounded our home, there was nothing but courage in him.

"Your daddy always held him a job. Nowadays, it looks like none of the boys can hold a job," my mother once told my brothers and me. "They don't make men like your daddy anymore." My mother must have been in one of her loving-Arthur moods. When she hated him, she used other words for other lessons.

She would sit in her favorite chair in the front yard, surrounded by children, thinking aloud, "Arthur done walked out of dis house and gon' over yonder in Kill-Me-Quick, and when he come back, he won't have no money." I thought the worst of Kill-Me-Quick, the most notorious section of town. What kind of place would call itself that anyway?

When he could no longer travel, not even to Kill-Me-Quick, it was my mother who traveled. She went to Florida and New York as a migrant worker, working in the fields alongside my sister Vera. These were the times that tried the bonds of our family more than any other and laid the ground for a culture of disintegration. It affected me because it affected Ozzie.

My mother, with so many children, appointed the older ones to look after the younger ones. I was to look after Ozzie Lee, but by the time I could help him, I was away at school in Tennessee. So Ozzie had to fend for himself. He coped by going about his business, surviving in a world full of thieves, and he became a man full of confidence tricks.

᛭ ᛭᛭

Unlike my younger siblings, I spent my time—lots of time—at odds with something, and eventually I had to speak out about it. Even when I went to the Valdosta Public Library to check out a book, I found myself having to argue with the librarian about the library's racist policies. I did not know at the time that I was preparing myself for the academy.

"How could you be about knowledge if you won't let me borrow books?" I said to the white woman at the desk. The readers, all white, looked up at me in the coldest stares I had ever seen. I was still in my teens, but I knew then that segregation was dead.

There was always the threat of violence, the possibility of insult, the danger of being chased and beaten by gangs of whites, but overall, we stayed in our world and they stayed in theirs. My neighborhood was stable and all black, and except for bill collectors and farm owners when we picked cotton, I rarely saw any white people. Occasionally, a white woman would bring over clothes because periodically my mother took in ironing to help pay the bills. White people were almost an invisible part of my life. I could see them if I went downtown to the stores or attempted, as I did, to go to the library. Only later would I see whites as the controlling force in the economic life of Valdosta. It was a gradual awareness, like opening a book one page at a time. Finally, the entire book had been read, and I had become a little boy with a clear understanding of the racial divisions in Valdosta.

Vera and I were the best of friends and often defended each other at school and at home. By the time I was ten we had become defenders of our mother as well. When Daddy was gone and mother was home with no money, Vera and I stepped up to the plate to stand between her and the white bill collectors whom we hated; they were like vultures, slinking around the black community, going from door to door it seemed, asking black people for money. Of course, they controlled all of the utilities and services we used. It was a continuation of the slave conditions my great-great-grandparents had known.

"My momma say she ain't home," we repeated once, when a tall white man with a blond crew cut came to our house. Fortunately, the man did not insist or threaten. He just left the porch shaking his head, like he was saying, "Them people are show 'nuff crazy, having children say they ain't home, when I know they are in the house."

So the petty racism that afflicted blacks who lived in more direct contact with whites did not bother or harass us in any immediate sense. I did not have to experience white people calling me "nigger" or sending me to segregated water fountains or doling out verbal or physical abuse every day. In this way, I was mostly protected except in rare instances.

Our world was one in which the structure of racism dictated that we would often not have enough to eat, that our clothes would be clean but tattered, that our illnesses had to be treated at home or by the root doctors. This was the socioeconomic dimension to the terrible burden of racism. But our resilience was acted out on the dirt road called Oliver Street that ran in front of our little house.

Oliver Street, with its twenty or so homes, all seated high on red brick pillars, was the whole world. Everything was on this street, and we found the world in our backyards and front porches as well as in the middle of the dirt road, where we played "London Bridge is Falling Down!" After all, this was the era of the world war, when anything could happen and did happen to London. But we were in Valdosta, thousands of miles away, at the edge of the pine forests near the Okefenokee Swamp.

I had gone about the father's business when I was ten years old, two years before the preacher said Jesus had done the same thing. It was something strange but necessary; in fact, when I went to church that Sunday, I had no intention of becoming saved or being baptized.

I sat in one of the long pews, alongside a row of children my own age. Several of them were taking their chewing gum out of their mouths and pressing it into the back of the pews. The church service was very long, and we all grew tired and bored. There had to be three or four full songs, scripture reading, two prayers, announcements, a sermon, and collections before the church service was concluded.

I was wearing my new white slacks and a new white shirt—my Sunday clothes. Now that I think about it, these were the colors of Obatala, and when I was in my thirties, the babalawo who read my cowry shells told me that I was a child of Obatala and that white would be a good color for me to wear.

The preacher was unusually emotional, flailing his long arms and stabbing the air with his fingers, feeling the audience's eagerness to get out and go home, so he kept walking up and down the aisle, shouting,

"Come to Jesus! Come to Jesus! If you are weak and heavy-laden, come to Jesus today!" He looked like he was talking straight to me. I felt uncomfortable, but the preacher would not let me off the hook. He kept his eyes on me, saying, "Come to Jesus! Come to Jesus! Little lambs, come to Jesus! All you that labor and are heavy-laden, come to Jesus!"

So magnetic were his eyes and so emotional was his plea that I felt myself getting up and going toward the front of the church. I did not feel saved, but I felt relieved that I was no longer under the glare of the preacher. As I walked, the church members exclaimed, "Thank the Lord! Thank the Lord!" They were happy that I had come forth to confess my sins and become a member of the church.

I was ushered to a seat on the front pew, and I waited there. Soon other people, older people, were coming to the front pew as well. They sat there next to me, looking like they were sorry for something they had done. I was the only one who wanted to be baptized; the others wanted to repent for their sins. I later discovered that they had already been baptized but had strayed away from the straight-and-narrow way.

A cadre of brothers and sisters came around me as I made my confession that I was a sinner and wanted to be baptized. They prayed—some even shouted aloud—and walked with me to the door at the back of the baptismal pool. Before I went into the changing room, I glanced up at the picture of Jesus, a white Jesus, hanging over the baptismal pool. Inside the changing room I took off my white Sunday clothes and put on the white baptismal gown. With the big exception that I was black, I looked like the Jesus in the picture over the pool.

When Brother Stanley stepped into the water and reached out his eager pink hand for my young hand, I could feel the seriousness of the occasion, as no one in the audience said anything. I could only hear the breaking of the water as I stepped in the pool. Then Brother Stanley boomed, "In the name of the Lord Jesus Christ, I baptize you," and he plunged me beneath the cool water, and when I came up, I was supposed to be a new person, but the only thing I felt was wet.

I came out of the baptismal pool, changed my clothes, and went out into the audience, where I was received as a new member of the church and a child of God. For the first time I had received the mark of difference from my peers. They were still just young sinners, but I was in the saved category. People came up to me to pat me on the back and shake my hand. Some even told me what I needed to do to remain faithful to my calling. I only knew that I was not a little boy anymore; I had confessed Jesus, and now I was on the road to heaven.

It would be a while before I realized how phony the system was, when white and black people served the same god and yet the god seemed to favor the white people. This was not a religion for me. The vestiges of racism, like appendages, are found in every sector of the American nation, including the church—evidence, it seems to me, that the system is bogus.

As a child, I did not know what purpose the church served—that is, why it was in our community or how it saw its role in the midst of the foul air of racial hatred. What was it meant to be, to do? How were we to respond to its existence in the midst of our weekly life? I could not ignore it because I was thrust into it by my mother and father, who did not make a big practice of going to church themselves.

Not long after I was baptized, I discovered a dead sparrow by the side of our house. I picked the stiff bird up and showed it to my brothers Esakenti and Paul. None of us knew how it had died; it was a mystery. Sparrows were plentiful, but this was the first time that I had seen a dead one. I surmised after a while that the bird had flown straight into the window, misjudging the glass for air. What poor luck, I thought.

There was only one thing to do: we had to bury the bird, just like people were buried. Someone had to read something or say something, and someone had to dig a hole in the ground, and we would have to bury the sparrow. My brothers and I carried out the funeral, but there were no great lamentations, only a sense of finality now that the bird had been placed in the earth to become dust. We were simply acting out the protocol that our church had taught us.

I was preeminently a child of the Westside Church of Christ in Valdosta, although I traveled with my grandfather to other church sites. As early as I could remember, I was in the midst of all the activities of the church; it gave me my early definition of the world, of Satan, of Jesus Christ, and of the painting of the long-haired white man praying at Gethsemane over the baptismal pool, who I swore looked like a

Ku Klux Klanner with a beard. Some Sunday mornings, I felt like we were all rejoicing in heaven—the righteous way the singing, preaching, and shouting came together in one Holy Communion of believers. But I don't ever remember believing in the "sweet Jesus" of the pictures on the church walls. I knew that Jesus could not have been white because I had never heard of any white person with the qualities of Jesus. The stranger whose picture was over the baptismal pool was as out of place as the green lightbulb someone had placed in the ceiling just over the water.

Because we were in the right church—that is, the Scriptural church—we were not supposed to get "carried away" like the Sanctified Church or even the Baptist Church people. No, the churches of Christ were serious about their religion and had to study the scriptures in order to keep on the straight and narrow; it just happened that most of the people I knew had a hard time keeping on the way. However, in Valdosta a famous preacher, Marshall Keeble, baptized the people in our church, which gave them a certain status in the community. Keeble was one of the most famous preachers of the time. My grandfather was one of those who had come out of the Baptist Church. Keeble was a soft-talking, short brown man with a sharp wit. His precise use of parables, anecdotes, and everyday experiences brought audiences close to him. He could charm a snake out of a hole with his humor, proverbs, stories, and down-home ways.

One old church member, Mrs. Gray, who had heard Keeble preach many times, told me, "I did not know Jesus, but I knew Keeble many years after his transforming presence in Valdosta. If Jesus was anything like Keeble, he was calm most of the time—that is, even-tempered—except when the stroke of fire that was his passion flashed out and struck those whom he believed had strayed." Keeble's quick change of temperament was legendary. He could be so calm that you could depend on him to be rational over most issues, but if something was contrary to his beliefs, he would react with definite condemnation. Yet he was not considered a hell-and-fire type of preacher. He was often called bold, by which people meant he might embarrass you with his utter truthfulness.

Marshall Keeble's appearance in Valdosta was monumental in the African American community; no more famous black person had ever visited the city. Keeble came into town with the charisma of his oratorical talents and reputation for debate on full display.

He came to the city in 1933 to establish the Church of Christ in the black community. He preached every night for nearly three weeks, and when they were over, he had made 266 converts to his brand of Christianity. My grandfather, Moses, was one of those who "accepted the Lord" during Keeble's revival. Our family was "Baptist born and Baptist bred," but by the time Keeble finished his tough preaching, Granddaddy Moses and his wife did not want to be "Baptist dead," or die as Baptists, because they believed that the Church of Christ was the right church. By the 1950s we were not Baptist in name, but there was still much Baptist left in us, so that when the singing and preaching got the church rocking, the sisters and some brothers in the amen corner shouted all over the church, saying, "Hallelujah! Hallelujah!" Shouters were usually looked upon with some disdain because it was contrary to the scriptural way Church of Christ people saw religion; it was not supposed to be emotional. Of course, it was hard to keep emotion out of the church because most African Americans had responded to singing and preaching with intercalations and shouts from the beginning of Christianity in the community.

I was awestruck by this phenomenon, believing it meant God had come right down in front of us in the spirit, because we couldn't see him, and entered the holiest people who showed his presence in the graceful African vigor of their spiritual dancing. I felt particularly righteous, blessed because of my easy access to the divine. I loved the virtuousness, the holiness of the women in the white shouting dresses, and the amen corner where bald old men sat and recited the scriptures as the preacher spoke for long rhythmic spans.

At the same time, with all the religiosity surrounding me, I was still uncomfortable with much of it, not knowing truly what was real and what was not, who was spiritual and who was a fake. I thought, however, that I was authentic, that even if I failed to live up to the high commands and demands of the faith, I could come so close that anyone looking at me would have to declare that I was next to holy. It was a child's wish.

My young faith caused my family and friends to honor me as someone who had been fortunate, perhaps born with a blessing, called forth from the ancestors as foretold by the caul. I accepted that uniqueness, believed it, and thought of myself as driven by supernatural energy. My blackness was my badge of adoration. It was because I was black that I was blessed. I was strong, I was intelligent, and I was predictably spiritual, perhaps even destined to be a preacher, the highest calling for the fortunate black male in southern Georgia.

In the earliest moments of my church experience, even before I had accepted Jesus and been baptized, I went to church with my younger siblings. Walking into the huge frame church building, I was always amazed at how many beautifully dressed people were packed inside. The building had been the greatest dance hall in the city; it was now the biggest church in the black community. I could point out the sisters who would do the holy shout that Sunday because they were all dressed alike in long white dresses. I found my seat near the front of the church building, among men suited down with black and brown suits that were accented with red and yellow ties. My joy at being among the elders was explosive, like peonies that come to life in a blaze of bloom, only to fall back to the common and ordinary.

I was clearly convinced that my own qualities as a spiritual person meant that my community would protect, appreciate, and accept me. It was not a false thought. Almost everything that I wanted came to exist. Of course, at that age most of what I wished, dreamed, or desired for was about my family. I wanted my father and mother at home together for Christmas. This may seem like a petty exuberance, but it was pretty important to me. My father, who had been staying away from the house, came home with gifts on Christmas Eve and remained with the family for several days before leaving again. I was ecstatic. My mother said that I was lucky, born with good fortune because of the veil over my face at my birth. Other people said it was the rabbit's foot that I wore around my ankle. Still others testified that the bit of tallow around the snake's tooth that my mother put around my neck when I was a baby was what did the trick. Even then, I was on the road back to Africa like the Ibo people who walked into the sea with chains around their ankles and wrists when they were off-loaded on the coast of Georgia. I just did not know it.

Of course, I had my moments of mischief, periods of trouble, and times of conflict. I was about nine years old, in the third grade, when I learned the lesson that good did not necessarily win out every time. One of my classmates, a girl, took her chewing gum out of her mouth and put it on my new oxford shoes. I told the teacher, Mrs. Gamble, who reprimanded her. When school was out, the girl tore my shirt and punched me in the face; I was twice humiliated in one day. I continued to always tell the truth, but I found it increasingly hard to deny the fact that telling the truth or being right did not mean that you could avoid attacks.

This was reinforced when one sunny day in the same year, Ms. Gamble was teaching us mathematics, and while she was writing on the blackboard, someone in our class threw a piece of chalk toward her. She looked at the chalk as it fell near her, swung around, and threw the eraser at me. It dusted my new gray sweater. I protested that I had not thrown the chalk, but it did not matter—she thought I had. It was one of the occasions on which I was accused of something that I did not do but had to accept the consequences anyway. My early commitment to religion would never have allowed me to conceive of such an action against the teacher, but alas, Ms. Gamble did not know that about me. I would become a true believer.

I came to love the moment of religious possession as one of the peak experiences of the African American culture in Georgia. It never happened to me, but one day it almost did. I could feel myself carried away on the wings of joy as the church sang, over and over again, "Were you there when they crucified my Lord, were you there?" Had I not been so concrete, so logical, so full of explanations, perhaps at that moment I would have gotten up and performed the Nigerian stomp all over the church. As it was, I just sat there with tears of ecstasy flowing down my face.

I later experienced the same emotion listening to Cannonball Adderley and Nina Simone perform. Cannonball Adderley died before I got the chance to tell him about the feeling his jazz had given me, but I was able to talk to Nina Simone when I gave her a reception at my home when I lived in Buffalo. Nina would often tell people, "I am not your therapist," and yet her music remained one of the most therapeutic interventions in the African American community for a long time. She was a black woman performing out of the depth of her soul. Her death was a great loss.

Perhaps the whitest man I ever saw in our church was Brother Stanley. In my mind, he was the Ashley Street priest, but he was also the most available and most loved stand-in preacher when the real preacher was out of town. When the Westside Church located on West Adair Street did not have a preacher, they did not call my grandfather, probably because of his eclectic African and Christian beliefs and his strict, hard, sometimes confrontational style, but instead they called Brother Stanley.

Stanley was a slight-built man, about five feet ten inches, who frequently appeared in church with his short, kinky blond hair shaved very close. Always with his Bible under his arm, he was the perfect, unthreatening example of the desexed African, even to other Africans. He was a plain, simple man, a straight, quiet person who spoke in a slow monotone that would generally put half of the church to sleep by the time he called sinners forward. He did not mind that he put us to sleep; his was the work of a journeyman who did what he was asked to do. He knew the scriptures well enough to quote many of them by memory, and although no one ever considered him for the permanent ministerial post, on more than one occasion when there was no minister, he had to step in and lull us to sleep with his monotonous voice.

I would leave Valdosta and return many times, each time becoming more convinced that had the whites been able to put aside their prejudice, Valdosta would have been a model city. There is a sort of infectious energy in the way the sun strikes the tall, elegant pine trees or tends to linger over the fishing streams and dance on the cotton plants. I did not find the land or the environment oppressive; rather, I found it pathetic, unfortunate, and sad. So beautiful and pregnant with possibilities for the human race and yet so tainted with a conspiracy of hatred, racism, and white hostility against Africans. Valdosta was not to be trusted with one's emotions.

Too many oak trees had seen too many murders; I was afraid to walk down the dirt roads at night because of the hanging bodies residing in the inner recesses of my mind. And, for reasons of safety and security, it was best that whites remained on their side of the city and we remained on ours. After all, there did not seem to be anything that they had that we wanted during my childhood. Later, however, would come the swimming pool built for white children and the library that did not admit black children, and I would understand more about the lingering nature of racism and the wanton demands of emotional and moral vulgarity in this azalea-laden town.

Years later Alex Haley came along and challenged us to think about the meaning of Africans in America. It brought me back to the superstitions, taboos, rituals of innocence, fights, dances, and ceremonies in Valdosta's dank cotton fields, wet with the thick morning mists. The world we lived in seemed so surreal, like it existed a million years ago, and yet it was only yesterday in the Deep South when we learned how to protect ourselves from misfortune when the sun went down.

There were so many things that we knew we shouldn't do that we could have created our own Bible from the old people's sayings. I was afraid to split a pole; that is, when you approach a tree or pole with a friend, each of you would go to a different side of the pole. There was something about the energy of that tree or pole that should not be separated or else your mother would get sick. I always looked out for black cats crossing in front of me. Even if the cat appeared dark brown, not quite black, that was good enough for me to go in another direction. I just knew it was bad luck! When the sun was shining and it was raining at the same time, I just went into the house and let nature run its course because the devil was beating his wife. It was not my fight, and I did not want to be caught in the middle.

We were surrounded, it seemed, by unseen forces out to get us. We didn't know where they came from, but there were enough of them to keep young people worried about the possibility of violating an unwritten law. Looking back, I find it interesting that this system ran parallel to biblical traditions, but the two were never integrated. The old people did not say, "The Bible says such-and-such" when it came to these beliefs. They just told the superstitions as if they were fact, independent of anything else. Of course, a lot of these traditions were based on the root traditions of Africa.

Children could be protected from evil spirits and bad upbringing by appealing to supernatural forces. We lived in the United States of America, but we were descended from people who had not been Christians long; most of the black people in Georgia had been Christians for less than a hundred years. In my family, on my mother's side, it had been less than fifty. So, beginning when they were infants, giving children something to protect them was a normal practice. The old people did not think it was against the Bible's teaching. They didn't even consider the Bible in the equation; it was just something that you had to do.

If you really wanted to protect a child, you had to give him some special amulet. From the time I could remember I had a rabbit's foot tied around my neck or my ankle to ward off diseases and bad luck. This was a ritual of innocence meant to demonstrate to the natural world that I was a protected child. I must have been around school age before my parents removed my talisman.

I came to believe that with so many infants dying, the African community had to devise a way of challenging the sickness. As my family saw it, sacrifice was the ultimate action a poor community could take, and therefore, they had to demonstrate their willingness to do something to appease whatever evil or disease lurked in the pathway of their young.

I have contemplated Valdosta many days and nights because there was something special there for me—something magical, playful, and happy, and in my limited community, though I did not know it then, I was confident, self-possessed, and smart. My mother said I was intelligent, that I could read at four; in fact, the midwife had seen the birthmarks in my eyes and declared I would be smart right from the spanking moment. She was also the one who removed the veil, the birth caul, from my face and declared that I would be able to see things others could not. I guess I felt an obligation from an early age to examine the history and heritage of my people. As soon as I could read, I tried to read everything, and what interested me most were the lyrics to the Spirituals and the blues as well as the poetry of James Weldon Johnson.

I soon mastered "The Creation," and became one of the best interpreters of that poem by the time I was ten. I was beginning to find a voice—someone else's voice but a voice nevertheless—that would inspire me with poetry and eloquence. I also read and loved Langston Hughes; he sang so purely about the things we felt, and although he was a northerner—that is, from Kansas—he seemed to understand the way African Americans in the South saw the world. Not since

Paul Laurence Dunbar had we seen a poet of the people like Langston Hughes. I remember my father and mother talking about "When Malindy Sings," Dunbar's famous poem. And when I was thirteen, I learned the poem, "The Debt" and forever held Paul Laurence Dunbar in my heart as a master poet.

Zora Neale Hurston was the Alexander Pushkin of South Georgia and North Florida; she was a master of listening to the voice of the people and making that voice serve a universal purpose. We could not exist without knowing that she existed; such had been the devastation of our existence in the deepest part of the South. The old people sitting around the canal pylon on West Street would say, "Dat ol' gal named Zora show done told dem white people the truth about how we is." Was this a type of redemptionism for us? Perhaps, because we truly believed that black people could do anything and be anything they wanted to be if it were not for racism and segregation.

I will never forget how proud we were when the Pompey girls went to Spelman College. They leaped ahead of the class. They could not attend Valdosta State College; it was segregated and off-limits to blacks. There was a rumor that they lynched a black man for walking on the campus. Even if this was not true, enough had happened to blacks in the Azalea City to make it true anyway.

Strident racist voices yelling "niggers" at us, like Viking spears attacking our bodies and our minds, and shouts of anger as we passed by indicated that they did not care if we were just children walking; as far as the whites were concerned we were in alien territory just walking on the sidewalk near the college. We counted the brutal dislike for us as one more indication that white people were crazy.

We learned early that there was lots of what my grandmother would call "educated fools." They were not all white, but it seemed that there were far more white "educated fools" in that part of the world than anywhere else. We didn't have too many other places to use for comparison, we only knew the white folks of Valdosta. There was no diversity in the white population: there were no Italians, Portuguese, French, Russians—only Anglo-Saxons. The Anglo-Saxons we knew usually had arrogant demeanors and were not educated. Nevertheless, they acted foolishly when it came to African people.

They would cheat us out of our money when we worked, they would curse our elders when they complained, and they would threaten us with death if we insisted on our humanity. They were callous, cold, and without passion.

Because I was considered a bright child, some of the parents on Oliver Street asked me to tutor their sons and daughters. Our street must have had the most beautiful girls in the world. When I was about fourteen and back home in Valdosta from NCI for the summer to pick cotton, I thought that the two girls who lived at opposite ends of our street were the most wonderful creatures on the earth. Gaynell lived to the east of our house, and Jackie lived to the west.

Tutoring the boys was alright, but I enjoyed tutoring the girls. They were lots of fun—giggling all the time, full of wonder and mystery, attendant to detail, and willing to listen. I did not see that at that age I had already formed a gendered socialization for the girls. They were not rough, did not like to fight, and were eager to do well in school. Boys just felt differently about the world—at least that is what I thought. So whenever I was around Gaynell or Jackie, I felt good inside. When the lessons were over, we played up and down the street, ventured across West Street, and dug for worms under the tall houses.

Girls always seemed to have such stunning powers over boys. I soon fell victim, and Jackie and Gaynell knew how to tease me with their charm. Gaynell was short for her age, almost a reddish tan, and already at twelve you could tell that she would be a beautiful woman. Jackie was taller, with a light chocolate complexion and a winning smile. All the boys seemed to like Jackie because it was rumored she knew how to kiss; I got slapped trying to kiss Jackie one night in the back of our house. Gaynell was just my friend. I took them inside our house for teacakes, and we played late into the summer nights until one of our parents would call us inside. The amber lights flickered like distant stars as we traveled home down the mostly dirt roads.

My father was a blues man, always singing the blues early in the morning to get the children moving. At least that is what he told us, but I always had my own beliefs. I thought that childhood memories brought on his blues. He would often sing Spirituals, but the blues took him inside his truest emotions and brought him face to face with the reality of being African in the American South. He was the blues descendant of Bessie Smith, Honeyboy, Big Joe Williams, John Lee Hooker, and Lightnin' Hopkins.

I grew up with the blues and Spirituals because the conditions in the South were blues conditions—in our house, on our street, in our community, all over the city of flowers. We were in a tragic situation as Africans in a country ruled by whites who wanted to keep us from advancing. The blues were all around us. On Sunday morning the Spirituals were sung in churches to ease the blues condition, but there was just more blues than Spirituals.

My father must have gotten the blues when he was about ten years old, during the depression of 1929. My father talked a lot about "The Great Depression" as if it were something epochal, and it was for most of the people in the United States at that time. It was worse in the South than in the North, and it was worst among blacks in both places. My father had lived only a decade when the Depression hit, but he always spoke of it and sang of it as if it had consumed all of his young adult life. He had to quit school to help his family survive; I heard the story many times. All of his blues singing had a stinging element of pathos that moved the slow cadence of his songs to a mournful tone. Nothing could release him from the essence of his life; that is, the overriding blues of his existence seemed to burden him all during my childhood, stamping him with a range of metaphors for dogged determination.

The basic pattern of my father's blues remained the same, but he could change his themes with the seasons. Sometimes he would sing summertime blues, and other times he would sing wintertime blues, all the while using his hands for percussion. I think there must have been only two seasons in Valdosta at that time. Even if he woke up happy, he would sing the blues because, as he later explained to me, if you don't have the blues yourself, somebody in your family or someone you know does. I do not know, even now, how I escaped the melancholy that comes with singing the blues or hearing it as often as I did. I guess I appreciated the artistic quality of the music, the nature of the repetition, and the texture of the blues voice without really buying into the lyrics except as poetry: authentic, but not necessarily something to which one could aspire.

My mother, however, loved the Spirituals. The rule was morning was for blues, and the rest of the day was for Spirituals. Night was for reading, studying, homework, and talk—lots of talk. I did not get a chance to hear any "sinful" music until my big sister April started buying a few records that we could sneak off to play. When she won the dance contest at a local circus, we became the "do the huckabuck family." We were celebrities, or at least April was a celebrity because she could "wobble like a duck," and I was her little brother. It was never rock and roll or rhythm in our house; rather, it was the down-home, gut-bucket blues or the rejubilated Spirituals à la the Fisk Jubilee Singers.

However, blues reigned in the household. "Ain' got no dollars, ain' got no cent / I said I ain' got no dollar, ain' got a cent / Well I ain' got no dollar, ain' got no cent / But Lordy, Lordy, I got to pay my rent." Arthur Smith was the king of the blues on Oliver Street and had the habit of making up songs as people walked into the house, in the tradition of the West African djelis—often called griots—the calypso singers of Trinidad, and the best of the discoursing rap poets. His songs were commentaries on everything and anything. If it could be discussed, it could be discussed in song. Nevertheless, I do not recall many overtly political songs or songs that attacked the system itself—the racist, segregated system that maintained white dominance. The songs normally spoke to the emotions of black people, to their cultural pathos. The conditions that brought about those bluesy feelings were never really examined.

My father's blues were indirect protest—not for the public but for his family. They were a narrative of what was and what could be. When I did think about the blues, I thought of them as literature, as narration about life, as someone being after something possible to attain but yet just out of reach. Whatever deprivations of spirit moved my father to sing, once he had finished his song, he was ready to confront the world.

Between my father's blues and my mother's Spirituals and both of them creating a spirit of song in the house, I got a good dose of African American culture off-key. I think I even understood how jazz arose from blues and Spirituals at a very early age because of the insistent pathos of just living with both genres. If blues were considered pursuit and Spirituals spoke of dreamlands, jazz was what was happening now.

I could hear my father at daybreak, sounding the alarm for people in the house to wake up: "Woke up this mornin' / Col' as it could be, woke up this mornin' / Col' as it could be, well I woke up this morning col' as it could be / And told my children, I might as well be free."

When I heard my father sing, my spirit would always fly out of the boarded-up windows and circulate among the tall pine trees and little squat oaks; conversely, my mother's Spirituals somehow kept my spirit right at home. There was peace in that quaint, worn, high-off-the-ground, shotgun shack in those early days. Later, when I was about fourteen, I could see a factor causing my father to sing blues and my mother to sing, "Steal away, steal away, steal away to Jesus": my father's son, older than me by one year, whom I never knew.

My mother would use him as ammunition when she was angry with my father. It didn't matter to me once I had heard it because I never saw the boy. Anyway, my mother had had three children before she married my father: having children had little to do with anything except living in Georgia and finding intimacy and love where you could, and children were the greatest blessings in the world. This was the African spirit asserting and, in the case of my family, reasserting itself. Again and again. Deep-down blues and high-flying Spirituals came out of these situations.

My father's family was a family of warriors and lovers. It was rumored that Plenty Smith's old man may have been killed near Andersonville trying to assist the Union troops. Plenty's son Moses's reputation as a "bad man" had come as a result of his adolescent and young-adult tussles over women and money. But Plenty had a more violent temper than his son and had killed a man over a woman.

My father told the story of his grandfather as if he had been present when all the action occurred. It was a steamy August evening when John—my father did not remember his last name—visited Plenty at his farm. He accused Plenty of sleeping with the man's lady, and Plenty never admitted nor denied it. John pulled a shotgun out of his buggy and told Plenty that he was going to kill him, but before he could get off a shot, Plenty shot him with a Smith & Wesson pistol. The man fell where he stood, dead.

When the sheriff, who in those days was always white, came to the farm, it was agreed that Plenty Smith had shot the man in self-defense.

He was never charged, and no one ever accused him again of messing with their women, which, I was told, he was known to do.

There had been so much blues in my family. My favorite uncles, blues lovers, had fought in America's wars. Moses Jr., like DeBuddy, decided to go to war right out of high school. Nothing could have kept them away from fighting the Germans, so demonic had the military painted the Nazis. My uncles felt that to fight to rid the world of Nazism was fighting to rid the world of racism. This was, of course, youthful exuberance. When they returned to Valdosta after the war, they went on singing the blues. So my father, even without military experience, came by his singing blues spirit righteously because it found its way to all the men in his family. They were confident, confrontational defenders of the underdog and were always willing to stand by their word, and they were tragically deep blues men who tried to understand their social and racial condition until each one in course found bitterness that needed to be expressed in song.

My mother's singing the Spirituals and my father's singing the blues almost every day had a lasting impact on me. So when I learned that my father had briefly lived with another woman in Kill-Me-Quick and was drawn to my mother by her physical beauty only to find that she had many other suitors, I understood another source of the blues and Spirituals. Kill-Me-Quick was legendary in my childhood imagination as a place where you could get killed quickly. It was a desolate area of shacks that slid under the south side of the railroad tracks like a Rio favela on the side of a hill, but there was no hill here—only twenty or thirty places of abode that housed the most destitute families. As poor as we were, we believed ourselves to be better off living on the west side. And yet my father found his way to some solace in the dark, dank, smoky backrooms of Kill-Me-Quick.

Of course, as my father told me later, he was crushed, saddened, and angered by my mother's freedom, though it could have only been a patriarch's regret. My mother, however, a remarkably attractive woman in her youth, had watched my father's antics with the young women of town—sporting his father's old car, dressing in the latest styles, and being "as free as a butterfly."

The Smiths were not rich, but they were thrifty and skillful, plus the three boys, Arthur, Moses Jr., and DeBuddy, all worked. Georgia, their younger sister, was studious and was often left to read and keep the house clean. My father, the oldest boy, was not wild, as the people say, but he was clearly into the ladies.

When she was in one of her talkative moods, which was often, my mother would enter the kitchen, push open the back door to let in fresh air in, and turn to April or me and declare her resentment that my father had continued his romancing long after I was born. Then she would break out singing something like, "Soon I will be done wid de troubles of the worl'."

Our house was not large: a front room, a back room, a kitchen, and a bathroom. You could hear conversations throughout; sometimes the marital arguments in the amber twilight produced by kerosene lamps or the one long electric light in the middle of the ceiling would be surreal, like you were in somebody else's passion. Sometimes the noise drove me outside, and I usually went to sit under the old, crinkled black walnut tree that stood on the edge of our property. April and Vera had formed a comfortable spot from cardboard and leaves there, and we often went there for solace from the increasing arguments between my father and mother.

It was hard for me, the eldest boy, to take the riveting news that came out frequently in my parents' arguments. They blamed each other for sexual infidelities, and this eventually led to separation and a split in the immediate family that would lead to a period of familial disintegration. Unlike some families brought to ruin by alcohol, wasteful spending, and physical abuse, our family saw disintegration because of mutual recriminations. Neither my father nor my mother drank alcohol or had money to waste, but both were consummate arguers. They took the art of stubbornness to the highest level of disrespect. To give in to the other was considered weakness, and in this family no one wanted to show weakness; perishing with arrogance and haughtiness was a more predictable outcome.

April, with a thirst for life—my mother's child—often found me in the yard. She was very close to mother and was at times our surrogate mother, so we called her "Little Mama." A riot of energy and spirit, she would grab me by the arm and begin to sing, dance, and laugh, cajoling me until we were both laughing hilariously.

April consoled all of us when we cried, wiping away our tears with her bare hands. She had always been the comforter in our family. Born with a keen sense of right and wrong and always supporting the underdog, April was eager to keep the children together. When she worked at S and K Restaurant as a teenager, we would all wait up for her because we knew she would bring food, stories about white people's habits, and laughter. My first French fries, onion rings, and shrimps were gifts from April's teenage job. She spent her childhood making other people happy.

So here she was, under the old walnut tree, as beautiful as any young woman in Valdosta, standing beside me with her arm over my shoulder, just laughing. My mother, far from pious, stood in the back door and, with a stern countenance, asked, "What y'all laughing at?" And we said, "Nothin." And my mother started to sing, "Swing Low, Sweet Chariot." My father's singing voice was silent; the argument was over.

Not long afterward I asked my mother if I could go over to my grandparents' house for the weekend. I knew the way by heart, like I had been born with the way; I never knew a time when I did not know the way to Gaynor Street from Oliver Street. I would go down to the corner and cut to the left, heading for the tobacco warehouses where the old white men who chewed tobacco spit out the auction numbers. Then I would cut left again, just before the Philip Morris sign, and then make a quick right that brought me alongside the longest warehouse, which was on my right side, and Uncle Alex and Aunt Sally's house was on the left. Then I would run across Hill Avenue and into the no-man's-land between the white folks' section of town and the railroad tracks. Once I got to the tracks I was home free. I could see the bend in Gaynor Street where the chinaberry and mulberry trees grew.

I enjoyed my grandfather's jokes and stories about herbs, his adventures in Dayton, Ohio, and my grandmother's cooking. I also loved going out of town with my grandfather. So any time I could I would ask permission to go to Granddaddy's house. Of course, he would put me to work on some project in the backyard when we were not traveling up and down Highway 41. I would cut the gourds from the vines along the fence, plant tomato seedlings, or chop wood. He always found something for me to do so that I would not have an idle mind. I loved it when he would say, "Boy, let's go." I do not think he ever called me by my name—maybe by my nickname a few times, but he could use "Boy."

Grandfather Moses would turn his long black Buick northward along the highway, through the heavy thickness of what was left of the American apartheid system. We couldn't stop at the restrooms in the small towns, eat at many of the restaurants along the highway, or get lost in a white neighborhood. We were heading straight through the regime of madness to Great-granddaddy's big farm, going to another "Second Sunday in August" meeting at the old family church in Dooly County. The county may have changed from year to year, but the change was imperceptible except in some cases of social change. In this county it was as if time were born here and did not leave. I always felt the old oppressiveness of the Spanish-mossed South. I felt tension in the air when the whites seemed scared to serve food to blacks, even from the side windows of white-only restaurants. I saw every white highway patrolman as a potential member of the Ku Klux Klan. It took a long time for bitter memories to fade.

Through time, I felt that many of the old attitudes remained, hidden under the smiles that were replacing the frowns when whites saw blacks. When we first started going to Dooly County, there were separate toilet facilities for blacks and whites. There were separate water fountains at the gas stations, and some places would only feed the whites but not the blacks. Soon, in the state of Georgia there would be no colored-only and white-only water fountains and no separate toilet facilities, but in the summer of 1958, those transformations had not yet come. The Civil Rights struggle would have to be waged to release us from the bondage of Southern custom.

We passed through Vienna, Lilly, and Montezuma, named for some Austrian or French or Aztec memory, to get to the old family homestead. Pecan trees and peanut fields rimmed Dooly County—our county.

In the backwoods of Dooly County, a forest of pine trees and quickly running streams, I found many sources of family lore. I met the Shines, my paternal great-grandmother's family, and I went to see the house where my father grew up. But the keeper of traditions was J. T. Spivey, whom I called Uncle, although he was really my father's first cousin. In keeping with the African tradition, first cousins were treated like siblings, so he really was my uncle. And like the other men in our family, he seemed to have avoided any direct contact with whites over a long period of time. They were not central to his existence, as they had not been central to Plenty's or to Moses's. The Smiths were farmers who worked their own land.

Like the Wolof, Yoruba, and Akan people of West Africa, the Smiths came to realize that land cultivation was akin to the very touching of the divine. The thick, black dirt, rich with minerals, was the laboratory for the morality, relationships, ethics, and productivity of the Smith family. That dirt was so rich that it looked like oil would come flowing right out of it. It was blacker than midnight, and we thought all dirt that was so black had to be fertile.

As I remember it, much of our dignity as a family was wrapped up in the 150 acres of land that Plenty had inherited. You do not understand how land can tie a family to traditions until you no longer have land. Plenty and Hattie Smith lived right in the middle of their land.

Just beyond the woods, behind the old, awkward, gangly, rambling, ancient house, flowed a cold, clear, silvery stream. It ran through the tall slender stand of pine trees that stole time from my youth and gave voice to the many years when my grandfather Plenty had hunted deer, rabbit, and raccoon in the thickets at the feet of the trees. I loved that nameless stream because somewhere in its ancient run over the dead leaves and stone-gray rocks were the memories of my ancestors' struggle against extraordinary inhumanity. It had seen everything that I had missed because it was running long before I was born. But now I was here, always in the summers of my youth, looking into its memorable mirrored body as a witness to my own time.

My cousins and I would run down to the stream and toss rocks into its murky bosom. We would count the ripples, watching each one fade. It was not large enough for swimming, but it was great for wading. The cocoa-brown sand would churn to the top as we treaded through the stream. It was the best of youth, unencumbered by worry, fear, or dread.

We marched uphill, back to the old house, and played in the big yard. Here we could have been in the rain forest near Tafo in Ghana. There were no white people to disturb our peace, demand attention, or threaten us if we did this or that. There was no fear, no frustration, no lies, no rumors, no worries that we as children knew anything about. The adults did not share their fears or shame with us; they protected us from whatever worries they had. Timelessly, we played throughout the day and into the dusk.

Years later I would go to Dooly County many times and meet with my uncle, who had become the real, official keeper of the family secrets. He rationalized all the things I experienced as a young boy. Uncle J. T. was about six feet four inches tall, wiry, and with angular features betraying what I thought was Akan background until the DNA test. Plenty was his grandfather, and I could tell that he relished the time he had spent sitting at the old man's feet, listening to him talk about how he came to own property in the middle of one of America's most racist counties. He could make the stories as exciting as Plenty had. Aunt Jessie Bell just smiled at J. T. as he rubbed the head of little Vickie, my cousin, while telling the family stories.

One day, when I was very young, he said to me, "Come on, boy, and go with me. I want to show you something." He drove me over a few bluffs, around some bends, and across a couple of bridges and then we stopped. Pointing to a long, shuttered building no larger than a small log cabin, he said, "Right over there was where the white man had his grocery store. Ol' man Lester. He was the one who all the black folk went to when they wanted to buy food. Everybody owed him. They called him Boss Man Lester, but he didn't do no work but run his store."

"Any blacks work for him?"

"No, they just called him Boss Man."

"Why Boss Man?" I asked.

"'Cause you had to show any white man respect, whether you worked for him or not, else they would mark you," J. T. answered.

"Did Great-granddaddy Plenty call him Boss Man too?" I asked, curious because Plenty was considered the leader of the black community.

"No, I can't recall Plenty ever going in there. If he needed anything, he would send me or Moses, but he would consider no white man his boss."

J. T. enjoyed the role of historian. Always holding the legacies of the people, he was the recorder and observer, the type of person the Mandinka call djeli, an African sage with the keen wisdom and insight of a hundred generations, as if he had always been here. As solid as the sycamore tree that stood in his backyard, J. T. Spivey was the prime example of a Yoruba-Muskogee mixture. One could see it all in him. The lines in his face told of his Yoruba past, like his forehead revealed his Muskogee background. His chiseled lips reminded everyone that he was also descended from Yoruba. His radiant handsomeness was legendary; he attracted people with his straightforward manner and gentle spirit.

He greeted me warmly when I visited him the summer of 1979. "Boy, look at you! Ain't you something now!" he almost shouted in that high falsetto voice that African Americans use to express happiness at seeing someone. Aunt Jessie Bell, her golden skin radiant with shea butter, stood next to him, a whole foot shorter, beaming with joy. When she said she was doing "tolerably well," I wanted to ask if she was sick but did not because I also learned very early to keep your mouth shut if you do not know how to ask something.

My Uncle J. T. stood to the side watching me as I talked to Aunt Jessie Bell. We embraced again and kept shouting in those falsetto voices that characterize real excitement. We took turns praising how the other looked and spoke about the family members who were off in other parts of the world, those who were making the family proud, those who were dead, and those who were in trouble with the law.

I wanted to become like him—the chronicler of the family, the one who knew the stories and could reveal the intimate details told by those who lived the lives of the countryside. But I knew I had to wait until my turn came. There were many before me all of my older sisters, Juanita, Lucille, and April, and others in my family who lived much closer to the soil than I ever did. They were the raconteurs who would define the meaning of family in its most reverent ways. There I was as a young man, sitting at the feet of one of the best. I could not tell what I did not know, and it would take many meetings and many conversations with Uncle J. T. before I could venture to tell his stories. So I sought him out and teased him to speak. And when Aunt Jessie Bell had left for the kitchen, I would urge Uncle J. T. to talk some more. And speak he did.

"You see, I was the one male child left on the farm when everyone had grown up. All the girls had left also, so it was me and Granddaddy working this farm. I was young, didn't know nothing but the fields. I believed that the hard work was what kept me sane. All the time I was plowing those fields, acres and acres of them, walking behind that old mule, I was thinking, reflecting, writing in my mind, plotting to change the world.

"On Sunday morning Plenty would go to church and make out like he was a saint, when in fact, during the week he had been quite mean, quite demanding of me. I loved that old man, but he had a mean streak in him. He didn't want you to slack up a bit when you were out there in that farm. I worked real hard, night and day, making something of those peanuts. When y'all would come up here, it made me happy because then I knew I could relax a bit, have some fun, listen to some people talk about what was going on in the big cities like Valdosta and Tifton."

At night Uncle J. T. and I walked the quiet road outside his house and talked. I was eager to tell him about what had happened to me since I left Georgia, but I was more eager to hear more about our family history from him. The road was dark; I had never seen it so black dark in the United States. Later I would find that Africa still had black nights, but here I was in Dooly County, Georgia, thinking that James Weldon Johnson's "Creation" song of darkness "blacker than a hundred midnights down in a cypress swamp" must have imagined this place.

One could almost feel that the universe was created in the black of night in Dooly County. I once heard it said that Dooly County was the most rural county in America, and I believe that it was the darkest county in America at night. If the moon was not shining, it was pitch-black. In Georgia that was the time for serious, authentic talk.

We walked and talked. Then we sat out in the darkness near a large rock to continue to talk. I sat on a small stool carved from a tree trunk, and my uncle sat in a wooden chair near the rock.

He rocked his chair back on its hind legs, rearing it like a Tennessee walking horse as he warmed up to his subject: Plenty Smith, born in 1862. He was "born in slavery" and was three years old when the Civil War ended.

"Yeah, old Plenty was something. You know, when I was a boy, I seen white people right here in Dooly County who brought their sick children to Plenty," said Uncle J. T., staring out into the night.

"For what?" I asked, incredulously.

"For healing, that's what. Plenty could heal the sick, or at least that's what people believed about him. He would chew his tobacco, and when they bring the little white babies and all, he'd spit into their eyes. Then the white people would leave him money, and thank him, and be on their way." I chuckled a "that's silly" laugh, and my uncle said, "Don't laugh. You know lots of people down here believed in old Plenty's power. They'd give him gifts, money, just to consult him."

"Did he practice witchcraft or something?" I asked, ignorant of the old ways.

"Naw, nothing like that. Your great-grandfather was a Christian, a deacon in the church. At least, he went to the church and held a position in it. He paid for the building of Mount Olive Baptist Church himself. All your cousins can tell you that he wasn't a believer in witchcraft; he just had these powers. He couldn't read nor write but he could count. Old Plenty was smart, always talking about Africa, the little he knew."

"Did you believe in his powers?" I asked.

"Well, I know what I seen. And I know that people down here believe that a male child who never lived with his father has powers to heal. The black folks believe it. The white folks believe it, and the few Muskogee Indians living around here believe it too. Plenty Smith didn't live with his father. He knew his mother, everyone did, but few people knew who his father was, and since he never lived with his father, he was thought to have these spiritual powers. So Plenty grew up, according to J. T., spitting in children's eyes. Yes, indeed, he was a real "spitter.""

I took it that Plenty was discreet in the use of his personal power. He was not an activist for social change. That would be left to his wife, Hattie Shine. She came from a family of pure Akans; there was never any question about Hattie Shine's African origins.

I remember being taken to her old home in Montezuma to meet my relatives when I was very young. A proud people with a dignified bearing, they stood like tall cypress trees, thickly grounded but swayed back. Hattie was just like them. She had the same triangled face, almost a perfect V from the chin up the sides of her head. You could tell that her small beady eyes saw everything, but she never gave the impression of seeing much.

One time, when the children were playing in the yard in front of the house, the adults said they wanted us where they could see us. Hattie sat with four or five other adults on the porch. She was in a swing; the rest sat in straight chairs. They were so engrossed in their conversation that we knew they were not looking after us. My sister Vera tried to go to the side of the house out of their view. As soon as she made a move toward the side of the house, Hattie shouted, "You make one step, and your behind belongs to me." We hadn't thought she was looking.

Plenty Smith was whispered to have been the oldest son of a black man held with the Union troops at Andersonville Prison and released when the Civil War ended. His last name was said to have been Smith, though no one seemed to remember his first name. In fact, his name may not have been Smith at all, but Smith was a fairly common name in Georgia, and to name a child born outside of wedlock Smith may have been a common thing to do. Plenty's mother, Frances, went by two other names, Henderson and Chapman, the names of two men she lived with after she had had four children: Plenty Smith, Elijah Simpson, David Turner, and Israel Horne. Ultimately, Frances would give birth to ten additional children. She was the earliest recognized matriarch of our family.

Her eldest son grew to more than six feet tall by the time he was sixteen years old. There was ample reason for his name to be Plenty. We sometime spelled his name Pleni and sometimes Pliny, but most people came to spell it Plenty.

Plenty never knew his father, and none of the members of the old Mount Olive Baptist Church ever spoke openly about the child's ancestry. What was known was known but not repeated. They all whispered that Plenty never lived in the same house with his father and so had unusual powers not possessed by his younger brothers, Elijah, Dave, and Israel, or the ten siblings he ended up having beyond the older boys.

Frances, my great-great-grandmother, was by all estimations a very charming African woman. She walked, they say, with the same grace as the West African women with bundles of wood or clothes on top of their heads. Her bearing was regal, authoritative, and charismatic. In her eyes you could see the coral, suggesting the depth of her soul. Her face—carved, chiseled, round, and full—gave her a sensuality that was haunting. The air of dignity around Frances was such that many men in Dooly County desired her. With skin blacker than the darkest nights under the Spanish moss along the Chattahoochee River, Frances glowed with internal and external beauty. She could work as long and as hard as any man. Her children loved her, and she understood and accepted their gifts as sent from the spirit world. Every African ancestor, deep in the forests of Georgia and, indeed, Africa kept faith with Frances.

By the time J. T. finished telling me all these stories, I felt I had flown a million miles into space. It was as if the darkness of the night had made it possible for me to see my relationship with my ancestors so clearly. I was bonded to history, attached to the invisible cord of blood lineage, an inaudible voice of being, the very meaning of my deepest identity. I held onto every word, listening through the nuances and discovering in the interstices the necessary reality of my selfhood. The words were magical. I was a victim of their magic.

I believed Uncle J. T. when he said Plenty was a modern-day African priest. Shango, the Yoruban deity, or some ancient Akan river deity had made peace with Plenty's soul in the hollows of the Chattahoochee and Flint rivers, and he poured forth his proverbs and dream interpretations like a man possessed. He told J. T. many dreams, and J. T. told me. Of course, I knew that my grandfather Moses was a dreamer and a dream interpreter, but I learned from Uncle J. T. that it all came from Plenty.

In one dream Plenty said he heard the rattle of a thousand snakes, and strangely enough, when he looked to see if he could discover the source of the rattling, he saw nothing—no snakes, no rattlers, nothing. As the dream progressed he heard the rattling again, and again he went to look for the source, but saw nothing. Just as he was leaving the place to which he had gone to look for the sounds, he saw a large green tree standing in the middle of the path back to his house. When he approached the tree to see if it was the source of the rattling, it changed to a huge black rock. Plenty said he approached the rock to see if he could find the source of the rattling, and when he got close to it, the rock was transformed into a river. He awoke, puzzled by the dream's meaning. It bothered him that he had not found the source of the rattling. Compelled to search his mind, to look into his experiences, and to try to fathom the meaning of this dream, he firmly believed that he had learned something profound. What was it?

One day, while walking in his peanut field, Plenty discovered the meaning of his dream. The shadows that hounded him like running dogs intrigued him, and he realized the lesson was the impossibility of knowing what a thing really is except as you experience it. He told J. T. that once you hear something, if you try to capture it, you will lose it, even if your hearing is very good. It will never be the same, and if you go to search for it, you will find that it has transformed itself from a tree to a rock to a river, and it is never what you thought it was in the first place. We could never know anything with certainty.

Plenty went on for more than ninety years, dreaming and interpreting his dreams. Moses, his only son, inherited the gift of dream interpretation and followed, albeit poorly, in his father's steps.

Plenty was like a true babalawo on Georgia soil, but he did not possess the thunder and lightning of Shango. He was rather gentlemanly—a kinder, more sensitive spirit toward children, perhaps with the exception of J. T.; he was also easy to laugh and display wit. I remember him and his many great-grandchildren running around in the big sandy yard, usually swept with *veve* designs, in front of the big house. My cousins and my siblings and I were all too young to understand or appreciate how this strong black man had carved out a piece of territory for himself in the midst of a racist white population, yet we loved him because there was nothing evil in his presence. He exuded love for his family, and his eyes danced whenever he spoke to his great-grandchildren, teasingly so, combative in a friendly way, almost as if he were preparing us for something. Then these traits became the traits of his son Moses and his grandson Arthur, my father. There was defiance, confidence, courage, and intelligence, all wrapped up tighter than a chinaberry in this one man.

"Bring that boy here," he would say to my grandfather, who would instruct me: "Go on over to your great-grandpa, boy." I would approach him, half afraid of him because he was so old and because I did not want him to spit his tobacco on me. He seemed to always have a wad of Brown's Mule Chewing Tobacco in his mouth and a spittoon nearby. "Boy, take a piece of this tobacco and chew it."

"I don't want no tobacco," I said, knowing full well that tobacco-chewing children were not acceptable in his household. At the same time, I was conflicted because everyone respected Plenty—no one talked back to him or told him what they did not want to do.

"You telling me what you don't want to do, boy?" he asked.

"G'won, take the tobacco," Moses said.

"Here, boy, take this piece." He handed it to me and I took it and put it in my mouth. It had a sweet but pungent taste. I did not find it as atrocious in my mouth as I had thought it would be, but I did not know if I should swallow the accumulating juice. Just then, my great-grandfather Plenty said, "Spit it out. Show me how far you can spit it."

I tried to spit the yellowish brown juice, and it fell right in front of me, some of it splattering my clothes. The adults laughed and I was embarrassed. My great-grandfather pulled me to him and hugged me. This was a child's performance, his great-grandchild's performance, and the blood connection was so strong that he felt pride at my tobacco-chewing accomplishment.

Plenty Smith was a fierce prophet. He held himself with nobility; there was nothing but freedom in his movements. No alien energies dared possess him, and no subtle forms of inferiority ever invaded his consciousness, as far as I could tell as an adolescent. Independent, proud, determined, no nonsense, and competitive—those were the words that walked into a room when Plenty walked in. In fact, those were the words that led the singing and the praying in Mount Olive Baptist Church on the second Sunday in August. He alone was the voice of God in that church while he was alive. He had given most of the funds to build the church building, made sure that preachers came and preachers went, and took charge of praying and lining the hymns. He also counted the money, but he could not read.

I knew my great-grandfather because of my grandfather, not because of my father. Going to Dooly County each year for the annual homecoming was my grandfather's purview. It was his responsibility, as he saw it, to take everybody back to their roots. Years later, before my son, M. K., went off to college, I would take him to Dooly County and let him walk the sacred grounds of Mount Olive Church to see the old land where his ancestors lived and worked.

Plenty's eldest child was Moses, my grandfather, whose own life rivaled that of his father's for color and excitement. Moses was to be the deliverer. He would liberate the oppressed, heal the sick, and bring peace out of trouble and stability out of chaos. After Moses married Willie Maud Anderson, daughter of the only black cotton gin owner in Dooly County, he moved to Columbus, Ohio, and then to Valdosta, establishing his reputation as a "bad black" that nobody bothered. Of course, Moses never created trouble for Willie Maud. Her family considered themselves a cut above the farmers. They were capital owners, as the cotton gin served black and white farmers in Dooly County. Willie Maud did not have to do a whole lot of labor in the fields; she was a favorite daughter who found the tall, handsome Moses a worthwhile partner. She probably had as much to do with their marriage as he did because she knew more what she wanted in a man than he knew what he wanted in a woman. They got married and moved in with Plenty and Hattie for a few years before they settled in Valdosta. Hattie Shine liked Willie Maud and taught her much about the Smith family. Willie Maud died in 1950.

By the time Moses married Corrine Bell in 1952, he had gotten in fights with both white and black men yet still maintained his church leadership as an elder and itinerant preacher, constantly guiding the black community while keeping far away from the white world. He buried himself in the traditions of roots and herbs, reading all types of dream books, almanacs, and the Bible as well as listening to the teachings of a couple of rural root men who lived on the outskirts of Valdosta. He told me, "Buddy, dere's something else dat you should know when you are older, and it ain't all in the Bible." I was curious about this "something else" because I had my own questions as well.

My grandfather Moses had a strong Asante head and cheeks that looked just right for the Asante ethnic markings (markings that I have always admired in others but that no one in my immediate family possessed); his complexion was a sort of Mauritanian bronze with a touch of black pepper. The old man—when I knew him he was already old—was a natural spiritualist. Not that this made him different from some of the other black men in Valdosta, but it underscored his solidarity with his ethnic tradition and with his own father. He had inherited from Plenty an interest in herbs, spirits, ghosts, dreams, numbers, symbols, and ceremonies. He was a man of the farm who believed himself to be of the city. He grew up displaying his talent for the spiritual elements that populate the African people's imagination, and he conveyed that gift to all who would listen to him.

Moses's ministry was personal prayer. You would call him if your mother was sick or you were in fear of death; you would call him if you couldn't pay your rent or mortgage. Whenever someone needed prayer, he was the one to call. People seemed to like to hear him go through his "Lord God of Abraham, Isaac, and Jacob." He would get into his old 1950 Buick with the soft velvet-like coverings and drive to their house, where he would tell them the religious facts of life before leading them in prayer. In Valdosta a lot of people seemed to need prayer. Destitution due to the lack of employment, poor welfare programs, racial discrimination, and poor health ate away at the self-confidence of the African American community.

When people were too sick to "cut up" or cause trouble, they needed prayer for all the cuttin' up they did before they got sick. My grandfather Moses was pleased at the way he could stop people from acting like "dirt-daubering rumormongers." You could pray that away from them, but the best thing to do was to prepare some roots and give them some special mint tea mixed with secret herbs. Then the "dirt-daubering" people would lose their interest in spreading rumors, though they might still cut up now and then. Valdosta would be less sinful and more righteous after my grandfather had made his rounds.

Cuttin' up was synonymous with keeping up a ruckus. It was usually done on the weekend at one of the local bars like the Blue Moon or the Right Inn, but cuttin' up could be done anywhere if the cut-upperer wanted to act the fool in public. Some of the people grandfather prayed for had even been brave enough to cut up downtown in the Valdosta Confederate Square, but most of the ruckus took place in the black community.

Like most poor African American neighborhoods in the South during the 1950s and 1960s, the white authorities basically left ours alone unless something happened that affected the white people. People could fight, drink, and cut up any time they wanted to in the black community, and the white police would not bother them. In such situations the black leaders—tough, spiritual, courageous, and authoritative—are the ones who had an impact on the troublemakers. You didn't want to be on the wrong side of the community leaders. They held their positions because of the respect people had for them—or at least for their ability to negotiate their own safety, security, and economic livelihood without anybody standing in their way. They almost always had a reputation for being willing to physically whup somebody if that was necessary.

Moses Smith was one hell of a praying man, and he was one of those leaders. He came by it naturally because his old man, my great-grandfather, whom I had the privilege of seeing pray when I was eleven, was also a masterful praying man. But Moses had inherited more than praying from Plenty; he also had the same keen sense of leadership, wit, humor, and fraternal spirit. His physical stature, tall and fit, combined with his know-it-all attitude about everything from religion to science meant that he was a shoo-in; without a hitch, he would be a cinch to become a community leader and perhaps even a preacher.

Although it seemed that preachers fell out of the sky as thick as South Georgia rain, not all of them were good preachers and most were jacklegs, preaching here and there for whatever leaderless black church would pay their automobile gasoline costs. Moses started out like a jackleg, taking me, my aunt Georgia, and, later, Esakenti, with him on spiritual missions.

There are, in the milieu of itinerant or jackleg preachers, certain protocols for participation that include lots of conversation, a proper understanding of the Bible, a knowledge of how racism affects every-thing, and a special bond with people. Human caring is uppermost, and an infinite consideration of the people whose souls must be saved and whose lives depend on the weekly sustenance preachers like Moses provide; consequently, it is a unique and special fraternity of people who do it. Granddaddy took it upon himself to involve his youngest child, Georgia, and his grandchildren in the protocols of preaching for small groups throughout the area.

My aunt Georgia, a beautifully svelte woman with high Asante cheekbones, small dancing eyes that glittered in the dark, and an even, pure, ebony complexion, would give me the necessary interpre-tations of my grandfather's sermons. He would stop at some random house—difficult to distinguish from any other in its obvious poverty except that the sinners' houses were better kept, with their lawns neater and the outsides freshly painted—and ask the occupants to come to church. They would often turn their backs and say they already went to church. My grandfather loved this life because it meant that church people didn't only come to his house to get him to interpret their dreams; he could do it at their houses as well, as a part of his religious mission.

As Valdosta's mystic, in the black sense of the word, Moses, always dressed neatly in khaki slacks and a sports shirt, could run a rather brisk business reading stars, moon positions, eyes, and his dream book. That was one reason many members of the church feared that Brother Nuddy Brown was obsessed with Moses. Nuddy Brown was a leading light at the big church where Moses was nominally a member and where we all attended.

If it were an obsession, it was one born of envy. Nothing Granddaddy did amounted to any reason for Nuddy Brown to be jealous. In fact, Moses deliberately kept most of his achievements to himself. He was credited with founding a church in Tifton, Georgia, but none of the Valdosta people would ever know that, if it depended on him. He was aware of the crazy response he got from Nuddy Brown whenever he would get up and say something in the church.

Nuddy Brown lived near the church. He had been nicknamed Nuddy because of his complexion, a soft pecan shade. Most people spelled it "Nuddy," but it probably would have been correct to spell it "Nutty." Others thought he was a little weird—hence, Nutty. He thought Moses was becoming too popular, with too much influence on the five hundred or so people who attended the church. Grandfather Moses could stand in as a preacher when the regular preacher was out of town and Brother Stanley was not available. I remember that he would ask for the tithes when the time came, and often he would be the one to make announcements. Moses was an influential layperson in the church, although he could assume preaching roles if necessary.

To counteract my grandfather's influence, Nuddy Brown went to the church early on Sunday morning before anyone else had even heard the call of the Sunday morning spirit. And because the church members drank Welch's grape juice every Sunday as the liquid part of the Lord's Supper, Nuddy Brown figured he could magically control the membership by "doctoring" the Welch's grape juice.

In a frenzied scientific creation, trying to finish before the congregation assembled, Nuddy Brown would piss in a pan and then pour the bottles of grape juice in the pan, mixing the liquids. Meticulously, he would fill each of the small glass cups with this mystic potion and place them into the communion tray. Reaching into the cupboard in the church's scullery, he would bring down the unleavened biscuits, break them into pieces, and place them on the bread tray. Satisfied that the "blood" and "body" of Jesus Christ were ready for the congregation, he would retire to his home a few houses down the street and wait for eleven o'clock to see how his magic worked on the people.

Many people believed Nuddy Brown had been doing this for five or more years before anyone even suspected. Because I was baptized when I was eleven, I partook of the communion like everyone else. The thought that I drank Nuddy Brown's piss as an act of piety when I was a child gives me an irresistible impulse to vomit. But my grandfather was on the case. He confronted Brown outside the church building one Sunday after the worship and asked innocently, "Did you change the grape juice?"

"No, it's the same Welch's I've been preparing for years."

"You think Welch might have changed the mixture?" Grandfather joked, half seriously.

"Why? What's wrong with it?" Nuddy Brown inquired, feigning innocence.

"Some people thought we'd switched over to real wine. They would have swore it was not Welch's if they were swearing people."

"Naw, it's the same old Welch's."

Moses hadn't liked Nuddy Brown from the beginning; there was something twitchy, fidgety, shifty perhaps about the way his head darted from side to side when he talked. Anyway, Moses was determined to get to the bottom of this Lord's Supper crisis.

On the very next Sunday morning, as a light rain was falling, Moses took my uncle Alex Anderson, a tough rascal by anybody's measure, along with him to the church before service began. They arrived just after Nuddy Brown had entered the little scullery, leaving the door open behind him. Grandfather and Alex stationed themselves so they could see straight into the scullery through the two windows in the front door of the building. And they saw what they suspected. Nuddy Brown unzipped his trousers and pissed in the pan, mixing the urine with the "blood" of Jesus and pouring it into the individual glass cups.

Terrified by the sacrilege, Alex dropped to his knees, cursing Nuddy Brown's desecration right there in Jesus' house. Moses, satisfied that Brown was a scoundrel, went home to ponder his course of action.

At worship, before the communion was passed, Moses stood his six-foot-four-inch frame up, walked over to Nuddy Brown, and grabbed his arm. "Before we go on, Brown has a confession to make, don't you?" Moses said, squeezing Brown's arm; meanwhile, Uncle Alex went to the back of the church, his pistol in his hand, to cover the action while Grandfather took care of Brown.

"What you want me to say?" Brown asked.

"Tell the people what you been doing to the communion."

"I've done nothing more than fix it for the last twenty years. That's all."

"What's in it?" This question caused a hubbub among the church members. "Quiet, let him talk. Go on, Brown."

"I'm sorry. I'm sorry," Brown cried.

"Not enough. Tell them what you did to the grape juice. We saw you do it this morning."

"I can't."

"You did, and you will tell them." Moses twisted his arm. The church was in a minor uproar until Uncle Alex called from the rear, waving his pistol in the air, "Let's have some quiet."

"I peed in the communion," he blurted. The church members gasped. Moses told the church that Nuddy Brown had done this in order to exercise power over them. Brown's reasoning, according to the unique interpretation advanced by Moses the mystic, was that if the people drank his urine, they would be under his influence.

Subsequently Moses's stock rose in the church and Uncle Alex became a respectable church leader. Not content to graze in the old pastures, Moses got a preaching assignment in Tifton, fifty miles north of Valdosta, where he did not have to share power with anyone, and yet his fame preceded him. He was the "big tall man who could smell out the devils." I loved riding in his long black Buick up to Tifton to hear him preach the word. It would be years before I realized how dangerously he drove on the two-lane highway, straddling the solid yellow line like you straddle a horse. It was fun going to the various church sites in the small towns where my grandfather practiced his jackleg ministry as an itinerant preacher.

CHAPTER 3

Passages

R ELIGION WAS AT THE HELM of my family's sense of itself. My enthusiasm for church was electric around our house. I would come
home every Sunday and imitate the preacher for my mother and
father's enjoyment. They would laugh and urge me to stomp my feet
and raise my voice, just like our preacher did. I was good—too good,
they said. The Lord must have called me to be a preacher.

They had to consult the preacher about what to do with me because I
had mastered the oratory of the mature preachers and had memorized
several sermons, almost verbatim. He recommended that my parents
consider sending me to the Nashville Christian Institute.

So in 1953, when I was eleven, my parents made preparations for me
to go on the long journey to Nashville, Tennessee. Of course, this was
a major decision for our family. Only my grandfather Moses and my
father Arthur had ever crossed the Georgia state line going north. They
had worked in Dayton, Ohio. Moses had gone first during World War
I to work in the war industries, and then my father had followed his
example in the 1940s. I, however, would not go farther than Nashville,
remaining in the South.

The Nashville Christian Institute was one of the few black boarding
schools left in the United States. Marshall Keeble was president of the
school. I had met him when he visited Valdosta in 1952 to preach. The
ability of the young boys who traveled with him to advertise the school
impressed me: they were polished, cool, gifted, and very intelligent.

My family and some church members wanted Keeble to hear me speak. He always had some boy preachers traveling with him, and the two who came to Valdosta, Floyd Rose and David Boatwright, were extraordinarily gifted speakers. Floyd would become a lifelong friend. He was more eloquent and capable as a public speaker than anyone I had met. His intuition for propriety, brevity, and directness escaped other public speakers, and he never gave a bad speech. David Boatwright was the son of the principal at the Nashville Christian Institute and had had the advantage of watching Marshall Keeble speak at many occasions. He could introduce Keeble like no one else. I can hear him now: "If I were asked to introduce a great orator, I would have to introduce Frederick Douglass. If I were asked to introduce an impressive educator, I would have to introduce Booker T. Washington. But if I were asked to name and introduce a great orator, educator, and Christian, I would have to introduce Marshall Keeble." He spoke with the gravity of one who believed in what he was saying.

When I gave my little presentation, Keeble was pleased with my potential and told the church that I should be sent to Nashville. Many people responded with applause. My parents were pleased that the church members promised to assist in paying the tuition—forty dollars a month. Keeble, a short, charismatic man, beamed when the church members spontaneously took up a monetary collection for the school.

A clean-cut man with a chiseled face, Keeble was the best promoter the Nashville Christian Institute had ever had. He was truly the soul and the brain behind the school. He had served as president of the school for many years, adding to its financial strength by securing private funding for the operations budget as well as church support for individual students.

Although it was five hundred miles away from Valdosta, my parents thought that the NCI was a good thing, getting me out of Valdosta for a proper education. How could any African American get a proper education in Georgia in the 1950s? This was the time when we found the word "niggers" written in our secondhand textbooks, after having been discarded by the white schools. This was the time when some of the country children who couldn't get up early enough to be driven into Valdosta had split sessions of school so that they could plant and harvest the white people's crops. This was the time when the most ordinary white person who decided to accuse a black person of a crime could turn a dream into a nightmare.

The Nashville Christian Institute was a glorious chariot to carry me away from sure trouble in South Georgia. Of course, I could and did return home in the summer, but I would never again live in my parents' home. They had never seen Nashville, but they acted purely on faith and the word of Marshall Keeble, the most famous African American preacher in our denomination. They knew lots of people who had seen the school, and graduates of the school were preaching and teaching throughout the country.

So early one Friday morning in 1953, during the dog days of August, our minister and his wife drove me up to Nashville, Tennessee, to enroll me in the Institute. It was the longest journey I had ever made, and it would literally be the changing point in my life and in my ambition. Getting out of South Georgia at that time in my life was one of the best things to have happened to me, and I believe that some of my siblings held it against me for a long time that I managed to escape the constant grind of misery measured out to the black people of Valdosta. I could never explain it to my satisfaction or that of my siblings; I was lucky, that's all, or else I would have remained mired in the same conditions as them. I felt cheated, however, that I missed some of the most precious moments of their lives, as when Ralph fought and won his first boxing match, or when Shirley brought her first boyfriend home to meet Mama, or when my nephew Abner started school. As I left Valdosta that August with tears in my eyes, I vowed to always remain close to the family. I missed them already, and we had not even left the county limits.

I went to the Nashville Christian Institute as a boy with a limited understanding of the world, but I returned to Georgia with increasing wisdom in the summers. I knew that even among family members, adults especially, life was no bed of flowers. Yet my childhood had been, until I left, a period of endless festival.

There are only a few details about my leaving that I have not repressed. The preacher and his wife, Brother and Sister Thomas O. Jackson, we called them, came by our house and packed my one tattered brown suitcase into the black Packard, and off we went to Nashville, Tennessee. What I do not remember is whether I cried or if my mother or father cried. Now it seems to me that they must have wept about the departure of one of their children. It seems that I must have cried, knowing I was leaving home for a long time. But I do not remember any tears. I knew I was leaving my best friend, Vera, behind, but no deep emotion came over me except uncertainty.

When the old Packard passed Adel and Tifton, I still knew I was in familiar territory because Granddaddy Moses had always taken us to Dooly County, and we had been up Highway 41 as far as Cordele. But beyond Dooly County, all was unknown, and I settled back in my seat in the back of the car, somewhat apprehensive of what was yet to come.

I didn't know then that some of my brothers and sisters would consider me fortunate to be away from Valdosta and would come to resent me for being selected to leave the Azalea City. Ralph, my youngest brother and the one that I did not spend a lot of childhood years with, became bitter as an adult. When I returned to Valdosta, Ralph would inevitably come to the family house where I was just deliberately to ignore me. In fact, I had begun after three or four times to ask my parents and siblings if something was wrong with him mentally. "Naw, ain't nothin' wrong wid dat boy. He jus' missed you. You his big brother, and he don't know you," my mother would explain.

It would be years before we reconnected at a family reunion. Abner, our nephew and Vera's son, insisted that we talk. We did, and we discovered that we had a lot in common, were really alike in many ways, and wanted to be closer as brothers.

Ralph felt that he had to be the protector of the girls in the family because his older brothers, Esakenti, Paul, Ozzie, Charles, and me, were often away doing our own thing. He was left at home to take care of many responsibilities until Charles moved in with Father. Ralph was considered athletic and handsome, and his peers admired his abilities in football and boxing. He became a cement finisher, which had a lot to do with his missing out on school opportunities. But he became one of the best cement men in Valdosta. He resented the fact that our parents always referred to me as the smart one and felt that, regardless of what he did, they did not give him any plaudits. "I tried to be like you. I got awards for football, boxing, and other things, and when I would bring those awards and plaques to Mom and Dad, they would just look at them and tell me what you were doing," Ralph told me at one of the family reunions. His witness to this familial play among children caused me to tear up.

"If I had known, I would have interceded with them, confronted them on this. I never felt anything but love for you," I told him.

The old Packard took US 41 through Georgia, from the pine-crowned plains to the rolling hills, farther north than I had ever been. Passing through Dooley County, Georgia, with its endless fields and muddy creeks I was in a world beyond belief. I saw Atlanta, to me the biggest city in the world, and then we drove up through the undulating hills of North Georgia toward the Tennessee state line.

The mountains of Tennessee astounded me. South Georgia was as flat as a pancake and smooth with an occasional dip that you could not even call a valley. I could not imagine that people lived on top of mountains. I could not imagine that cars could travel safely over them. I could not understand how they were formed. The only thing I knew when we came to Lookout Mountain in Chattanooga was that I was out of Georgia.

I had grown up in the coastal plains of Georgia, the epitome of the flat earth, or nearly the epitome, because I later saw the infinite plains of Kansas. The vastness of the experience agitated my senses, and travel humbled me, broadening me far more than anything else.

By the time we completed the five hundred–mile trip to Nashville, I had left the deprivations of Valdosta thousands of miles behind. I took in everything. While the preacher's wife slept, probably having seen the sights many times, I kept my young eyes wide open and saw different types of houses, people, schools, cars, and landscapes. I was prepared to be educated, but it did not occur to me how deep the education would go, how profound the transformation would be just in the ten or twelve hours it took to get to Nashville.

When the large luxury car in which we traveled entered the parking lot of the brick-and-tile building that was the Nashville Christian Institute, staff members came out to greet the preacher and his wife. He introduced me as I surveyed the old building that rambled on like a huge ranch. It spread out for many feet, occupying the corner of 24th and Herman. I was amazed that people actually lived on the campus.

A few of the boys and girls, also newly arrived, came to assess me. I greeted them and took measure of them as well. They seemed like normal children. They were well dressed; each of them had on new shoes. This occurred to me because though I had brought money to buy some new shoes, for now I was still wearing last year's school shoes.

The preacher took me into the dormitory where we unloaded my one suitcase, in which everything I owned fit. I eventually got a trunk after being there for a few semesters. The preacher and his wife said their good-byes, and I felt a sense of loss; they were my only connection with Valdosta. They knew me and they knew my family, my church, my needs, and my possibilities, but they could not remain with me.

All alone with my memories of Valdosta and the journey north, I sank into depression. It was a depression that would invade my thoughts many nights when I would think of my brothers and sisters, my mother and father in Valdosta. *What are they doing now? What new discoveries have been made in the backyard?* Nevertheless, here I was in the Nashville Christian Institute, and sure enough, they had enough to occupy your time so that you did not have to think too much about home.

The staff was generally warm and helpful, though there was one member of the staff that had a bad reputation until he was fired. Jimmie Lymon, the dean of boys, lived with his wife and two young daughters in one of the small apartments on campus. Lymon had married Marshall Keeble's daughter and therefore had secured a good position in the school's hierarchy, although no one knew what credentials he had other than the fact that he had married the school president's daughter. He was probably in his early thirties when he got the job at the Nashville Christian Institute. He was rumored to be homosexual; he was definitely a child molester.

Lymon always wore soft shoes and had the habit of coming into dorm rooms to wake up sleeping students. We called him "Soft Shoes," and whenever we saw him coming, we would wake our sleeping roommates with, "Wake up, Soft Shoes is coming." Lymon would enter a dorm room and go over to the two sets of bunk beds, saying as he walked in, "Wake up! Wake up!" Almost with one movement, he would run his hands under the covers, supposedly to wake the young sleepers up. He would start at the top bunks and go to the bottom ones. Some of the students complained that he fondled them. I had no intention of finding out by letting him catch me asleep. I always said, "I'm awake, I'm awake!" as soon as I heard him walk into our room.

On one occasion, when I was not awake in time, I felt his hands on my genitals, fondling me. I leaped out of the bed and said, "What are you doing?" "Just waking you up. I'm sorry for touching you. I didn't mean anything by touching you. I apologize. I am very sorry," he pleaded. The other boys watched the entire episode.

I was only eleven years old, but I told the principal, Otis Boatwright, that Mr. Lymon had touched me and other boys on our private parts. Otis Boatwright was quite methodical. I had to go over the whole thing again, repeating word by word what happened while he wrote everything down. He needed all the facts he could get to bring a case against the school president's son-in-law. Boatwright did his own investigation and must have amassed enough information to make a solid case against Lymon.

I do not remember saying anything more about the situation to anyone. I just made sure that I was up early in the morning, before Soft Shoes came tiptoeing into the dorm rooms, probably fondling young boys at will. I believe that my report to the principal had something to do with Lymon finally being terminated; even Marshall Keeble could not retain his son-in-law. To his credit, he did not defend Lymon. I think he felt that Lymon had betrayed his trust and his mission for the school. No one could be harder, tougher, sterner than Keeble; he was about discipline above all else.

At about this time the school rented several buses and took the entire student body out to a huge park on the outskirts of town for spring break. It was a festive occasion, with all types of soft drinks, hot dogs, hamburgers, French fries, and several athletic activities, including baseball, football, track, and basketball. For several hours we ran, played football and baseball, ate our food, and had loads of fun. When it got dark and everyone got back on the buses to leave, little Alexander Lovell was missing. The adults counted us two or three times, trying to figure out if they had missed him. They had indeed, because he was not on any bus.

The fact that he was missing consumed all of us. Several of us volunteered to search the park, even though it was getting darker. We walked two-by-two, looking for little Alexander, then returned and walked in the opposite direction. He was nowhere to be found, and we asked, "Where could he have gone?" There was no public transportation and few cars passing by, and he could not have walked by the large mass of people without someone seeing him. It was strange, bizarre even.

We did not find him that night. I remember well how the azaleas seemed to be coming out in the park; unlike the ones in Valdosta that were already in bloom, these seemed to wait, to pause, before they gave a full blossom. I do not know what happened to them, as I do not know what happened to little Alexander that day.

It was one of the saddest days in our school's history. Teachers cried. The principal cried. My friends cried. I cried. We could only think the worst because there was nothing else to think—little Alexander had drowned in the lake. Sure enough, a few days later the authorities recovered his body. He had no bruises or injuries; it was as if he had wanted to walk into the water and disappear. Little Alexander always seemed to be disappearing and then reappearing. He was quiet, nuanced, and subtle, and perhaps we thought of him as weird or different and did not pay as much attention to him as we should have. His voice was quiet, almost too quiet for the tough and rough activities of the rest of the children. He was a very pleasant person—unassuming, kind, gentle, intelligent. His clothes were always too big for him, almost as if they had been purchased that way so that he could grow into them, but he never did.

Perhaps the administrators and teachers knew that Alexander always wandered off but thought he would always return. This time he did not return, and it was a moment of utter terror for me. I knew little Alexander like he was my brother. I was older by a few years, but little Alexander from Indianapolis was a presence on our campus, and we memorialized him in our hearts and in the chapel of our school.

The Nashville Christian Institute had many rules. One was that we could not leave the campus without permission. Even if we went to one of the two churches that were approved for the students to attend, we had to have permission from the dean of the school. We were on a rigid regimen every day: up in the morning at six, breakfast at seven, and class at eight. We had to take showers, iron clothes, shine shoes, make our beds, and clean our rooms before breakfast. We got out of classes at

3 p.m. There was time for play, fun, and basketball, and then the study halls opened, and we had to spend two hours with our homework. This routine taught us discipline and gave us a real sense of work.

This discipline had a decisive impact on my capacity for work and determination to succeed at what I chose to do. Among other things, I credit NCI with instilling in me my ability to stay dedicated to a cause and have the energy to carry out my duty. Discipline was the school's motto, and every young man or woman who entered felt a strong commitment to the institution. The boys outnumbered the girls about five to one, but no one could say that the girls had any less discipline or any less sense of their mission than the boys. We were all in it together.

We brushed our teeth, took our showers, combed our hair, Vaselined our legs to hide the ash, and went to chapel every morning. Chapel could be a real bore for everyone except the person who the rather somber, pious Principal Otis Boatwright called on to read the scripture. If you were chosen, it meant that you had been under surveillance and were judged to be either potentially successful or potentially disastrous. You could be asked to read the scriptures as a reward for your piety, or you could be asked to read because it was one last attempt to save your soul.

I must have been in the pious category, because I really wanted to be a preacher. There was historically something noble in preaching to the black community. It was the one job that depended on black people paying you. You did not have to ask white people for nothing if you were a preacher. Your living came from the people for whom you preached. It was a form of independence, it seemed to me. All of the revolutionaries in the black community had come from the preacher class. They weren't necessarily any more committed to freedom and equality than those in other professions, but they were more independent of the white-power elite. So whenever I got a chance to read the scripture in chapel, I eagerly accepted the task as preparation for the preaching profession. It would be years before I understood how this class of leaders was trapped by its own profession of religion, the tragedy was that we were often unable to effect change outside of the church.

However, at the Nashville Christian Institute, reading the scriptures was your time to shine. If they thought you showed potential, it was your chance to remain on the A-list, and reading the scriptures eloquently could redeem a potential failure. Few managed redemption, however;

Boatwright had pretty much predestined all our futures, and each of us was either good or bad.

The "bad" students could drop out or be asked to drop out. I saw quite a few good-byes in my time at NCI, but the dismissals had little correlation to the reality of anything remotely evil. Most of the poor dismissed, banished creatures had failed to "join" the church, or decided not to attend chapel, or chosen some other such "evil" practice. We were stuck with a set of narrow, provincial, petty pedagogical magistrates judging our every move.

"Now, when are you going to let the Lord call you, Johnson?" They were sure to use our surnames. "Not *let* the lord call, but hear the Lord's call," some theologically righteous colleague would correct the first teacher. The pedagogues would smile at each other with satisfaction that they had once more put the question to Johnson or some other poor fool, who would try to offer an answer acceptable to the moral magistrates.

I always had an irrepressible impulse to argue with the teachers after there was a diatribe against someone for not joining the church. I learned the techniques of debate in order to be able to defend the "truth" and deliver the knockout blow to evil; I was on the way to becoming an astute polemicist. My presence as a student grew as I took more and more interest in the church, and I was often called an "asset" to the school because I demonstrated to many visitors what we could do as students and orators after attending the school for a little while.

Visitors to the school were important, and Marshall Keeble was not one to keep any rich visitor waiting. Billie Sol Estes, the Texas millionaire and entrepreneur extraordinaire, was a friend to Keeble and our school. Estes appeared at the Nashville Christian Institute in 1956, when he and his entourage stopped by during a visit to see Governor Frank Clements.

I remember the morning well. It was raining, and the wind was blowing hard. The old wooden school creaked and rocked, beaten for the thousandth time by the elements as the rainstorm raged. It was my morning to say a few words of meditation in chapel; each student had been assigned a day during the semester.

Our school building was in a dilapidated state on the outside, although it was always clean on the inside: the wooden floors were scrubbed, oiled, and buffed twice a week. I found myself thinking that Estes, who was seated on the platform next to me, must have been surprised to find that the interior of the old building was impeccable. I noticed he was not such a good dresser. His tie was crooked and his brown suit was rumpled. Perhaps the rain had caused him to be a little ruffled looking. Yet he sat on the stage and gave full attention to the chapel program like the potential philanthropist he was.

President Keeble introduced him to the student assembly in his typical fashion: "Brother Billie Sol Estes is no respecter of persons. He is as true as they come. He has made contributions to NCI in the past, and I am sure he will make them in the future." Keeble had learned from listening to Booker T. Washington how to set up the big donors. He told us he had learned that much from Mr. Washington in his early twenties. We all applauded when he finished setting Estes up by introducing him in such a positive way. What could the man say but something good about Keeble and our school?

I had never heard of Billie Sol Estes, and his name meant nothing to me until Keeble's introduction. Here I was, a fifteen-year-old from a dirt-poor Georgia family and seated next to the first millionaire I had ever seen. But I am not sure I really knew what "millionaire" meant except, as President Keeble explained in his uniquely blunt style, "Mr. Estes has plenty money."

Keeble was quite intelligent. He did not want Estes to get up to speak after he had made his remarks; he wanted him to hear from the students. I was the student on the spot that day. It was my lucky day. I was nervous, but all the training in Sunday School and all the practicing I had to do before going to speak at churches with Keeble to raise money for the school would have to pay off.

When I walked across the platform's hardwood floor to the podium, almost slipping on the polished wood that some of us had buffed the night before, all I could think about was doing well with my little speech. NCI pushed us to always perform well so that visitors would be inclined to contribute to our building fund. It was a ruse, but a proper American ruse. It was like when enslaved Africans worked intensely to be seen to be working because they might accrue some value with the lazy whites who drank their mint juleps and talked about the next harvest while the blacks labored in the hot sun.

I had to do good. I had to be good. Being good was doing good.

My speech on patience was well received by the audience, all of whom were my peers or teachers. Estes looked like he had enjoyed my speech and engaged in animated conversation with Otis Boatwright as I was concluding.

As soon as I finished Marshall Keeble got up and reiterated some of the points I had made in my speech. He said I had come from dire economic circumstances. He had repeated this often enough that everyone in the school knew that I was one of the poorest boys attending NCI. I sometimes felt uncomfortable with his public articulation of that poverty. Nevertheless, it was one of his best tropes for appealing to whites for money. He used it often—I thought too often—but I endured. He repeated the story again that morning.

Keeble could tell my story in such a way that you would want to cry. "This little boy's father had to use a cane, then crutches, and now is in a wheelchair, but look at this boy, he's a genius." He said my mother had always worked as a domestic, working for whites as a housecleaner or taking in laundry and ironing. Keeble would pause for effect and then continue the story of my family's poverty and my determination to be a good student. "His poor parents sent him to us for education, and they can't keep up the tuition. Do we send him home? A boy like this needs support; he is the reason we exist, and I believe that he will make a great man of the Lord. Yes, the economic situation is hard, but if there is a will, there is a way."

When Keeble finished speaking, he asked Billie Sol Estes to respond. Estes's cherubic face lit up, and he looked somewhat surprised. His dark brown suit looked even more disheveled; it looked like he had slept on a Greyhound bus all night. Of course, as we later learned, he had flown on his private jet to Nashville. His gaze was direct, and you soon forgot that he looked like an overweight teenager. The thick, dark-rimmed glasses that allowed him to see his audience rode his jolly face tightly.

Estes's speech had a profound impact on the course of my life. He was not eloquent, but he was sincere and, for an African American audience, credible. Estes turned to Keeble, and in his West Texas accent said, "Now this here boy [he tilted his head in my direction] is going to be something great. You can already see that." I felt rushes of blood in my head, a momentary chill came over me, and I tried to become invisible, sitting on the platform in full view of two hundred students. Yet I felt pride that I had succeeded in making my school look good in the eyes of Estes and the people who had come with him.

I do not know whether or not Keeble, an astute administrator and fundraiser, had privately informed Estes of my plight. Yet Estes turned to me and said, "Young man, I'm going to pay your tuition and see to it that you finish NCI and college. I'll pay the tuition of any other boys who need it also." He ended up paying the tuition for thirty-nine boys plus me. A few years later, as a college student, I tried to repay Estes with my own kindness when he was experiencing financial difficulties. But on this day, I was just pleased that Estes had selected me as one of the boys on his list. He never got the chance to pay my college tuition because by the time I went away to college, the federal government had indicted him on several charges.

Keeble was right about the condition of my family. My clothes and shoes were usually hand-me-downs from some white family my mother worked for as a domestic, and when I was finished with them, I would pass them on to my brothers if they were still useful. I had never had a pair of shoes bought just for me until I went to NCI, and then I only had one pair of shoes.

There were many items that I did not have, but my desperation never consumed me because I still had more than my brothers and sisters had, who remained in the South Georgia town of Valdosta. Nashville gave me sight and insight. I knew that there was something more to life than trees with colored bottles hanging off of them to prevent evil spirits from entering a house or the community, or the mysterious veves in the sandy yards of the shotgun houses. I felt I had been exposed, given a view of something powerful and electric when I could read any book and dream of traveling to the far-distant place. I was born poor, but I was not poor in heart, in spirit, in soul, in aspiration. It helped that every summer I journeyed back home to work in the fields alongside the other children, and I made my pocket money then. I could always go back to NCI with some money in my hands.

When Billie Sol Estes agreed to pay the tuition for forty of the poorest children at the Nashville Christian Institute, it relieved the pressure on my parents and made the president of the school very happy. Estes was the single most important contributor to the school during the 1950s.

He was an involved benefactor in many ways. I would send him letters periodically, reporting my progress and expressing my gratitude. He would always write back in his own handwriting, thanking me for the opportunity to help. The most he would ever say was, "Pass on what you've received." I tried hard, always rising to the top of my classes, reading widely, absorbing new ideas with enthusiasm, and sharing my knowledge with my peers and family.

Increasingly, I grew to challenge ideas students and teachers presented in the classroom, but my family's training forced me to be polite and correct, to pull back without going for the kill. Thus, I allowed a lot of nonsense to pass, although I stamped out more than I let by. I could never write to Estes to tell him that I considered some of the arguments the preachers of the Church of Christ made to be full of bologna. He was a devoted follower of the church's teachings, and I found myself increasingly skeptical.

One thing Estes did have was a dislike for racial prejudice. On this point he often went against the common behavior of the churchgoers. Billie Sol Estes, arrayed in the mantle of a modern-day Jeremiah, spoke bitterly against racial prejudice in Texas and anywhere else he saw it. His jeremiads were delivered against all forms of discrimination in and outside of the churches of Christ. When he was indicted for financial fraud for claiming collateral that he did not have for millions of dollars' worth of loans, his assets were frozen and he needed money. I sent him four or five letters with money in them in order to help his family get over the difficult times, and other black people mailed him money as well when they heard of his plight.

Billie Sol Estes never forgot those black men and women who believed in him and prayed with him during the worst periods of his life. But he had alienated enough white people with his championing of black and Mexican American causes that his support from whites was lukewarm at best. At least Estes seemed resigned to his destiny; he was not resentful of those who criticized him and was careful not to throw stones at the glass houses of his white critics. His quick fall saddened me, probably not so much because I knew him—after all, I did not really know him—but because he had shown himself to be a compassionate man when he agreed to pay the tuition of forty students.

My data was limited. I had only seen him once and had corresponded with him several times a year before the crash of his economic empire.

I completed high school and sent an invitation to President Eisenhower.

During the months between high school and college Mrs. Kennedy, a member of the Jefferson St. Church of Christ who suffered from high blood pressure and diabetes, "adopted" me. She was a kindly, graceful woman with a good sense of humor. She and her husband were extraordinarily committed to education. That was all they talked about, explaining that Jefferson St. Church of Christ was more education driven than Jackson St. Church of Christ, the home of the president and principal of Nashville Christian Institute. They liked me because while most of the students attended Jackson St., I had chosen to go to the educated church. When Mr. Kennedy passed, Mrs. Kennedy wanted to do something with the insurance money she had received. And because I would mow her lawn, clean up the lot, and run errands to the pharmacy, grocery store, and laundry for her, she decided she would pay my first year at Southwestern Christian College.

By the time I entered Southwestern Christian College, Billie Sol Estes's fraud trial had begun. I attended the trial in Tyler, Texas, and comforted Billie Sol, his wife, Peggy, and their family during the trial by telling them the story of the good man Job who had been tested by evil and yet never gave in to defeat. Billie Sol was very appreciative, but he was sentenced to federal prison nevertheless.

When I left Southwestern Christian College to attend college in Oklahoma, I promised to keep in contact with the family, and that I did. His children were younger than me and had lived a far more privileged life, but I felt deeply for them, though I believed that they had no understanding or appreciation of the revolution their father had brought to race relations in Texas and throughout the South.

Years later, when Billie Sol Estes got out of prison, I reestablished contact with him and thanked him for giving me the opportunity to finish at the Nashville Christian Institute. Tears came to his eyes as he reminded me that he had wanted another boy, Floyd, and me to excel in business. I told him that thanks to him, both of us had discovered other paths to excellence.

∞

Southwestern Christian College was my training ground, responsible for sharpening my political wits and growing my inherent dislike for racism. It was a small college in Jamie Foxx's hometown of Terrell, Texas. Terrell had a mental institution and a college, and at times, one could easily mistake them for each other. I would go to the mental institution as a part of my social service—ministering, singing, handing out gifts, and reading verses from the Bible to patients suffering various forms of dementia. There was pleasure in this type of service; it was more selfish than altruistic perhaps, but I enjoyed the feeling of doing something good.

A group of black preachers led by J. P. Bowser during the 1940s founded the college. However, it was financed mostly with funds collected from churches of Christ. Because the denomination was largely white, most of the donations came from white people.

At the time I attended the college, the president was a large, square-jawed southern white man named A. V. Isbell. I met him on the first day I landed on the campus. I could tell right off the bat that he did not like me. I was neither docile nor withdrawing; instead, I was opinionated, talkative, and quite self-assured. I was the opposite of most of the other students—assertive, direct, and straightforward. I knew that this white man was going to have a problem with me, and my only way of surviving would have to be avoidance. But how do you avoid the president of the college when there are less than three hundred students? All the students were black, but we had a white president and two or three white professors, including Isbell's wife.

Mr. Isbell's wife taught literature, one of the subjects in which I had excelled in high school, and I was her star pupil until I wrote a paper on existentialism that questioned the value of religion. She gave me an F on the paper. I went to her and asked her to explain, and she could only say, "Mr. Smith, this is a Christian college, and I do not appreciate your writing on an atheistic topic." I protested, stating that the paper followed all of the technical points that she had explained in the classroom, pointing out that nothing was marked off for grammar or style. I could tell she would not be moved, and I accepted the F, believing that it was an excellent paper, and I managed to get out of her class with a C, the lowest grade I had ever received. This was to be iconic of my life. I would always speak my mind, and some people would seek to punish me, but I would remain free, and as Shirley Chisholm had said when she ran for the presidency, "unbent, unbossed, and unbought." No inducements were so precious as my own ability to speak without sanction. My word had to be a free word.

It was not my encounter with Mrs. Isbell that would almost ruin my future; instead, it was my inevitable clash with her husband. Each week there was a large assembly for all of the students and faculty. On one particular day President Isbell delivered a lecture to us about responsibility. In the middle of his talk one of the black freshmen students, Mack Dillingham, raised his hand. Mr. Isbell failed to recognize Dillingham's raised arm for several minutes, so finally Mack stood up, and Isbell said, "What do you want?"

Mack said, "May I be excused to go to the bathroom?" Isbell was angry and said, "You stop me in the middle of my talk to ask if you could go to the bathroom. That's what is wrong with you people. You can't hold yourself. You've got to learn to contain your urges," whereupon I leaped to my feet in the third row and shouted at Isbell, "You cannot talk to him like that. He was just trying to be respectful. We are not on a plantation here. We are all human beings and demand to be treated like human beings." I was so hot that steam must have been coming from my ears.

Isbell shouted back, "Dean Sams! I want this student expelled from the campus immediately." Dean Sams, the highest-ranking black official in the school, was a weak, basically powerless man who was grateful just to have his job. He got up and motioned to me to follow him downstairs to his office. Leaving my seat, I thought that this must have been what it was like when Nat Turner stood alone at the gallows. I can't recall any student coming to my assistance or demanding that I be allowed to graduate the next month.

"Mr. Smith," Dean Sams said, "you have put us in a tough situation. The president wants me to expel you. I have got to do it. I don't want to, but he is the president of the college." I thought Dean Seams was a good man, just incapable of confronting white people who mistreated black students.

I was adamant, saying, "Dean Sams, you must do what you have to do. I know your position is at stake. I take full responsibility for my actions, but I will never allow a white racist to speak to a black person like Mr. Isbell did to Mack Dillingham without responding. He had no right to paint an entire race with a broad brush."

So there I was, an overall "A minus" student with a scholarship to Oklahoma Christian College, a popular leader of the student government, and a well-respected student among my peers, kicked out of junior college for standing up against an attack on black people. There were only three weeks before graduation, and I was out of school.

I immediately called some of the members of the Board of Trustees of the college. There were a few black members who held power over the president. If they did not like his management style, they could get him fired. I told them as precisely as I could what had happened, knowing they were fierce opponents of racism. These were the champions who came to my aid and had me back in college within a week.

Isbell, however, never said a mumbling word to me again, which, of course, was fine with me. He knew me and I knew him. I could almost feel the presence of my great-grandfather Plenty whenever I saw Isbell. How many times did my ancestors have to hold their words because they were speaking to whites? How many times did they have to bow to white privilege that did not want to listen to the voices of blacks? Yes, I knew that A. V. Isbell had thought of the school as his plantation, but he discovered that I was an incorrigible who would not allow him to run roughshod over me or any other black student.

I left Southwestern and entered Oklahoma Christian College in Oklahoma City in 1962. I spent my two years there listening and learning about white people; I was the first African American to graduate from that college, in 1964. Once I left I did not set foot on the campus again for more than forty years. I graduated near the top of my class, although this was the first time that I had been in a school with a majority of white students.

I found the students at Oklahoma Christian College to be average. I say this because I was rather apprehensive at first. Perhaps all of the white students were smarter than I was, and I would have the burden of my entire people on my back. After all, there were only two blacks in the school, William Muncy, a basketball star, and me. To my surprise I did not find a Wendell Wilkie Gunn, the genius with a photographic memory who was my academic rival at NCI. I also did not find a Roosevelt Robinson, my chief competition at Southwestern, an Ebonics-speaking colleague from Valdosta, Georgia, who later became a judge in Oregon. No one actually stood out academically. I think it was the religion thing. Students were not very well exposed to the horrors of their own people or of the American government. They were not well read about the world; they were, in fact, sheltered, protected from knowledge.

Although I graduated with a high distinction, and my godparents, Willie and Mamie Hambrick drove from Nashville to see me graduate, I have tried to blot the entire experience out of my mind. George Benson, a self-righteous archconservative, gave the commencement address, and I disagreed with almost everything he said. It was then that I realized I had little in common with the majority of my peers graduating from OCC.

During the summer of 1964 I drove to Los Angeles to see my then-fiancée, Hattie Hilliard. On the way to California I stopped off in Abilene, Texas, to see Billie Sol Estes. He had been indicted and was waiting around for sentencing. His wife, Patsy, was very upset but kept her pain even-tempered, mostly as an inside hurt. She didn't complain a lot, but I could tell that she was worried.

When Billie Sol entered the room after Patsy called him, he didn't appear the least worried about the trouble he was in. He came forward with a young, clean-cut white man at his side, embraced me in a big bear hug, and said, "I want you to ride with me and Frank to El Paso."

"I had no plans to drive to El Paso twice," I mumbled. If I went with Estes to El Paso, I would still have to return to Abilene to get my car and then go back that way when I left to go to Los Angeles.

"Got something I want to talk to you about. If you drive your car down there, then we wouldn't get to use all the time," Estes said.

We got into Frank's car after lunch and started out on Highway 80. Estes was a little nervous, though I didn't know why. It could have been that the judge had ordered him to remain in Abilene or it could have been anxiety over the sentencing. Without hesitation he started talking as soon as we got out of Abilene and did not stop until we reached El Paso.

When we got there, we turned off of the main highway, drove into the city, turned down an alleyway, got back onto a main street—and were stopped by the police. Two uniformed and one plainclothes policeman got out of their car and approached us, guns drawn. The plainclothes one was white and the other two were Mexican Americans. "Out of the car!" the plainclothes cop shouted.

"What did we do, officer?" asked Estes, immediately taking charge as he had since he was a rich teenager in Pecos.

"You're Billie Sol Estes, aren't you?" the other Mexican American, with a short goatee, asked.

"I am." Estes was always polite and definite.

"Well, spread eagle against the car. You too," he said, turning to me and Frank. And there we stood, the three of us up against the car like common criminals, being frisked.

Estes turned to one of the Mexican Americans and, in his most solemn and pious voice said, "I've picked your people up out of the gutters after they've been spit upon by others. Given them jobs when they were begging in the streets. Why would you treat us this way?" He sounded so innocent it was almost funny to me because I had seen police manhandle black people for most of my life.

The Mexican American policeman to whom Estes had directed his comments walked over to Estes and said quietly, "I only do my job, sir."

After what seemed like an hour, they finally released us, and we went on to Jack White's house in El Paso, where White was to open an import-export business. We sat in his lavishly decorated living room discussing politics, courts, finances, and Democrats most of the evening.

On the way back to Abilene Estes told me that he wanted me to keep a folder with his personal mementos in it. Naturally, I was overwhelmed. It seemed that there were so many other people who could have safely guarded his letters, telegrams, photographs, and documents. At the time I had written only one thing in my life, *The Break of Dawn,* a book of poetry published by a vanity press. Yet this was sufficient enough for Estes to ask me to take notes toward writing my own portrait of him as an individual. I was stunned, overwhelmed.

He gave me documents, including letters from senators, congressmen, Lyndon Baines Johnson, and some millionaire friends. A sizable number of letters came from people seeking funds to get married, start businesses, or take trips. However, the most interesting items had to do with Estes's personal road to wealth.

He started with one lamb at age twelve, fifty sheep at fifteen, a thousand pigs at nineteen, and $38,000 in the bank when he twenty. His first million at thirty and the ease with which he attracted more money and awards—all of this was in the documents. A great part of his growth in wealth came during World War II, when he received a contract to supply meat to a military base.

I simply kept the documents with me and returned them to him years later when he came out of prison. I would keep coming back to Billie Sol as the one example of a white person that I trusted, but he was obviously one not too many southern whites trusted: he had too many African American and Mexican American friends for them. They simply called him "a nigger lover" and dismissed him as a serious white person. Of course, Estes was nothing more than a man trying to live by the principles his parents taught him. He respected all human beings, and he felt deeply for those who had been harmed by the aggressive, often devious attitudes of his own people. Hypocrisy was often wrapped in the swaddling clothes of the manger baby, and racism was planted in the soil of the inferiority-superiority lexicon that he had rejected to the best of his abilities. I say to the best of his abilities, because there were times when he simply did not know how to act in the presence of black people. He tried to melt into the group, to listen to the common-folk wisdom of the black grocer who owned the main store in the black community of Pecos, to talk to the Mexican American cotton pickers with the same respect and dignity that he would have given to the local banker. That was the Estes that I had come to know as a young man.

My faith in him had to do with the intrinsic qualities I saw in him as a human being. He was truly one individual who tried his best to treat everyone right and equally, but he especially loved African Americans and Mexicans because, as he once told me, he heard the racist comments whites made about them all the time and believed that what was wrong with America was not the African Americans or the Mexican Americans but the racism he often found in white people.

I do not know any African American or Mexican American who felt he was patronizing, chauvinistic, or simply ingratiating himself. He honestly believed that African Americans and Mexican Americans had been mistreated, and he wanted to be fair. Perhaps it was the way African Americans responded to Estes that also eventually sent me searching for a psychological liberation for African people. Too many southern blacks responded to him as a great white father, something he hated but could do nothing about because it was something the society had created in blacks. That is why I would later say that African Americans were responsible for much of the negative image others had of us; we had so often internalized inferiority. Estes felt uncomfortable with the way some African Americans seemed to defer to him and would often say to Floyd Rose, another young African-American scholar Estes had educated, or to me, "A man is nothing but a man, whether black or white."

Two months after I saw Billie Sol I entered graduate school at Pepperdine College. By this time my relationship with the school teacher Hattie Hilliard had waned, and I was seeing Ngena Scarber, a beautiful ebony-complexioned woman from St. Louis who had moved to California to go to college. I was taken by her incredible beauty, self-confidence, and intelligence. I was easily won over by intelligence, and it remained one of my weak points when dealing with women. But she was also physically quite beautiful. Her skin was the smoothest I had ever seen. Her stark blackness, something pure and perfect, was straight from the hand of nature. She was an academic achiever and had won a scholarship to the University of Illinois from her St. Louis high school before moving on to UCLA.

I finished a master's degree at Pepperdine and applied to UCLA. I was admitted and immediately learned that the university was on an entirely different level from the sectarian schools I had attended.

As a graduate student and the only black student in my department at UCLA, I naturally gravitated to the company of the Jewish students who seemed to have a better grasp on racism than anyone else. Marilyn Kourilsky and Andrea Rich were in the same class with me and sort of introduced me to university procedure. They seemed so much more comfortable with the thirty thousand–student campus than I was, as I was coming from a school with barely three thousand students.

Fortunately for me, we were soon joined by Dennis Ogawa, a cheerful, bright, and delightful conversationalist who had been born in an

American concentration camp during World War II, when Japanese Americans were picked up and placed in internment camps to keep them away from the California coast, where it was believed they could send signals to the Japanese Air Force. Here was someone who had actually lived the racism that I had lived. It was different, but it was still the same kind of thing; whites felt they were superior to us, and some whites really believed that they had the right to persecute us, to intern us, to segregate us, to discriminate against us. We were not having it, and soon Dennis and I were the best of friends.

Only one white male seemed to want to join our group—Dick Erickson, the son of a Christian missionary to the Congo who had come to UCLA from Minnesota with a fairly positive impression of Africa, although he knew next to nothing about African Americans. He grew up in the Congo and had probably been among the whites who had to leave the country when the battle between the Congolese and Belgians intensified.

We knew that we would one day be the leaders in the communications field. We had all been accepted by one of the top universities because we were clearly the best students in the country. UCLA gave us that feeling. It was a good feeling, but it was not always the reality. We found that out as we met intelligence elsewhere, in other colleges and among our friends at home.

Andrea Rich and I wrote a book, *Rhetoric of Revolution*, which was published just after we got our doctorates. I wrote a book called *Transracial Communication*, and Andrea Rich wrote a book called *Interracial Communication*, making UCLA the first campus with an entirely new area in communication studies. She had married John Rich soon after entering the doctoral program in communication; Rich was one of the directors for the series *All in the Family*. After graduation Andrea had a stint at home, taught at the university, and then became an administrator at UCLA en route to heading the Los Angeles County Museum of Art. Marilyn Kourilsky went on to become a major scholar in education. Dennis Ogawa is a distinguished professor at the University of Hawaii and one of the leading interpreters of Japanese culture. He is right up there with Ronald Takaki and Harry Kitano, who in fact both taught at UCLA in the 1960s and 1970s. One of my first classes in African American history was with Ronald Takaki, and Harry

Kitano, the social administration expert, was a confidant and friend. I also counted as friends two other professors: Gary Nash, the young Princeton graduate who came to UCLA with a crew cut hairstyle when everyone was wearing long hair, and Boniface Obichere, the happy, folksy, story-telling historian from Nigeria who drove a huge Cadillac but had the most generous heart of any professor on campus. He would give you the shirt off of his own body if you needed it. Takaki, Nash, Kitano, and Obichere were a formidable team of brilliance. I learned a lot from them. Although Obichere, Kitano, and Takaki are deceased, I had dinner in Philadelphia with Gary Nash in 2009. I think what I liked about all of these people was their integrity; they had the ability and courage to speak without fear, to be direct without equivocation, and to correct themselves if they felt they were wrong.

Meanwhile, Ngena Scarber and I had plans to marry by July of the same year I entered UCLA, in 1966. My marriage to Ngena had all of the early marks of a successful long-term relationship. We were from the same cultural background, possessed similar ambitions, and were considered exceptionally bright by our peers. We had come from similar circumstances, though I was not nearly as gifted as she was in mathematics.

Our fields of interest were so substantially different that we had neither involvement nor much interest in each other's preoccupations. Mine had always been the cause of African liberation at home and abroad, the possibility of fighting in the military wing of the African National Congress, and resisting the anti-Africanisms I saw in American society; hers were perhaps more immediate, domestic, local. And although I thought of her then and think of her now as a fine individual, there was no basis—no functional or psychological basis—for marital longevity except, as is often the case with such marriages, a perfunctory, nominal relationship. Both of us deserved better, and so did Kasina Eka, our only child, a daughter, who was born in 1970. She would prove to be a unique spirit—complex, thoughtful, troubling, creative, curious about genealogy, and loving toward family members. I have always loved Eka, particularly with the winning ways of her smile as well as her deep emotional attachment to my mother and father, Aunt Georgia and Howard, and her own mother.

I have loved several women, but I married three. Ngena, the first, was a stunning beauty who turned heads when she walked into a room. Her deep, dark-chocolate complexion epitomized the "black is beautiful" era. She had a perfect Afro and the walk to go with it. An accomplished certified public accountant, she seemed passionate only about numbers.

Kariamu Welsh, the second, was the best dancer I have ever seen—charismatic, daunting, electric—and probably one of the most creative choreographers in the country. When I met her, I could see elements of her North Carolina African and Native American origins, but her education and training soon turned her into pure Brooklyn, which had been her home until she moved to Buffalo, where I met her. Moods of artistic complications, combined with financial and social entanglements, nearly squeezed both of us to death.

When I married Ana Yenenga, I married my greatest friend and the most perfect woman I have ever met. There may be better scholars, professors, artists, scientists, accountants, and, certainly, cooks, but I could not wish for a more perfect partner in our common mission to teach others that it is possible to be truly human. She is not only brilliant and accomplished in her own profession, but she is also the quickest study of anything that has to do with family. I learned from her the meaning of commitment, loyalty, openness, and affection. Her parents, Delroy and Euphrizine Hunter, born in Costa Rica, moved to the United States when Ana was ten, with eight children. They were a remarkable family with an admirable closeness. Trained as a registered nurse, Ana has never allowed her profession to prevent her from mastering the world of politics, art, culture, science, and literature. She is more knowledgeable about the lives of Zora Neale Hurston and Hugh Masekela than I could ever be because she reads more collateral material than I do. Then she forces me to be taught. In many ways she is the consummate African American—of Akan ancestry but born into a family that had moved from Jamaica to Costa Rica over a hundred years ago, and then to Pasadena, where she grew up and absorbed African American music, religion, and customs.

I met her in Egypt in 1996. I cannot recall if she was coming out of the Karnak Temple or sitting in a café on the Nile when it finally struck me that here was the most beautiful woman I had ever seen. But it was more than physical beauty that stunned me—it was her character, the sense of confidence and destiny that make a person impervious to the world around them. She had that quality of mind and presence that is magnified by subtlety.

To say I met her in Egypt does not mean that I had not seen her before. I had seen her at the JFK International Airport in New York, standing with her son, Mario. He had just finished graduate school at Texas Southern, and Ana was taking him on an African trip as a gift. A year later I saw her briefly when she came to visit a friend at Temple, and they stopped by my office. Two years later, in the winter of 1999, when I was in Los Angeles reviewing black studies programs, I called her, and we met for dinner. It was then that I truly met her mentally and emotionally. Unassuming, direct, and without shallowness, she sat with me for hours, discussing everything from Mugabe to Mbeki, from affirmative action to Marcus Garvey.

Ana eventually became the coordinator of the Cheikh Anta Diop International Conference, an annual gathering of scholars from across the globe, and made it a destination point for many Afrocentrists, those scholars and researchers who believe that African agency is important in interpretation and analysis of African and African American life situations. She claimed the mission of making the world better by being better as a human being and by running the Cheikh Anta Diop until it was turned over to a cadre of my former graduate students in 2008. These students were Adisa Alkebulan, Katherine Bankole Medina, D. Zizwe Poe, Christel Temple, Suzuko Morikawa, and Jahwara Giddings. Poe and another former student, Virgilette Nzingha Gaffin, also became experts on ancient Egypt and organized groups of scholars and lay people into effective travel-research groups to Egypt as I had done for twelve years.

Ana and I continued our travels to Africa, Europe, South America, Antarctica, and around the world, and we have underscored our commitment to be out front on issues vital to humanity, whether regarding the environment, HIV/AIDS, Pan-Africanism, hunger, genocide, racism, or sexism. With a cadre of intellectuals on every continent committed to our mission, Ana and I have worked to create an international network of conscious individuals who are prepared to create transformations in people's lives.

∞

Before marrying Ngena, Kariamu, or Ana Yenenga, I had found my calling in UCLA student politics in 1966. At UCLA I joined student government and became a member of the Board of Governors and a member of the Golden Bruins. I maintained leadership in the UCLA chapter of the Student Nonviolent Coordinating Committee and eventually became president and worked with the Harambee group to bring Black Studies to campus. Jackie Robinson, Rafer Johnson, and Ralph Bunche had already established their reputations at UCLA as outstanding student leaders; I felt that it was my time to extend that tradition. Not long after I entered student government I encountered the brothers from the Black Panthers and the Us Organization, two groups that had competed for UCLA student members. I had friends in both groups but had my hands full with SNCC. Early in 1967 I drove up to the mountains just outside of Ventura, California, into the then-smog-free air of the stubbled countryside. Pilgrims with backpacks and sandals passed me, walking down as I drove up. At the top of the hill, overlooking four valleys, was a shrine, a place of peace in war, of summertime during the blizzards of life. This was Ojai's spiritual center, perhaps for me at that moment, the spiritual center of the whole wide world. I was thinking about the young hippie-looking white woman I had met at UCLA.

She soared in her mind and sat at peace amid the turbulent student discussions we were conducting at the food shack outside Campbell and Rolfe Halls. When I finished making a particularly decent point about the presence of Nazis and Ku Klux Klanners on campus, having managed to get Dennis Ogawa's and Marilyn Kourilsky's assent, she spoke and we were stunned; her silence had been so foreign. "You've got to visit Ojai," she said. That is all I remember her saying, though possibly she said more. There was much more to say, but I heard Ojai.

Now here I was, visiting the shrine at Ojai—mind open, expectant, embroidered emotion worn on my countenance like so many rough spots needing to be smoothed out. I parked the car, walked over to the edge of the cliff, and looked for miles around at the surrounding terrain, bush, sagebrush, arid earth, and not another building in sight except for a small house about a hundred yards away, which belonged to the caretaker. Years later, when I stood atop the Matopo Hills in Zimbabwe,

I would sense the same immensity of nature, the same serenity, the same voices of the silent terrain.

There was nothing impressive about the Ojai shrine. It was small, of contemporary glass and stone, an American original bent to some Eastern attitude. Inside the shrine sparkling light reflected from the colored glass gave the sensation of a conference with spirits. The Tibetan, an Asian mystic, I soon discovered, held the place of spiritual honor. Sprinkled around the shrine, I saw books by and about the Tibetan, his system of telepathy, his understanding of peace and consciousness. I remained in the shrine for a couple of hours, waiting. And then it occurred to me that I could never fully meditate for a few hours; it would take a lifelong commitment.

The peace of the summertime, I thought, is no different from the peace of the winter. And so, after speaking to the caretaker and taking one more look over the valleys, knowing that somewhere below and around some mountains was Los Angeles. I took the peace I had and reentered the crazy world of four million maniacs raving for peace. I stopped on Fairfax Avenue and bought some cheese, got a bottle of wine from my favorite La Brea supermarket, and headed home to Redondo Beach Boulevard off of Pico.

About this time I had another revelation, one that would stay with me for the rest of my life. What about African religion? Here a sense of spirituality and origin, actually identity and knowledge, became a mélange of existential quests. I had never even thought about the spiritual energies of my Georgian ancestors in terms of contemporary African religion. I knew they were different energies from those whites exuded, but I did not have a real name for them. I did not even understand the meaning of the religion that my mother *really* practiced. I had long left the daily preachments of Hattie Hilliard and the familiar sermons of the evangelicals, but I was, for the first time, interested in African religion. Yes, what *did* our people believe before the enslavement? Ojai had brought me to my senses, and I could not turn back now. I know about the Tibetan mystic, but what about the Yoruba or Akan mystics or philosophers?

I joined a group of seekers in search of the nature of African religion. When I went to their meeting place, a little bungalow in Watts, somewhere off of 103rd Street, I sat on the sofa next to an attentive man dressed in a full agbada, three flowing pieces of colorful fabric, listening to the teacher, a babalawo, speak in English and Yoruba about the seven powers. That was it! Everything that I remembered from my childhood had congealed in the presence of the other attendees as the babalawo spoke about Shango, Obatala, Oshun, Eshu, Oya, Yemenja, and Ogun.

I do not remember the babalawo's name—it was a Yoruba name—but he was tall and thin, with a light cashew complexion and a beard. His words were quiet, different from those of the black Baptist preacher, but effective nevertheless. Here I was, a university professor, hearing for the first time something I should have known years earlier. Indeed, I believed that I had been diverted from this course several times in my life. The revelation came to me starkly, singularly impressive. In the small living room the babalawo took me by my thoughts, and I soared to spiritual heights that I had never known.

Somebody played the music of the crossroads in the background, saying it was the sign of Eshu. The polyrhythms bent my thoughts until they curved into a circle, and I joined the dancing of the orishas. *Have I really found what I was looking for, right here in this room?* I asked myself.

Connecting the dots once I had the religious lines straight in my head was easy for me. The babalawo explained to me that the orishas are the emissaries of God Almighty, whom he referred to as Olodumare. These orishas control all the forces of nature and humanity. One can recognize them by their colors, their numbers, and their personality traits.

We all bent over, our chins on our thumbs, listening to the thin man. He said that the orishas have their own food and like certain gifts and offerings. If we respect the orishas' wishes, they will always come to our assistance. He said that we forgot the orishas during slavery, and now that African people were remembering again, we would be blessed.

I soon learned that I was attending a Yoruba bembé, where the ancestral spirits would appear and we would see the priests mounted by the orishas. I felt that the babalawo was speaking directly to me when he revealed all of the traditions of the Yoruba during the bembé. I could not help but be struck, as a university professor but with limited knowledge because of my own upbringing, by the fact that my colleagues knew almost nothing about African cultural life in the United States. They were far worse off than I was, although I knew only a little bit of information. For example, they did not know that Eshu, or Elegba, as he is also called, owned all of the roads and doors in the world. Eshu holds ashé, power. He is the repository of ashé. His colors, red and black, or white and black, show his contradictory nature.

As the babalawo spoke, I thought of two people in my family who fit the description of Eshu. They were always trying to create opportunities for other people. The first was my father's maternal grandmother. Georgia Anderson, whom we called Mamie, stood at the door of all family decisions. Her role in life seemed to be giving advice. When I was about eight years old, her daughter, my Aunt Vanessa, and Vanessa's husband, John Henry, were debating about buying a house near the canal that ran through West Valdosta. They went over every argument, for and against, back and forth, until finally Mamie said to them, "We gon' buy the house tomorrow." That was the end of it. There were no more questions. She was the decider, the decision maker.

The second person was my niece Debra. We came to depend on her for truth telling even when we disagreed with her. So in one sense Debra, four generations removed from Mamie Georgia Anderson, had collected her spirit, and both were Eshu.

In Yoruba mythology Eshu stands at the crossroads of divinity and humanity, and his job is to forge a relationship with Orunmila, the deity of divination. The late Babatunde Olatunji, drum and music master of Yoruba, saw Eshu as the opener of ways, the forger of our truths and identities in the midst of confusion.

I now knew why the music of Elegba, Eshu, had been playing as the entry into the meeting. Indeed, nothing can happen without Eshu, who opens the door between the worlds. He is the opening and the closing; he is the way right and the way left. Without Eshu's permission, nothing that humans plan can be achieved, so we must always listen to his music.

The thin man said that Ogun, the deity of iron, labor, and war, was special for black people because he was the owner of technology and was the one orisha who people always appealed to in warfare. He clears the roads with his machete and is recognized by the colors green and black.

When the babalawo moved on to talk about Ochosi, I realized I was getting hungry, having been in the room for a couple of hours. He said that Ochosi is the hunter and the scout of the orishas and that he assumes the role of translator for Obatala, with whom he has a close, genuine relationship. Ochosi's colors are blue and yellow. He takes the lead in situations that demand leadership, and he is the orisha of leadership, of questing, of searching for the meaning of life.

The babalawo seemed not to get tired while talking. In fact, he seemed inspired when he talked about Obatala, the kindly father of all the orishas and all humanity. Listening to the babalawo, I learned that this generative, productive orisha was the owner of all heads and minds. In fact, although it was Olorun, Olodumare, who created the universe, it was Obatala who created humanity. Thus, he became the source of all wisdom, peace, purity, and compassion. His color is white, and those who are called to him wear white clothes. Furthermore, Obatala is also the only orisha who can demonstrate feminine and masculine characteristics. All other orishas are either male or female.

The babalawo spoke of Oya as the spirit of the winds. Indeed, Oya is the ruler of the winds, the whirlwind, and the gates to the cemeteries. Nothing escapes Oya, whose number is nine and whose color is maroon. She rules over the egun, or dead, and is a fierce warrior who rides to war with Shango, sharing lightning and fire with him.

A few years after listening to the babalawo, I visited Nigeria and went to the secret and sacred forest of Oshun, who rules over the sweet waters of the world, the brooks, streams, and rivers. Oshun rules over love and fertility, and I felt her presence, or what I thought was her presence, down beside the sacred river flowing through the sacred forest. I met Twins Seven Seven and the Austrian mystic, Suzanne Wenger, there, seeking to discover the peace at the Oshun River. There you learn something about the orisha who is the Iyalode, the great queen, embodying love. Oshun heals with her sweet waters and with honey, which she also owns. The femme fatale of the orishas, Oshun once saved the world by luring Ogun out of the forests using her sensuality in order to soothe him and claim him for humanity. Oshun clothes herself in the colors yellow and gold, and her number is five.

I realized the babalawo was older than I had first thought when I entered the living room. His voice broke a little as he spoke of Yemenja, but it was not in nervousness but reverence. He said that Yemenja lives and rules over the seas and lakes, and she also rules over maternity. I thought he would cry, but he composed himself and went on to say that she is the mother of all and that her name, a shortened version of "Yeye Omo Eja," meaning "mother whose children are the fish," reflected the fact that her children are innumerable. Like the sea, she is vast and unknowable.

Just as I was getting acquainted with Yemenja, the babalawo went on to explain Orunmila, the orisha of wisdom and divination; then he revealed that he was a priest of Orunmila. Indeed, all priests are "fathers of secrets," who devote themselves entirely to the practice of divination. Orunmila's colors are green and yellow, reflecting the fact that he is very close with Oshun. Orunmila is wisdom and Oshun is knowledge, for wisdom without knowledge is empty form, and one who has knowledge without wisdom is dangerous.

I could not believe what I was hearing for the first time from the babalawo. Here was an African system of thinking, believing, and myth making that had both logic and passion. Later, when I talked with Wole Soyinka, the Nobel laureate for literature; Adeniyi Coker, the playwright and actor; and professor Toyin Falola, the most prolific African writer—all Yorubas whom I had known prior to my own discoveries—I told them my story, and as contemporary and urbane as they are, they said to me, "You have found a home, you have a place, you must now sing the songs of Eshu."

Not long afterward I had this incredible sensation. Here I was, living in Baldwin Hills next to the reservoir and around the corner from Ray Charles, Ike and Tina Turner, and Nancy Wilson. I had been transported to a different reality from my siblings and peers, and I was a long way from Valdosta. I often thought of my friends from my youth: Bro Boy, Dimp, Gooseneck, Red, and Cootie. They too wanted to get out of Valdosta. But I got out, and I went to Los Angeles.

My early work experiences were periods of intense reflection on the nature of the black condition in South Georgia. At the age of ten I entered the complex realm of farm fieldwork, common work for blacks in the South during the 1950s. In fact, after the end of the Civil War in 1865, farm labor provided the most extensive employment for African Americans in the South. You didn't need experience, you didn't have to be paid minimum wages, and you didn't have to be eighteen to work. All you had to do was get up in the morning and go to the fields.

I believe that I have always liked the mornings because of those early experiences with the cool air, the initial quiet of the cotton and tobacco fields, the chatter of the workers once the work had started, and the isolated time you could find to reflect, think, meditate, and dream. My energies are more direct, concrete, genuine in the mornings; in the evenings I wane, lose focus, seek the bed. This is all the result of those early mornings on the old hired trucks carrying black people to the white people's fields.

As I sat in my office at the university, assessing what I knew as a child became one of the games I played with myself. For example, I knew at ten years of age that black people worked and white people paid. It was the logic of white rule in the South. I knew it was not right because great-grandmother Hattie Shine Smith used to say, "Dem dat works oughts to get somethin'; dem dat's not, oughts not." She had always been like the rest of the Shine family—practical, analytical, efficient. You did not find her in any type of religious fervor. She believed, but she was as rational as her condition would allow her to be. My grand-daddy Moses thought the Black Communist Movement in the 1930s had influenced his mother; he had seen some old documents around the house that looked like "propaganda" about the rights of workers. I only know that she would come out with some pretty intelligent sayings about work. Seeing the way we worked, particularly Vera and me, made me think that religion was a waste of time because black people still worked, and the white children still swam in the pond. My mother and father, I thought, had every right to enjoy life as much as the whites. And Vera and I had every right to have a childhood free of the drudgery of cotton fields.

Of course, I did not spend all day thinking about what happened to me as a child. I thought about it some of the time, and in thinking about it I realized that some times were quite refreshing. You could say that I often found the tobacco fields particularly joyful places, where I could hide under some of the thickest stalks of the stuff and write poems in the sand. I must have written more poems in the sand than anyone—all of them to vanish with the first rain or the coming of the tobacco sled. When you lose a poem, obliterated by the rain or a tobacco sled, you just move on and await the return of the Muse. Sometimes the Muse came, and at other times I was left with the hard realities of the physical labor itself.

Our family was a family of very capable and independent women. I was lucky to have such sisters. Two of them I knew more intimately than the others because we were raised together in Valdosta. Vera was the younger of the two and April, the older, but both had a profound impact on the way I view the world. I could never do enough for them and could never forget their sacrifices, their love of family, and their commitment to harmony. They must have been priestesses because they knew better than anyone how to mediate the energies flowing between people in times of stress. They were like the New Orleans Seven Sisters; they appeared where you would least expect, and they always had the same expressions on their faces.

April left Valdosta and moved to New York. I felt that she was alright, but we only heard from her intermittently, and this worried my parents. When we had not heard from her in about three years, we knew that we had lost her to the North. She had gone to work and then to dance professionally, but we lost her. I was only seventeen and a senior in high school when Mama gave me the last address she had for April and told me, "Go find your sister up there in Buffalo, New York."

I boarded a greyhound bus in Nashville, Tennessee, and went to Buffalo, looking for my sister. When I went to the address I had, the landlord told me that she had moved to Brooklyn, New York. He gave me another address, and I caught the next bus for the four-hundred–mile trip to the other side of the state. In Brooklyn I found my sister living on New York Avenue, just like the man had said. She recognized me immediately. We embraced, spoke of the past in Valdosta, and I caught her up on all the family news. She looked good, like a celebrity. She told me about her life and why she had not written. "I travel a lot, don't have much time to write," she said.

It sounded okay, but I could never fully understand it because we had been taught that nothing should break us away from our family. However, I was so happy to see her that I did not want to do anything that might disturb her line of thinking. Right then, I just wanted her to contact Mama. April was found, and we never lost her again. I have always felt that her and Vera's spirits are the two abiding presences in my life.

In May of 1985 my sister Vera, who had almost been my twin, we were so close, died of cancer. The day of her death was the worst day of my life because for the first time I felt the pain of regret—the gnawing, biting distress that comes over you when the finality of never seeing a loved one again really sinks into your mind. Regret, for me, was an utter sense of helplessness when I knew that I could never spend the time I had wanted to spend with the sister nearest to me in age.

Relief did not come, even though I had been with her a few days before her death, having gone to Georgia to see her one last time. She said, "I'm fine, I just want to rest." Her illness had slipped into her body and stolen her will to go on. A few days later she died. It affected me profoundly. I knew I would never be able to replace her as a friend.

Her children became, according to family custom, my children. The three youngest children, John, Leroy, and Nigel, remained with their father, Johnny, my brother-in-law; Debra and Abner were both adults, and I became their adviser. They loved their mother because she stood with them when times were hard. Debra had gotten married a year before Vera's death, and her son, Greg Jr., was born the day before Vera's death. Abner married the next year. Both were mature and had their mother's spiritual outlook: favor children, love family, and seek to be the best example of good citizens.

Vera lived a short but dynamic life. In many ways she remains the most vivid memory I have of a beautiful teenager. Her bronze skin shined in the Georgia sunlight under the hot sun when we picked cotton. More beautiful than any of the children on our street, she attracted young men much too early and had her first child at fourteen. Vera was without politics and without theory; she was practice and love, pure and simple. We loved each other so much because I was just the opposite. Vera brought purity and simplicity to all of her human relationships, whereas I was too early involved in the metaphysical, political, philosophical, and magical. I would say that I inherited my grandfather Moses's love for ideas of all kinds. But Vera—she was innocence itself. I would argue, interrogate, speak up even before I was given permission, but she would sing and enchant the listener.

Then, when we were older, I sat in her hospital room, staring at her frail body shot through with erratic cells, and I remembered our youth. Disorientation and nausea took hold of her as the pain tore through her body; the cancer that would take her did not wait long. She had suffered for more than five months; when they discovered the disease, it was too late for the doctors to arrest it, but she kept a smile on her face even in her weakest moments.

As I sat with her she told me that she was all right, that she was at peace. I was not at peace, and I cried. Although she remained in frightful pain and terribly disoriented from the medicine, she stayed calm throughout the last days of her ordeal.

When the pain and nausea were too much to bear and her face was contorted with each wave of discomfort, she turned to the other side, tuning out the distractions of family and friends. Death came and touched her gently, canonizing her as one of the great ancestors. Her voice became a memory to be spoken of with awe, and every time I thought about our youth, I thought of her joy.

I was robbed of my closest sibling, left to travel alone through my years without her wonderful laughter. As much as I worked to understand the intricacies of African politics, the absolute humanness of Vera, a soul so pure and free of striving, made me stop often to reflect on all of my strivings. Of course, I kept on striving.

Vera was always eager to work to better her condition, and she knew that I had the same drive, the same energy to do something rather than wallow in need. And our daddy had taught us to depend on nobody else, and we didn't.

My academic career began in the context of the emerging cultural struggles of the late 1960s. My first job after completing my PhD at UCLA in the summer of 1968 was at Purdue University. I arrived about the same time as college students were protesting against war, poverty, and racism. In the academic year 1968–69 news magazines called Purdue University the "hotbed of rest." William Gass, a sneaker-wearing philosopher who later became a very famous professor for his essays, was trying to raise the consciousness of his students to the crimes against the poor while I, the only black faculty at the time, on a tenure-track professorship, was tapped by black students to be their adviser. Nothing happened much on the campus until Fred Hampton and Julian Bond came to speak about the struggle against racism. They lit a fire on the campus that black students used to build a huge Black Student Union movement that would later see the university creating one of the first Black Student Cultural Centers.

I found it difficult to take the quiet of West Lafayette after the years in Los Angeles and was ecstatic when the associate vice chancellor at UCLA, C. Z. Wilson, who had been one of my mentors when I was a graduate student, called me and asked, "Do you want to come back to UCLA?" Wilson, UCLA's first high-level administrator, had studied in Switzerland, earned a doctorate in economics at Illinois, and chaired economics at SUNY Binghamton. He and Charles Young, the chancellor at UCLA, had established a Faculty Recruitment Plan that would give hiring positions to any department that could find an African American or Mexican American. It was one of the most successful of such plans: nearly fifty African Americans were hired as professors. A few—perhaps six—had graduated from UCLA. As Wilson put it: "If someone gets a doctorate at UCLA, why should we send our best students to other universities?" However, most of the young professors and a few more mature ones, like Thomas Sowell, had come from other universities. I was in the recruitment class with Angela Davis, James Pitts, John Davis, and H. V. Nelson.

I returned to UCLA as an assistant professor of communication and Director of the Center for Afro American Studies. My appointment by the chancellor to the directorship of the CAAS was a popular one, as I had been off campus during the fatal shooting of Bunchy Carter and John Huggins and had no proven alliance with either the Black Panthers or the organization Us, whose members are said to have fired the shots, during a mass meeting in January 1969. I had left UCLA in August of 1968 and did not return until July 1969. The shootings had occurred in January 1969 at a meeting on campus. I knew the parties to the events because I had been the leader of the Student Nonviolent Coordinating Committee on campus for two years.

The FBI had infiltrated both the Black Panthers and the Us organization—and probably SNCC—and whether the shootings were spontaneous or ordered by the agents' provocateurs is not known for certain. One thing we do know for certain is that Maulana Karenga, the leader of the Us organization, was not at the UCLA meeting, although the press sought to muddy his face and blur his reputation by claiming that his rhetoric was what created the climate for the killings.

As a compromise candidate, one accepted by the Black Panthers and organization Us, I sought to steer the Center toward academic research. I believe that when I left the university in 1973, I had set the CAAS on a proper and important goal of becoming one of the premier centers in the nation for African American research.

Furthermore, I had good relationships with all sectors of the black community and had published two books, *The Rhetoric of Black Revolution* and *Rhetoric of Revolution*, which gave me legitimacy with some segments of the faculty. The troika of black faculty, Henry McGee of law, Boniface Obichere of history, and Douglas Glasgow of social work who served as Executive Council during the time Robert Singleton was acting director, was retained when I became permanent director. The fact that Singleton was a graduate student in economics—and without the doctorate—meant that the university sought to strengthen his base with faculty by creating this cadre. When I took over as permanent director, I kept the troika in place as a necessary buffer to any agitation.

I set out to create the first truly Afrocentric center in the nation. I envisioned a center that would take the idea of African agency as the keystone of research about black people in the United States and the rest of the world. What could it mean for a research center at a major university to shift the paradigm of black research? The piece I wrote was called "Toward a Black Perspective" and was published by the center as its first paper, but at the time I had not settled on a name for this perspective. I would refer to "afrology," "africology," but I finally decided on "Afrocentric" as the designation of the theoretical orientation. I wanted to see African people "re-center" themselves into our own historical experiences. I wanted to see scholars who asked questions of black agency in social, political, and economic situations. I tired of the old paradigm in which blacks were problems, issues, burdens, and deficiencies and in which everything was seen from the viewpoint of white people.

This would take lots of work, alliances, colleagues, and a strong sense of mission. When I took my office in Campbell Hall, I immediately went to work to achieve several goals, which included:

aligning the Afro American Studies Center to the University of California, Los Angeles system of research centers, including changing the name to Center for Afro American Studies. This may appear like a small matter, but it had symbolic significance because UCLA had many Institutes and Centers, and our name would appear alongside other research centers;

negotiating with Sage Publications for editorial control of the *Journal of Black Studies*;

selecting an editorial board for JBS from eminent scholars, including Vincent Harding, Martin Kilson, Boniface Obichere, Harold Cruse, and Gary Nash;

resolving lingering conflicts between students who were partisans of Black Panthers, the Us organization, Nation of Islam, and Student Nonviolent Coordinating Committee. I held several meetings with student and community leaders regarding relationships with activists who maintained daily contact with their followers on campus;

publishing the UCLA Center's first monograph, *Toward Transracial Communication*;

establishing Grant-in-Aid for professors working on African American issues. Small grants were made to a number of faculty members who wrote proposals for research;

receiving outstanding visits from Muhammad Ali and Wilma Rudolph;

creating the distinguished lectureship program and inviting Janheinz Jahn, Arna Bontemps, and others to campus;

supporting the UCLA Afro American Library;

writing an interdisciplinary Master's Degree in African American Studies; and

establishing Community Outreach to Watts Poetry Workshop.

Two years after returning to UCLA I made Associate Professor in Communication by maintaining what David Saxon, the Executive

Vice Chancellor, called a "sit your butt down and write" attitude in an environment that was "publish or perish." By 1973 I had built such a reputation through my publications in the communication field—and Ronald Reagan was about to wreck the California university system—that I was open to the possibility of working in a communication department. Fortunately, I was given the opportunity to rebuild a communication department and simultaneously strengthen an African American Studies department, so I left for the State University of New York at Buffalo. Breaking with the West Coast was difficult, but I was to be head of the Department of Communication, and they gave me a tenured full professorship. I was thirty years old, the youngest full professor in SUNY history at the time.

My youthful zest for change and my moral outrage about racism may have outrun my patience at times. I immediately sought to increase the number of black students, bringing into the department Louis Browne, Fran Dorsey, Fidelis Amatokwu, and Ellen Gant. I reached out to women students and brought in Diane Hope, Erika Wenzel Vora, and Eileen Newmark. They all became successful in various fields of communication, rhetoric, intercultural communication, and information systems. SUNY Buffalo gained a reputation for innovation, vitality, and intellectual curiosity. Students like Erika Wenzel Vora, originally from Germany, established an early reputation with lectures and writings on intercultural diffusion of information. Diane Hope became a major theorist. Louis Browne went on to become the senior professor in communication at a major university. More than thirty students, from every continent, received doctorates during my time at Buffalo. I count the time, especially the winter with cross-country skiing and cold downhill, with special joy.

My tenure as professor and chair at Buffalo lasted ten years. After the blizzard of 1977, I acknowledged that I did not want to remain in the wintry climate of the Niagara region, yet I hung on for a few more years. The emotional climate wore on me as well; as a black person in charge of an all-white department, I experienced constant disputes, political intrigues, and attempts to subvert my objectives and the personal ambitions of black students. After I hired Cecil Blake, a Sierra Leonean, and Mary Cassata, an Italian-American from the Department of Library Sciences, the old white male club lost its grip, and the department became friendlier to women, blacks, and Chicanos. Nevertheless, I was already fed up with the fights and bitterness when Gerald Goldhaber, a businessman turned professor, headed a recruitment team from the University and then lied about interviewing African American candidates to fulfill an affirmative action requirement.

He told the university that I was on the committee that interviewed candidates at a convention in Washington. I had never left Buffalo and was not on the interviewing committee. I discovered that my name had been used in the report when Jesse Nash, the affirmative action officer, called to ask me about the interview. I told him I was not in Washington and had never interviewed anyone for the department, but I knew that with the existing white privilege, nothing would happen to Goldhaber because other departments had also faked their affirmative action reports. Hearings were held, evidence was presented that the documents were fake, and the University officials merely gave him a reprimand for the action.

It was time to move on, so I applied for and obtained a position as chair of the Department of African-American Studies at Temple University.

Buffalo had its moments, however. The winters were bitter and unforgiving, but they provided me with lots of solitude and time to think and write. Like the Niagara Movement, which led to the National Association for the Advancement of Colored People, you could say that, although the word may have been in my vocabulary, the Afrocentric Movement was really born out of my thoughts in the Niagara region.

In the late 1970s I perfected my arguments for an analysis of African life founded upon the idea of African agency. In the Center for Positive Thought on the corner of Utica and Main streets, I tested my theories on the artists, would-be revolutionaries, Kawaidists, and Sunni Muslims who came to the weekly Nommo meetings. Some resisted, others stopped coming to hear me, and still others took the arguments to new levels, exploring the possibilities in art, literature, and architecture. In those intense meetings with would-be revolutionaries who had inherited the wind of the 1960s, my most profound philosophical discoveries emerged, and I found the infinite possibilities within the struggle between marginality's savage brutality and the empowering virtue of centricity. Now this was an engagement to which I could devote my time.

While I was lecturing and writing on Afrocentricity, I was working with the anti-Rhodesian forces and the anti-apartheid forces to bring about freedom in southern Africa. A small group of committed intellectuals and activists gathered around the Center for Positive Thought to provide money, materials, and medicines to the resistance forces, advancing the liberation of Zimbabwe and South Africa. Naomi Nhiwatiwa Oseni, who became a minister of government in Zimbabwe, was active in the Buffalo group, as were Vimbai Chivaura, a literary critic and culturalist who became a professor and farmer, and Japhet Zwana, a political philosopher. Zwana remained, when sober, the clearest interpreter of southern African politics long after we disbanded. Ngarsungu Chiwengo from the Congo and Maraka Standa from Kenya rounded out my "committee" for African renaissance, as we talked and laughed and cried about African affairs while dancing the nights away in Buffalo.

There was an amber light in my Uncle Moses's hazel eyes, brightness from imbibing too much Scotch too fast, with not enough food, and for too long. He was a slight man now; I remembered him as a large, muscular man when he would come home with his smart army suit on and his sergeant's stripes telling the story of his rise through the ranks of the American army. But I was younger then; now liquor had stunted, bent, and reduced him to a slight pencil of a man.

"Boy, what you doing in Valdosta?" he asked, his breath heavy and foul with cheap whiskey.

"Visiting the people," I said, which in our vernacular meant the family.

"So here's where I live." He flung his arms around the shambles of a room with a fallen picture of President Nixon on the floor.

"How are you doing?" I asked, looking around. Newspapers and pillows were strewn on the floor. The sofa was a stationary cargo ship with all kinds of bottles, Ritz cracker boxes, and potato chip bags on it. "How you doing?" I asked again after surveying.

"I'm fine," Uncle Moses assured me.

"You taking care of yourself?" I would not have dared to ask a few years earlier, for fear he would snap my head off.

"Look at me." He beat his chest and almost stumbled over the pillows scattered about the floor.

"I see you."

"Don't mock me now, boy!" He pointed his finger.

"No, I wouldn't do that, Uncle Moses." And I wouldn't have. He would have known that much about me had he remained sober long enough to really get to know me. I always respected my elders, and especially him because of his kindness toward me and my siblings when we were small.

Uncle Moses looked me up and down, trying to get a hold of himself, sort of dodging the alcoholic lapses in consciousness by asking questions. "How long you here for?"

"One week." I indulged him.

"Then where you going?"

"To Africa." I said, knowing I baited him.

"Africa? What's in Africa?" he asked, his pitch-black skin turning red. "What the hell you left in Africa?"

"There are people there, black people, new countries, history."

"You ain't left nothin' in Africa, boy."

"I'm going on a study tour," I said, wishing that I had the courage to tell him that we black people in America had left our minds in Africa, just like Malcolm X once said.

"Africa, shit, Africa. What's a black man doing going to Africa? You're an American."

"Yes, American by citizenship, but black people came here from Africa, you know."

"Naw, the Smiths came from Dooly County," he said, jabbing the air with his right hand.

"But before that, where did we come from?" I asked, smelling the whiskey on his breath, we were so close.

"Don't matter before that, don't matter." He had given his final declaration.

Seeing my Uncle Moses, listening to him, feeling his alienation from Africa helped me to see how deeply distressed African Americans are about their African origins. Every discussion would come right around to the topic of African identity; we were stuck on this point, and there was to be no moving off of it. Of course, I was convinced that African Americans' real problem was the denial of our ancestors' origins, language, religion, customs, traditions, and gods. The only thing we had managed to keep was the music, and this in spite of the early criticisms of it.

"Have a drink?" Uncle Moses asked.

"Uncle Moses, I got to go now."

"Too good to drink with your uncle, huh?"

"No, it's not that."

"Well damn it, have a drink." He offered me a fifth of J&B. I took a small sip, and as the smooth Scotch tingled down my esophagus, Uncle Moses took the bottle and drank a large swig. He took me by the shoulders and, rocking back and forth like a swaying palm before a hurricane, said, "Tell my people in Africa hello for me." The truth of the matter was that Africa was not on his mind, and yet there he was, blacker than Alabama coal and lost in the wilderness of alcohol. What he needed was a good swig of self-esteem; had he been interested in Africa, he may have found a new lease on life. Instead, he withered more and more away, a crusty shell, an olive, shriveled.

When I told my father what had transpired, he shook his head. "He used to be a fine man. The Army destroyed him. Took his life and gave him the bottle."

Even as a young man Moses Jr. was always handsome, intelligent, and industrious. But as it turned out, he was the least successful of Moses Sr.'s children. In the Smith family Moses Jr. was the favorite. Although my father was the oldest, Granddaddy Moses thought to name his second son Junior. This was troubling to my father all of his life. He could not understand the rationale for it, so he created all types of scenarios in his mind. Some were far-fetched, but his childhood fantasies shaped the strained relationship between my father and granddaddy.

Years later I reflected on my earlier experiences and the youthful wonderment of my uncle Moses, my daddy's youngest brother. I was not good at singing, but I could recite poetry, and Uncle Moses would always show me off to other people. "Go on, Buddy, recite *The Creation*, by James Weldon Johnson," he would say.

Uncle Moses's love of poetry often came to me when I was in graduate school, years later. Like the time I felt his presence with me in South Central Los Angeles while I lay on my small bunk bed with the rust showing between patches of aluminum paint. Then I thought that I had actually become a poet like my father. I had a collage of memories, a recollection of childhood that had pounded itself into the secret moments of my relaxation in that 53rd Street bungalow. I would never describe myself again as an aspiring writer. I was a young writer, but I had been organizing the symbols in my head since I was ten. Nothing impressed me more than the concrete experiences of the ordinary black people in the South. I was one of them, like Uncle Moses and my father, even though I had moved to California for graduate school.

CHAPTER 4

DESTINATIONS

I N 1973 I CHANGED MY NAME OFFICIALLY from Arthur to Molefi while living in Buffalo, New York. My father was so pleased about it that I was shocked, surprised—I had experienced some trepidation about doing it because I wondered how he would feel. After all, I had been named in his honor: Arthur Lee Smith Jr. Like his name, mine had all of the anonymity an African could wish for in Georgia. Arthur was clearly European, Lee brought to mind the Confederate general who fought to keep us enslaved, and Smith was an authentic nonname in America. Perhaps Smith was the European equivalent to the black Muslim's X, the unknown. Well, I wanted to be anonymous in neither Christian nor Islamic circles; I wanted to claim my African heritage and legacy, and the place to start was with my name. Thus, a Georgia boy headed toward an African destination.

My mother was perplexed by the change. She had always called me Buddy Boy, never Arthur and never Junior. Years later, when I got married, she dropped the "Boy" and just referred to me as Buddy.

In some ways, to change from Arthur Lee Smith Jr. to Molefi Kete Asante was to blossom like a flower. What had been dormant during the terrible ordeal of oppression in America—the nightmare of suffering, the loss of identity—was recalled in the names of the nananom nsamanfo, the ancestors remembered, as I became "keeper of the traditions." I had no intention of being an invisible person in the midst of a society where people were looking for authenticity.

The fact of the matter is that I was not alienated when I changed my name. I was not angrier than I already was about racism in the universities where I studied and taught. I did not feel that I was reacting to white people when I changed my name; it mattered very little, almost not at all, what other people thought about the underpinnings of my name change. I was finally running toward Africa.

I felt as if the entire 246 years of enslavement and the numerous indignations that had been heaped upon my people's heads were gone, vanished. I did what the African American women had done during the 1960s, when they revolted by wearing their hair in its natural state. Changing my name was a relief, a celebration of my Africanity, and an honor to my ancestors because whenever someone called my name, they would be remembering the ancestors' names.

∽

Not long after I changed my name, I began to reflect on Ralph Ellison's *Invisible Man*, which I discovered while I was at the Nashville Christian Institute. What fascinated me about the book was its size—after all, I had never seen a book written by a black person, and I had never had but one other book, Charles Dickens's stories. I must have been fourteen or so when I first read some of the book. Later, I read it and read it again; such was the power of Ellison's prose.

I do not think I had enough experience as a teenager to understand all the nuances, innuendoes, metaphors, and tropes of Ellison's large work. Some books are like that; you have to read them in different life stages until you get that "Aha!" feeling. When I got it, I joined the chorus celebrating the gifts of Ralph Ellison. Of course, in successive readings I began to have my own questions about the book. It remains a classic, but perhaps it represents more the limitations on the black writer than anything else.

One day, while in Boley, an all-African town, it hit me like lightning: I really had to be a writer. As I drove slowly through the main street, the intense black faces stared at me from the hardware store, where ten or twelve people were assembled on the porch. They looked like tough, strong, and resilient souls—these were survivors. I could see how Ellison penetrated the intricacies of these souls and saw something that was invisible to the average person. I could see the invisibility of Africans in American society. I could also see the racism in Oklahoma; Ellison would have remembered the bombing of the black business community in Tulsa during the 1920s race riot.

Many African families had come to Oklahoma with the native nations that made the great trek in 1835 on the "Trail of Tears." Perhaps some of my ancestors on both sides went with them. This strange land laid claim to powerful spirits. I wanted to spend a lot of time in Boley and the other all-African towns in Oklahoma, but I was only a student, and did not have time to do all the things I needed to do.

I sought to break out of the bondage of my routine. Writing appealed to me because it gave me a way to order the chaos I saw. The murder of blacks in the South by anti-Africanists had a profound effect on me. The Birmingham church bombings as much as the 1964 murders of civil rights workers James Chaney, Andrew Goodman, and Michael Schwerner as well as the 1965 murder of Viola Liuzzo were psychologically scarring. Madmen who knew no respect for decency had killed them.

The murders of the 1960s reignited the psychological hell I had experienced after the death of Emmett Till in 1954. I had just gone to the Nashville Christian Institute when the lynching of Till happened. White men kidnapped the fourteen-year-old Chicagoan from his cousin's house in Money, Mississippi, and tortured and bludgeoned him to death in one of the most heinous crimes committed in the 1950s. Money became synonymous with the worst crimes of whites against blacks.

My daddy called me on the phone and said, "Boy, you all right?"

"Yes, sir, I'm all right."

"You hear about the killing of the little black boy who they say whistled at a white woman?"

"Naw, sir, I ain't heard nothing."

"Well, they killed little Emmett Till." After that conversation, I learned as much as I could about the event. I told my brothers about it, giving them all the details, particularly after I saw the mutilated face of Emmett Till in *Jet* magazine. It was gruesome. Who could protect me, an eleven-year-old black boy, from such a cruel fate as that which happened to Emmett Till?

My brother Ozzie knew so much more about ordinary things than I did, but he still said to me, "You got book learning. This here is folk learning. I know a whole lot of these folks who ain't been to no college, ain't been to no school, ain't been to kindergarten, who can run rings around college people." It was true that I was good in schoolwork.

"Yes, I know. They my people too," I replied, to let him know that I recognized my own background. I wanted to know more than Valdosta, than Georgia, than the South, but I never abandoned my roots. The South was the South, and Emmett Till, Ozzie Lee, and I were all children who knew something was not right in the way our lives were going with all the segregation and discrimination.

As a young person and later as a college student, with little to protect me from the vagaries of the system of oppression that I saw all around me, I grew to believe there was only one orientation for me, and that would be to swear an oath to always oppose injustice. And Ralph Ellison always lay at the back of my mind. I couldn't truly identify with everything in Ellison; yet *Invisible Man* perplexed and challenged me.

My professors at Oklahoma Christian could not deliver the explanation, solace, or counsel I needed; they would have had to condemn themselves because their own people—white Christian Americans—were the cause of the South's turmoil. I started to think that white people and the Bible did not add up, as it made no sense to me that the most murderous people I knew were Christians, and this overwhelming realization disturbed me.

During the period when I was in Oklahoma I turned to my own history with greater intensity. I wanted to know all of the great works: Langston Hughes, Paul Laurence Dunbar, James Baldwin, John A. Williams, Richard Wright, and Ralph Ellison—these writers were my heroes.

I had little knowledge of literary heroines, as this was before the feminist or Africana Womanist awakenings. It would be several years before Zora Neale Hurston and Margaret Walker would truly burst upon my consciousness. The women of struggle were seldom the literary women: Harriet Tubman, Sojourner Truth, Mary McLeod Bethune, the Grimké sisters, and Ida B. Wells. Then the new lyrical voices, Mari Evans, Sonia Sanchez, Maya Angelou, Nikki Giovanni, and Toni Cade Bambara, rose in the 1960s. When I was a student at UCLA, Gwendolyn Brooks also encouraged me to continue to write, and I found in her history the most eloquent expression of nobility in the race.

I also came to see Richard Wright's *Black Boy* as a significant contribution to my understanding of what it is to live in an oppressive society. Wright's portrayal of the quality of the black male's sojourn through identification and rejection was akin to my own journey to manhood in a racist society. I identified with his characters, and I understood their logic. By the time I was in college Wright was one of the deities in my growing pantheon; he knew how to tell my southern story. There were many stories about northern urban communities, but few about the many southern towns that gave birth to so many of the northern folk. Wright showed us the drama of the myths (some called them the superstitions), the songs, the magic of meetings, and the ghosts that hovered over the cemeteries. I knew those ghosts, haints, and places darker than a score of midnights, and no one could tell the stories I felt in my heart better than Wright. He also demonstrated the intensity of the contradictions in our lives, the distortions and wisps of fortune that appeared and then disappeared as quickly as they showed themselves. We were southern blacks who knew the time to plant, the time to harvest, and the color of the azaleas and the camellias that grew around scores of Confederate monuments in our small Southern towns. And like us, Wright had discovered his own demons.

What I did not understand was, How could a black person write like Wright had and avoid being killed in the 1940s? It was still dangerous for black people to speak the truth to an ignorant society, and so the courage that Wright exhibited caused him lots of pain and suffering until he escaped to Paris. He found his freedom in Montparnasse and Montmartre and the Latin Quarter.

Ralph Ellison, who won the National Book Award, seemed to eclipse Richard Wright; however, James Baldwin, in some ways Wright's true successor, received no such honor. His writings, like those of Wright, were much too pointed, too strong, too bold and on the mark for the general American audience. Meanwhile, Ellison saw himself in the larger role of writer—and not as a black writer. He was running to claim an illusion—a poor illusion at that—to escape from his blackness, his identity, his oppression. And with the National Book Award, he had to deny that his work was antiwhite, antisystem, anti-oppression. With the acclaim of white critics resounding in his ears, he felt the need to deny his kinship to Richard Wright. As a young man watching, all

I could do was take in the experiences of these writers and witness the battle. Wright and Baldwin went off to Europe and Africa, but Ellison remained stuck in the sands of another time, a victim of his own invisibility.

Many years passed before Margaret Walker's *Jubilee* entered my life in the 1970s, and I would understand how close she was to Wright in her sensibilities as well as how close he was to her. I got to meet her when she visited Temple University in the late 1980s to accuse Alex Haley of lifting material from *Jubilee* for his book *Roots*. When she talked, even about the things she hated, you did not get the impression that she was angry. But you could tell that she had a lot to be angry about; it swelled in her, but it came out in steady streams of pure rationality. A steel cage could not contain her pitiless anger at unfairness or injustice. Just as tough as nails in her mild manner, Walker seduced the unsuspecting readers of her poetry and novels and poured disdain on racism, discrimination, and sexism. Unfortunately for Alex Haley's history and for Richard Wright's betrayal of her personal affections, she was a ferocious lioness. I remember being in awe of her presence when she spoke and wanting to imitate her sense of outrage at insincerity.

Although I came late to her work, it influenced my thinking about Georgia. She did with Georgia what Richard Wright did with Mississippi: painted such an evocative picture of reality that it seemed even the pitiless oak trees, upon whose branches many black men had hung lifeless, would have to cry out for freedom.

In college I had studied Marcuse, Lukacs, Habermas, Sartre, Memmi, and Hegel, among other European writers, but I loved Fanon, Diop, Baldwin, Wright, Achebe, Ngugi, Du Bois, Carter Woodson, King, Zora Neale Hurston, and Paul Robeson—the black writers that ordered so much of my reality. I read them for fun, relaxation, and any evidence of Africa. And of course, there were other guides for my education. I was inspired by participating in the civil rights discourse of the day, marching, selling buttons, and going to Venice Beach to read poetry that protested the Vietnam War. Richard Erickson, Dennis Ogawa, and I sat in Royce Hall studying to become communicationists only to find the drumbeats of the communes in Venice Beach interrupting our time. Yeah, I planned my time to dip my feet in the Pacific and to inveigh against aggression and invasion of the Vietnamese lands.

Like my poetic heroes, I committed myself to suffer for the truth of my calling, even without knowing what my dedication might bring. While Sholokov's *And Quiet Flows the Don,* Wright's *Native Son,* and Ellison's *Invisible Man,* which I read and loved as a teenager, were beckoning me to step toward writing novels, I declared myself a poet. My personality and my patrilineal Yoruba ancestry may have led me toward drama, like Ola Rotimi and Wole Soyinka, or history, like Jacob Ade Ajayi or Toyin Falola. I was clearly addicted to the art of writing anything.

When I lived in Los Angeles as a college student, I would climb the flight of stairs to my cramped room to write a poem, correct a poem, or listen to the Yoruba orishas beating in my heart, because I was a poet, an ancient warrior-poet-lover, and I had been one since I first spoke words of power on Sundays after church.

In the winter, the California rainy season, I would often lie in my bed—a young, broke poet, pen and notepad in hand—and listen to the steady percussion of liquid nature against the clay tile roofs. I believe this meditation prepared me for the out-of-body experience I believe I had, years later, on a rainy day in Ibadan, Nigeria. So here I was in California, preparing for the night in Nigeria. I would turn to watch the apartment gutters behind my room weep rain, and I would study the flowers, begonias, geraniums, and azaleas turning limp with the weight of the watery curtain.

Back when I was a preteen in Georgia, in just such moments, with nature as a witness, I had learned that the poetic sensibility was close to my soul. "No poet can ever really poet without an appreciation of nature," Melvin Tolson, perhaps the most intellectual of all African American poets, was credited with saying.

At the same time, a poet in America is a lonely person, and an African American poet walks an especially lonesome road. With every stroke of the pen he or she creates something antagonistic, lovely, just. I had imbibed so much poetry from watching Toni Cade Bambara, Amiri Baraka, Quincy Troupe, Haki Madhubuti, and Ishmael Reed perform their work that I was drunk with this wine of the word. This was, in itself, provocative, transforming.

So I have always been a poet, but as I got older I also discovered I leaned in the depths of my heart toward being a dramatist, where I could join the fraternity of those who knew the value of good and the quality of beauty. The dramatic and poetic spirit lived in the character of my Georgia and Tennessee upbringing.

I did not shy away from either gift and felt comfortable with both genres. So many observations and experiences colored the way I saw the world that I could only choose a few moments for concentration—I could never write everything. What my father did not write, I would try to write. If I could not write something, then it would be up to my children to write it because somehow it appeared that the ancestors had declared that we would write. I welcomed all my experiences.

On one of those rainy days in Los Angeles I thought a lot about home, about Valdosta—not so much about the physical place but about the people, their simple understanding of good and evil, righteousness and unrighteousness, justice and injustice. The things I had heard as a young boy and the experiences I had as a young man, when I returned to Georgia in the summers, crowded themselves into my mind.

Wright's *Black Boy* captured the essence of what I had learned as a young black boy in South Georgia. He depicted the whole host of prohibitions, truths, and regulations under which we lived, including:

> If a black cat crossed your path, you'd have bad luck.
> If you were good to your mama, you'd grow old and rich.
> If you covered a mirror while a storm was raging, lightning would not strike you.
> If you spat on corn as it was being planted, it would grow tall and have good ears.
> If the sun came out during a rainstorm, then the devil was beating his wife.
> If you broke a mirror, you'd have seven years of bad luck.
> If you mocked a crippled person, then you would become crippled.
> If your nose itched, you'd have a visitor.
> If your hand itched, you'd have money.
> Whites would do anything for money.
> Whites loved to see blacks fight each other.
> Whites could not be trusted to support blacks against evil whites.

Whites thought we were animals.

Whites were curious about our sexual habits and the size of our
genitals.

Whites didn't think we would be in heaven, because it was only
for whites.

Wright was gifted and significant because he saw the novel as a weapon for challenging and changing—granted it was a literary instrument, but no less a weapon.

Ellison too, showed some truths about our Southern existence: life was to be lived openly and with a good dose of respect for reality—after all, in the Deep South, racial reality was always brutal. And at the same time, like Ellison, I could not get the beauty of its blooming flowers out of my mind, although I had traveled extensively by the time I was twenty-five. The daffodils, lilies, birds of paradise, and other colorful flowers gave my early life an abiding appreciation of diversity, the dance of life, and the ever-changing nature of our reality.

Thus, Ellison was not an end for me, but a beginning. Ellison prepared me for deeper moments of spirit and soul, and I would later fly off to Africa, both physically and intellectually, as I found myself in the midst of anomie in America.

And yet I found myself inside the head of Richard Wright's characters and kept my distance from those of Ralph Ellison. It is not so much that I found Ellison's characters ahistorical; it was just that I discovered something in Wright that was much more African to me, something that tapped into the wellspring of my ethical motifs, my relatives' behaviors and sensibilities. I loathed injustice, despised segregation and discrimination, and plotted to destroy every vestige of racism in America. At the time this mainly consisted of daydreaming about what it would be like to live in a country where there was no doctrine of white racial supremacy. Little did I know in my early twenties that the quest was more difficult than I imagined.

I did have a few nonliterary role models earlier while at the Nashville Christian Institute. Fred Gray, who would become Martin Luther King's lawyer, was one; another was Obie Elie, the Cleveland, Ohio, master of deconstructing buildings; Franklin Florence of Rochester was my hero for justice and dynamic ethics; finally, there was Floyd Rose, the most gifted orator I have ever heard and an early influence in fighting for civil rights.

Florence helped organize FIGHT, a direct-action group that moved on issues of discrimination with intelligence and vigor in Rochester, New York. Florence was always in the front of the group. A protégé of community organizer Saul Alinsky, Florence became the voice and the vision of Rochester as he rallied group after group in the fight against racism.

He always sought to keep me in the circle. I would get a phone call from him, and I knew that it was always regarding some activism that he wanted me to be involved in. Some actions I could take, and others I could not, but I learned much about organization from Minister Florence. I came to believe that this short, strong black man with a square jaw was the essence of boldness, a quality that I admired more than any other except character.

I have always been attracted to the bold—those whose passions are so strong that they are willing to risk career, position, and even their lives. There is something sacred in the strength to speak one's mind; that must be the reason in some societies the freedom of speech is protected by law. If it were not for such protection, and in countries where one cannot find this protection, people are silenced.

Like Franklin Florence, there were others that had the same strength like Chinweizu, the slender, determined Nigerian philosopher who carried the same fire that must have burned in the hearts of Zumbi, Sengbe Pieh, Nat Turner, Martin Delany, and Marcus Garvey, the precursors of Harriet Tubman, Nanny, and Maria Stewart. Chinweizu and I crossed paths in Buffalo, New York, but I did not get to know him until after I read his book, *The West and the Rest of Us.* I met him after that, and we would hold conversations about all things African. He wrote on Arabs and their agenda for Africa, Wole Soyinka and the corruption of Yoruba literature, and African American reactionaries. He could see no way out for Africans but to turn to themselves. We would eat chicken, collard greens, and sweet potatoes and then solve the problems of Nigeria, the giant of Africa. We would almost always end up in some argument, however, that we could not resolve but that we left with due respect for each other. With his thin frame, almost Lumumba-like form, Chinweizu did not seem threatening. He was not angry in his demeanor,

nor was he strident. Chinweizu was deliberate and cautious but direct and clear. You did not come away from a meeting with him trying to figure out what he said or what he meant. His language was always about the future, and I cannot remember him ever talking about any future except one in which African people would do for themselves, act in their own interest, reward their own geniuses, grant their own writers the freedom to speak their minds, and create conditions for the masses to gain true national—even continental—consciousness.

Years later, in 2004, I drove Chinweizu from my home in Philadelphia to Doylestown, Pennsylvania, on a cold winter night in the snow, after my wife Ana fed him and the Gambian ambassador the best chicken ever eaten in our house. Chinweizu never tired of talk, and he had also written some scholarly papers that he promised to send to me once he got back to Nigeria and to his house at Festac City. "Asante, you are a good African man, my friend. On to victory," he said as he got out of my car.

"Africa will be free from mental slavery, brother, one day. May it be soon," I said. However, the next time I heard from him, he was in a hospital in London. He had had a massive stroke on the way back home. He remained recuperating in England for many months, and then he finally made it to Nigeria, where he underwent more intensive medical and physical rehabilitation. I had been writing to him periodically with no response, and then one day, unexpectedly, an e-mail came from him: "Molefi, where are you? Do you plan to publish the papers on ancient Egypt?"

I knew then that we would resume our intense discussions on the politics and culture of Africa. We were at war with hegemony, and sometimes it seemed that only Chinweizu and I knew it. To be quite honest, I had once known nothing about it. I was a victim of ignorance, just like the rest of my brothers and sisters who sought to confront racism, we were flying by the seat of our pants.

A couple of years after Chinweizu returned to Festac City, Lagos, I went to give a speech at the Nigerian Communications Conference, and we arranged to meet at my hotel. Just as before, with Chinweizu now able and mending yet slight and deliberate in movement, he and I started over again on the Arab agenda for Africa. We disagreed over Gaddafi, the intentions of Islam, and the United States of Africa. I wanted a total united Africa and he wanted a united black Africa. I wanted a secular, opened Africa that could accommodate a multicultural and multiracial population. Chinweizu wanted a black population that would exclude Arabs from citizenship because he feared that they would push Sharia law on the entire continent. I told him I did not fear that 800 million blacks would allow 160 million Arabs to dominate them. If I had that fear, then I would say that the change had to come from the way Africans saw themselves, their own philosophies, histories, values, and religion. "No one can dominate you unless you are dominatable," I told him. I did not convince him, and he still writes strong critiques of the Arab threat to Africa.

Years earlier, while I was a student at UCLA, I had talked to Beah Richards and Maidie Norman about discrimination in the theater industry. I had heard the lectures of Robert Farris Thompson, Maulana Karenga, Janheinz Jahn, and Arnaud Bontemps, but I learned my real lessons from the bold band of brothers who took revolution and change so seriously that they were ready to lay down their lives for the liberation of black people. I know now that the same boldness inspired Chinweizu. Of course, Maulana Karenga would lead his own organization called Us and establish a cultural philosophy referred to as Kawaida that would challenge us to rethink everything we had thought about black nationalism, culture, and identity; he would become the embodiment of many of the ideas of Marcus Garvey. At the same time, he sharpened his logic and the rhetoric of victory that made him the most dynamic young leader of my generation. Few understood him, perhaps, because he was so deeply conscientious and so thoroughly committed to black transformation in a way that could not be done by the church or the Nation of Islam. He would later write the *Introduction to Black Studies* and become one of the champions of the field.

One spring day, as the sun crept over the Los Angeles Basin, a group of us black college student leaders went somewhere in the Angeles National Forest high above the brownish thickness of the smog to a lodge secured for us by the rich white girlfriend of one of the brothers.

We sat down together to eat steak sandwiches and a few bagels in revolutionary secrecy. I have never been in any place so peaceful, so secluded, with brothers who seemed so determined to overcome all resistance to our progress. We all felt invincible yet ready to organize for action—any action.

The meeting had been called for all of the black student leaders at southern California's colleges and universities. As the head of the Student Nonviolent Coordinating Committee (SNCC) at UCLA from 1966–68, I was one of the representatives from my campus. Along with me were other student and community leaders, young people old enough to have lived three lives, though we were all between twenty and twenty-five.

There were other students from UCLA; a few brothers were students from Jamaica, Nigeria, and Kenya who attended college in the Los Angeles area. They were intense, agitated, and easily angered. It seems like Ayuko Babu was there, John Huggins may have been there, Forest Davis must have been there—and maybe not, maybe others, I cannot remember everyone. About thirty representatives were piled into the room, sitting in a circle, African-style. Some of us were friends, but our political views, or at least our senses of what was tactical and what was strategic, were different. Some of us did not like each other, socially or politically. Everyone seemed uptight, on edge, ready to go off. Some kept weapons discreetly out of sight.

The meeting was intense, the atmosphere explosive, with gunpowder for air. Representatives from every black "militant" organization were present. I am sure the Black Congress had representatives, maybe even the Black Panthers, and, certainly, the Us organization.

There was friction between a brother from San Fernando Valley State, later called California State University at Northridge, and the USC brother whose girlfriend had secured the lodge. "How can you be a revolutionary, sleeping with the enemy?"

"She's not the enemy," the USC brother retorted. "She's a victim."

"Shit, you're the mother fucking victim. You gon' lead the revolution with your dick?" The San Fernando Valley representative was getting really hot. There was nervous laughter from some of the brothers.

The brother from USC ignored him, turned to a representative from Occidental or Pepperdine—one of those palm-league private colleges, you could tell by the expensive way he was dressed, the colors and all—and said, "It's not about race at all, man. It's about class. White people are not bad because they are white; they're the way they are because of capitalism."

"Nigger, where you from? Gitaway from here." The San Fernando Valley student responded disgustedly. The preppie-looking representative said nothing; he just smiled a broad, beautiful smile, as though to say, "This is not really happening." I think it was half about fear and half about tension.

You could hardly live in Los Angeles in those days without belonging to some society, self-help organization, community club, gang, or church—such was the fear of the negative accent of isolation, the sound of aloneness that was first captured for television by Tony Brown, the television producer. Change was the watchword of the day, and everyone wanted to be a part of transforming America.

The clean-cut middle American black boy that made UCLA look wholesome became one of the university's signatures. I had once aspired to that tradition, but I was too poor and too southern to really make the optimum cut as a preppie. Then I became head of the SNCC, which stamped my Order of the Golden Bruin, Democratic Club, Graduate Student Council, and other memberships with second-class status. I was fully committed to changing the racist regime. I was not only committed; I had also become one of the leaders of change by assuming the role of SNCC's head. I was a member of the inner circle, the students who had come to discuss the role students had to play in the liberation struggle.

The meeting lasted five hours, a marathon session in emotion-bending, hair-splitting, and name-calling arguments. Everyone was angry, more at our condition as blacks than at each other, yet we took enough hide off each other to settle all doubts about commitment.

"America can't be a nation for white people only—our blood enriched the soil of this nation as well. We must fight for what we want," I argued, sounding sometimes, I thought, too much like I was preaching.

"We must be ready to die for the truth, to fight to liberate ourselves, to make the enemy pay for oppressing us," said someone else, in the manner of Fanon, one of our intellectual heroes. Everyone considered radical was quoted: Nkrumah, Mao, Malcolm, Castro, Cabral, Nyerere,

Guevara, and Mandela. I could feel myself becoming more radical through the process of discovery.

Not hearing myself talk but instead listening to the brothers expound on the nature of the struggle that we had to confront really brought Uncle DeBuddy's words back to me. His shadow never left me. My father's brother said things to me that reverberated through the years, and I thought of him, as the Akan people later taught me to, as one of my fathers. I did not have a maternal uncle to give me advice and guidance, and so my paternal uncles became for me the compasses with which I found my political direction in the mountains. I sank into thoughts of Valdosta, sitting there in the rarefied air of the Southern California mountains. What was America, really, to me?

However, my mental wandering off did not last long, as each argument, each statement, each proposal, each criticism was a dagger into the heart of any sense of fear, inferiority, or negativity that we may have held before we went up the mountain. In the end the blood and the water that constitute our lives won out over every other element, and we were truly brothers, a long way from Oliver Street, and though they were not Willie James, Dolan, Esakenti, Ozzie, or Bro Boy, these were brothers nonetheless.

"Malcolm died for us. Freedom has to be by any means necessary," said a brother from California State University, Long Beach.

"We shall overcome," someone shouted.

"We have overcome," someone else corrected.

I thought a long time, and without speaking aloud myself, I agreed with the first brother.

Some moments were clear, others were opaque, but always our discussions were passionate and sometimes made radiant descent, with colorful language, into real quarrels.

When we came down from the mountain, I did not know if we had decided anything, resolved anything, or made a difference. I knew only that we had merged our agendas, gotten some idea of who was potentially a liability and who was willing to lay down his life. I could not have imagined how exhausted I would feel after the marathon arguments and debates.

In the days that followed I had to deal with the inauthentic nature of my own path to activism. Actually, I was meant to be a preacher like my grandfather, to walk in the way of "de Lord," but I had met my destiny in the varied harbors of racism that existed in the 1960s. Valdosta and Nashville had not prepared me for the agony and havoc that confrontations with racism would produce. I knew when I came down from that mountain that I had grown as Uncle DeBuddy would have wanted me to grow. I also knew that there were pockets of African Americans who were willing to give their last measure of strength for our total freedom, and I was one of them.

Africa was always on my mind. I do not know if I could ever say that it was not present in some cultural, political, or spiritual way most of my life. I recalled that when I was an undergraduate student in Oklahoma, one of my white classmates and I deliberately went to a restaurant that had an antiblack policy, the only restaurant near our college. The local bowling mothers would dine there, and guys in red pickup trucks would gather outside just to have a chance to talk to the ladies. A big sign inside the restaurant said, "Negroes are not served here."

My friend Guy Ross and I were young, assertive, and creative. He didn't like racism any more than I did, and he had the same messianic flair for taking on institutionalized racism. At the time I thought of him as being "just a little bit crazy," but now, looking back on the incident, I think I was the one who was crazy. Imagine, there I was, a young black man with long hair sitting in a working-class restaurant in a nearly all-white part of North Oklahoma City in 1963.

The Russian-looking waitress came over to the table where we had positioned ourselves and said, "We don't serve Negroes in here."

Guy looked up, his red face dancing with excitement, and said with a smile, "My friend, Bubacar, is an African who is studying at the college."

She said, "Oh, I'm sorry, I thought he was a Negro." Looking straight at me, she asked, "What can I get for you, sir?"

Guy stepped in and said, "He does not speak English, but he would like a hamburger and a Coca-Cola." The waitress rushed to get my order.

I was intrigued that white Americans had respect for Africans from the continent that they did not have for African Americans. On the contrary, I found that many African Americans had little appreciation for or knowledge of Africa. I had vowed two years earlier while at Southwestern Christian College, where I met Essien Essien, a Nigerian, that I had to visit the continent for myself, see the land of my ancestors, and understand something about the relationship between Africa and America that made the idea of Africa so controversial in America.

∞

I have visited Africa many times, somewhere between sixty and seventy times, over the past thirty years, but no visit was as instructive and inspirational as when I lived in Zimbabwe after the independence war ended in 1980.

Salisbury, the capital, had not yet been changed back to being called Harare. When I arrived, time had stopped; the Second Chimurenga, as the revolution was called, was in slow motion. The war had ended in April, several months earlier. On that July day the sun was high in the sky, but the weather was pleasantly cool. Zimbabwe's weather was totally different from Nigeria or Senegal or Ghana, where I had also spent considerable time. Zimbabwe lies in the Southern Hemisphere, south of the equator, and the winter was mild, with no humidity as there usually is in more tropical lands around the equator.

As I had done in so many African cities before, I got out on the streets almost as soon as I checked into my hotel—my practice since the first time I went to Africa as a young UCLA professor and director of the Center for African-American Studies. There is always such surprise in African cities.

I wandered lazily around the city, looking for signs of the revolution, for signs of liberation, or at least symbols of struggle. Dressed in my West African multicolored outfit, I recognized after a while that I was the only person wearing African clothes; all of the Zimbabweans had on European suits. There were few outward signs that a terrible war had been fought; I later learned that there were few internal signs in the local attitudes. Whites still acted like they had won the war, and Africans, although in charge of the government, were still tentative.

"I can't believe that the kaffirs are in charge of the government," an old white Rhodesian woman told me as I handed my traveler's check and my passport to her at one of the largest department stores in town.

The word "kaffir" was as bad as "nigger." I wondered what she believed about me—although I carried an American passport, I was certainly no different in color than the Zimbabweans she had just referred to with the most vile derogatory term.

"Well, they are in charge now," I said to her, and took my change.

A few stores down from the department store, I met a young man who had just returned from London. "When I left seven years ago, there were no black faces to be seen in the ministries other than servants'. I feel so strange now that we are the government," he exclaimed, and I could see the tension in his handsome black face, hear the quiver in his voice. I could not tell if he was afraid of failure or afraid of responsibility, but I did not get the idea that he was quite comfortable with the transformation. It would take time. Rome was not built in a day, and certainly Zimbabwe would take years to overcome the one hundred years of European rule.

Sitting in the Monomatapa Hotel's modern lounge late one evening in Harare, with the rain falling gently outside, I thought back on my arrival and my initial disappointment. How could the poor people of Zimbabwe have fought for so long and so hard and yet ended up with so little of value? The whites still owned the land and the stores downtown, they were still rude to black customers, they were still the bosses. They still had their private, all-white clubs, and they were still arrogantly racist.

Uptown, along Manica Road, the Indians dominated the markets and shops as their brothers and sari-clad women did in other African countries. They were the in-between people, a role they shared with the coloreds, who were mixtures of African and European. But the coloreds had no stores: they were the secretaries, the bus drivers, the mechanics, and the office managers. Conversely, the Indians were a commercial people, and they sat on the same gold mine as the whites, just further toward the underbelly of the city—but always on the black people's backs. When they entered the old Rhodesian economy, they entered with the permission of the whites so they could sell to black people. They were allowed to participate in commerce as the retailers of small appliances, some furniture, and fabrics.

During the first winter after the Second Chimurenga, Salisbury was tensed. The authorities saw spies everywhere, and spies probably were everywhere. It reminded me of UCLA in the early 1970s, when we knew COINTELPRO, the counterintelligence program, was on campus, but we could not tell who the spy was. In Zimbabwe white South Africans mingled easily with the local Rhodesians and then caused havoc by leaving bombs around the capital city and escaping to South Africa. Only seven months after independence, a young British woman was arrested for espionage after taking pictures of the parliament building with a Kodak camera. I told the editor of the *Herald* newspaper, the major news source in the country, that white people could take pictures of the parliament building from the air and that it did not make sense to arrest the young English woman. I do not know if I had any effect, but at least I do know the young lady was released a few days later.

Sabotage was still rampant throughout the country, and soldiers from the three armies that had fought in the war frequently clashed—the Zimbabwe African National Union (ZANU), the Zimbabwe African People's Union (ZAPU), and the Rhodesian Army. Roadblocks dotted the city, and army officers guarded every entrance into the metropolitan area. Security personnel not only stood guard at the principal public buildings, but they also accompanied all members of parliament while carrying Kalashnikov-47s, visible for everyone to see when they drove around town. The entire capital district was a military camp. Many of the former guerillas had no formal education, and consequently, integrating them into the society after five or seven years in the guerilla armies was no easy task. They now held down jobs as chauffeurs and night guards.

At independence, Robert Mugabe, the thoughtful and deliberate prime minister who was later to become the first president, inherited two armies—ZAPU's Zimbabwe People's Revolutionary Army (ZIPRA) and the white-controlled and -dominated Rhodesian Army—in addition to his own forces, the Zimbabwe African National Liberation Army (ZANLU), the military wing of ZANU. The forces of ZAPU were folded into the ZANU forces.

There were lots of guns in the hands of trained fighters and apparently untrained fighters as well, given the fact that so many people were being killed. Fighting in the streets between blacks and whites occasionally flared up, the result of the shifting power bases. White farmers, already armed, sought more weapons to protect their farms because the Rhodesian military had been disbanded and could no longer offer assistance. Angry Africans who had worked for years on large estates often slipped through the barbed wire fences and the dog-guarded compounds to lay siege to the whites who cowed behind their iron gates and reinforced doors. The newspapers were full of anxious letters from whites about the lax security. Living behind the walls of a beautiful condo in the Avenues, as the quaint residential streets, not far from downtown, were called, I ventured out frequently to get a sense of the place. I was at the museums, the university, and the Zimbabwe Institute of Mass Communication called ZIMCO, and I felt quite comfortable in town. I had neither apprehension nor fear, but this was perhaps because I did not speak Shona and could not understand all the events that were happening in the country. I only knew what those who spoke English told me and what I read in the English newspaper. I knew that violence was occurring but had no sense that it would occur near me or to me.

I met Robert Mugabe before he was president and during the time he was still prime minister. He had been a determined guerilla leader, a fierce competitor, and a student of Kwame Nkrumah. His first wife had been a Ghanaian, and he had mastered the intricate lessons of Pan-Africanism. He wanted me to help arrange opportunities for some of the young men and women who had fought in the war to attend school in the United States. With a halo of integrity and sincerity, Mugabe was overwhelmed with the burdens of office in a way that he had not known as a guerilla leader. How do you read telegrams from Japan, Bulgaria, and Greece if you do not have anyone in the government to perform those duties? These were some of the issues that he discussed with me. Yet I sensed a moral commitment and a historical consciousness in Robert Mugabe that I had not seen in many other leaders of African nations; it was this commitment to peace, to reconciliation, that convinced me that he would become one of the most dominant influences in African renaissance. His first declaration was that the first year of his government would be "the Year of Reconciliation." However, forces that he could not control would soon challenge his olive branch with bombs, intrigue, and conspiracies to destroy the economy of the country.

Incidents of terror did not diminish with the coming of an elected government. Landmines exploded, killing innocent children near outlying villages. Two white fishermen were found drowned in the Pungwe River. Armed robbers held up a black farmer who was accused of siding with the Rhodesians in the recently ended war, and they terrorized his family; whites who refused to change their behavior toward Africans were pulled out of their houses and beaten. The air was thick with revenge and fear, curses and incantations. I prayed for true peace.

"God has visited his wrath upon us for neglecting to do his will," preached a white minister to his all-white congregation in downtown Salisbury, now known as Harare. The Africans felt the power of jongwe, the rooster that was also ZANU's election symbol, and the whites in the country felt fear and helplessness perhaps for the first time since Rhodes sent his columns north from South Africa.

However, the blacks saw the new dispensation as the answer to their prayers, so the leadership pleaded for calm. "We must not do to the whites what they did to us," shouted the ZANU revolutionary who had been asked to calm a crowd gathered in front of the parliament building. The people had gathered to protest the fact that land had not been redistributed and that there was a continuation of white landowners' arrogance. Whites still had the luxury of a judicial system that was nearly 95 percent white.

Immediately after independence in Zimbabwe, unjust court proceedings demonstrated the deformity of the political situation. Africans who were apprehended for attacks on whites were still brought before all-white judicial officers and sentenced to long prison terms. The whole place was crazy—not on the outside, but deep within. You could hear the fury left over from the war in the clipped tones of the settlers: "The blacks can't run a government" and "The economic well-being of this country depends on us." They had been defeated militarily and politically, but the fact that they held economic control gave them at least one of the three important sectors, perhaps the most influential. They were still bizarrely arrogant.

One bright Thursday morning I sat eating breakfast at a downtown restaurant with Kariamu Welsh, whom I later married in Zimbabwe, and we both remarked on the eerie atmosphere. We heard no laughter. Harare was not Dakar or Lagos or Abidjan, where you could hear laughter and see people dancing in the streets; Harare was tepid, cautious, vigilant, and had the feel of stealth, and you could not tell what was to come next. I had been to Kinshasa, yet even with the sadness and poverty of the Congo, Kinshasa still danced. Harare was tensed and staid, tentative and cool—a deadly combination for melancholy. In Harare the people drank and drank in ways that I had never seen before and would never see again until I later visited the shebeens of South Africa.

The city's colors were monotone—evidence, I thought, of white rule and control for too long over a population that could not express its own color and joy. I later discovered, however, that it was like that because the Shona culture privileged the colors white and black, not meant to stir strong sensibilities or create improvisations of style.

Africa's irony struck me that day. Richard Wright, one of the few important black writers to comment on contemporary Africa before the 1960s, wrote in *Black Power* that he left the Ivory Coast as soon as he arrived, asking how you would feel being discriminated against in an African county. His trip had awakened Wright to the shock of white racist colonists occupying principal seats in African nations. These racists made Africa look bad to the African Americans who came seeking a refuge from prejudice.

Fortunately for me, although the entire situation was absolutely insane (being denied an apartment because of my race, being abused as a "cheeky kaffir" because I refused to allow a white driver to back his car into a parking space into which I had driven headlong), by the time I visited Zimbabwe seven previous trips to Africa had blunted the edge for me. Richard Wright was not quite so lucky. I knew that wherever the white man had been in Africa, you would find an unequal distribution of power and the residuals of discrimination against Africans in one form or another. I also knew that Africans would find African Americans bold, brazen, even impudent when it came to interactions with whites. They would be terrified when I refused to allow a white man to skip to the front of the line in the post office or to be served first in a restaurant where blacks had been waiting long before.

I bristled at discrimination of any kind, toward anyone, and especially toward me. But here I was a black man, a person of African descent, being treated with hostility in Africa by Europeans. The settlers' aggressive behavior appalled me. They had neither fear nor respect for the African; in fact, the general sentiment among the Europeans was that the Africans were docile, servile, and obedient to whites. Their attitude reminded me of the African enslavement stories in America, when the "good slave" was considered the one who expressed his subservience in the most gratuitous manner.

The European used the African's courtesy, good humor, and harmonious nature as a way to destroy the African's confidence, to show him as weak—as Ralph Ellison objected—to show him as a chump, an object to be taken, used, and dispensed. All of this was contrary to the history of the Mashona or the Matabele people, who had been a proud, determined, and courageous people, but one hundred years of white brutality took the swing out of their walk. Like Karl Peters, the nineteenth-century German commissioner of East Africa who fired his pistol point-blank into village chiefs' heads to subdue the Vagogo people of Tanganyika (Tanzania), the white Rhodesians had humiliated the chiefs and common people of Zimbabwe so much that the masses could hardly think of revolting. Of course, the ZANU and ZAPU forces had begun the process of rebuilding the people's confidence. In fact, the guerilla war itself was the first step in demonstrating to the masses that whites died just like they did. Yet to my eyes, repairing the damage done to the Africans' psyches would take a long time.

My American consciousness and behavior saved me on several occasions when my African consciousness would have counseled me not to make a big deal of the slight, the abuse, the ignorance. Having lived a defiant battle against racism as well as class struggle, I was able, after a few months, to completely disarm any potential attacker of my psychological or physical person. There can be no attitude of superiority unless there is an attitude of inferiority, which I did not possess, and I made damn sure no European racist could catch me with my guard down.

I acted like I was back in the Mississippi of the early 1960s, and it worked. I gave no place, out of natural courtesy, to whites. I made no move to give the racists any comfort; I spoke to them directly and matter-of factly, looking them straight in the eyes. The crispness of my tone, snapping like the falling icicles of a Buffalo winter, often gave me pause to ask what was becoming of me—this was not my normal behavior.

Whenever I was approached in a threatening manner, I would say immediately, "I'm not from here; I am from Chicago," and each time the Rhodesian white would head in the other direction. I came to believe that "Chicago" was a magic word because every white person in Zimbabwe reacted negatively when I mentioned I was from there.

Nevertheless, as long as I lived in Zimbabwe, I could not allow my guard to drop. The racist vultures would have pounced on me as they did every poor, slaving black Zimbabwean who tried to raise his head. A culture of domination, so deeply grown in the whites, caused them to look upon all blacks as servants or potential servants. The old Rhodesian whites maintained their arrogance although they had relinquished political power. I took their behavior as a regressive trait, an anachronism, but one that had to be addressed with sense and forthrightness.

Barely a week after I arrived in Zimbabwe I encountered a person I had assumed, because of my American sensibility, was African. He looked like my brother Paul, but he lacked Paul's freckles or red hair. As we stood outside the H. M. Barbour's department store, he said to me, "The Africans are hopeless."

"But aren't you African? Why would you say that?" I was hoping to get a detailed analysis of the social and economic conditions of the country.

"No, I'm colored."

"You were born here, weren't you?" I asked, not knowing the complexity of the peculiar system of racial classification in the old Rhodesia.

"Yes, I was born in Rhodesia, called Zimbabwe now."

"It's in Africa, isn't it?" Trying to use clear logic, that being simple, basic.

"Sure, but you can look at me and tell I'm not African."

"Well, I can't," I replied honestly.

"Don't you see by my complexion that I'm not *black*? Africans are black."

"Oh, I see what you mean." I recalled that in southern Africa, beginning at the Cape, the whites call offspring of blacks and whites "coloreds."

"We're coloreds," the man said. I thought that no one ever told my brother Paul that he was anything other than black. He would have been shocked to discover that his race was different from mine. Even "colored" in the American South meant of the same race as those who called themselves black, African, African American, or Moorish.

"To be 'African' here means you have to be purely descended from Africans, and coloreds are not, right?" I asked.

"Now you've got it—we're coloreds, a different race," he said.

"Where's your continent of origin?" I asked, remembering the argument we used in SNCC in the 1960s to browbeat those few blacks who continued to call themselves coloreds or Negroes.

"Coloreds were born first in the Cape and then spread to other countries as whites interacted with Africans."

"But the Cape is in Africa?"

"Oh yes." He seemed a little embarrassed. "It's the bottom tip of Africa."

"Depending how you look at the globe," I said. The Mercator Map is arbitrary in what is considered up and down because the earth is spherical, and what seems "top" or "bottom" depends on where you are in the universe.

"They used to call every colored person 'Cape Colored,'" he said.

"All born in Africa."

"You bet."

"Africans." I had the last word and went down to Wimpy's to sit in the sun and have a cup of coffee, playing a game with myself, telling the colored from the blacks as people walked past on the sidewalk. I found the game fascinating because the only criterion for being colored or black seemed to be how you lived. If you lived black, you were *black*; if you lived colored, you were colored. To live black meant to eat African food, sing and speak an African language, and have relatives you regularly visited in the countryside. To live colored meant something like enjoying *Ebony* magazine, liking African American basketball and music, and distancing yourself from African cultural behaviors. You could be coal-black and still be colored if your behavior was colored. I felt myself wishing my mother could see this because she had a real problem with dark skin and would have wanted to challenge the darker-complexioned coloreds about their identity. That would have been funny. White racial hierarchy creates such ugly parodies of humanity.

In the United States, if you were of African descent, you were black. In England you were colored. In South Africa, Zimbabwe, Malawi,

Botswana, Lesotho, and Swazi, you were black or colored depending on the degree of white blood in your veins. Because most races are mixed, including the European race, the whole system in southern Africa was racist madness, brought about when white settlers and missionaries had children by African women and then taught the children to hate their mothers.

The coloreds are the descendants of the Moffats, Selouses, Livingstones, Rhodeses, de Villierses, Schoemanns, and Baineses with their African mistresses. In South Africa there are some three and a half million coloreds; in Zimbabwe, a mere one hundred twenty thousand. For the most part they are a tragic people—without cultural, political, or social direction, often hating their mothers and the Khoisan, San, Xhosa, Zulu, or Shona blood that courses through their bodies.

No longer are coloreds in Zimbabwe valued because of the lightness of their skin or the straightness of their hair. Color gives no advantage; commitment to Zimbabwe and Africanization are the twin constituents of acceptance. Whites can often make the change to this way of thinking more easily than coloreds. The colored person in Zimbabwe has no tradition, no custom, no particularly heroic history but rather a pedestrian existence on the dirty underbelly of society. But because these are constructed identities, there are some "coloreds" who have worked to construct themselves as blacks by choosing their African heritage and discovering the lost signs of their African language.

What I saw, however, was that many young coloreds have become the flesh peddlers of twentieth-century urban decadence in Africa: the bridge between the sophisticated drug culture of the West and the local dagga-smoking population; the big-time prostitution catering to South African nighttime liberals who find their way, like their fathers before them, to the darker women; the petty criminals who rob and steal, oblivious to cultural prohibitions inhibiting the African or embarrassment that warns the European. The dismemberment of the African's psyche continued unabated.

Among Zimbabwe's coloreds, unlike in the South African colored population, one finds few bright spots, no intellectuals, and only a handful of professionals. Their commitment seems to be in keeping the colored race pure—an impossible task, bound to fail because of their insatiable thirst for European values and blood. What they mean by pure is avoiding blackness.

Because there are few like Alex La Guma, Dennis Brutus, Billy Kie, Allan Boesak, Thelma Ravell-Pinto, or James Ravell to preach on loving their past, both the black and the white, they are rudderless, wandering on the troubled sea of life, blown by the foul wind of their own antiblack racism. You see the wrecks of this psychological game when the mental casualties among "coloreds" increase as some of them reject their black side altogether and claim various immaculate conceptions.

Just as the jacarandas began to bloom, I met a colored woman who seemed promising in her consciousness, wanting to break free from the shackles of self-hatred. She came to meet me and Kariamu because she had read about us in the newspaper, and black Americans fascinated her. To her, we who would be classified by the Zimbabwean coloreds as coloreds (a large percentage of African Americans, according to Lerone Bennett and Henry Louis Gates, are of mixed African, Native American, and/or European ancestry) remained passionately African and black. And the coloreds pattern much of the superficial elements of their lifestyle, such as clothing, language, and music, on black America. So Norma came to question us about blacks in America. She was eager to know about the National Association for the Advancement of Colored People (NAACP). I tried to point out that the name was an anachronism because there was no separate "colored" race in the United States. She found it difficult, almost ludicrous, to understand how the "most sophisticated nonwhites in the West" could identify themselves as blacks or Africans.

She told me that her mother was a pure African and her father a colored whose white father raped his mother and never claimed him. Norma was twenty-five, slim, of dark-cashew complexion—an average African American hue—intense, and talkative. Her sister, darker than she, also a colored, had married an Australian mercenary during the liberation war. He hated all Africans, parading around his house referring to them as "kaffirs," "baboons," and "apes." One day their mother, blacker than last night, went to see her daughter, only to be told to enter through the servant's entrance. When she remained more than twenty minutes, the Australian racist cursed the mother and sent her running out of the house, threatening to kill her if he ever saw her around the house again. Norma said her sister did not say a word because she loved the Australian.

"More than her mother?" I asked.

"I guess. They're in Australia now," she replied, her eyes small masses of water. "Mama was too dark for her."

"It is so crazy," I said, not having anything else to say.

"Yeah, I guess so."

"Well, it would mean splitting up so many black families in America. You know my family ranges from vanilla to chocolate in complexion, and we're all black. We call ourselves African Americans—used to be negroes, used to be colored, but it always referred to the same people of African ancestry."

She then told me of a colored man who had three daughters, one cream-colored and two cocoa in complexion. When visitors came to his home, he would have the daughter lightest in complexion, though the most homely and clumsy, meet the guests while he banished the darker, more beautiful ones to the kitchen, out of sight of the visitors.

I repeated, "It is so crazy." Even to myself I was sounding like a battered, tired, monotonous record player. "It's absurd," "It's crazy," "It's so ridiculous," "It's unbelievable." After three hours of disbelief, Norma took her guitar and left. I sat in a psychological stupor for another hour, trying to ascertain if I understood what the hell had happened and was happening in Zimbabwean race relations.

Sure, it had crossed my mind that we had colored people in the United States, but they were clearly not a race of people, even in their own mind. Henry Louis Gates had written a book entitled *Colored People*, but he was not implying a race like the people of southern Africa—or was he? Gates's colored people were black in any legal, social, or American sense, regardless of the confusion he may have created by using the terminology.

So in Zimbabwe I was perplexed by this "colored" business and asked a lot of questions. Of course, the white population saw the transgressions of their fathers every time they saw the coloreds, and the blacks saw the subjection of their mothers. Perhaps love had blossomed in a few of the past encounters, but the history did not speak of that in any mythical or real terms. The coloreds were children or grandchildren of the fathers, and often they hated the mothers. In some senses this was the case in the United States, where the large mulatto population during the seventeenth through nineteenth centuries was the result of white slave masters having children with enslaved women. One could safely say that what the Zimbabwean coloreds would deem "coloreds" in the United States are derived from the white men who raped African women on plantations. It is a reality, a history, but certainly nothing for a black man or colored man to take pride in.

The one colored person in Mugabe's cabinet when I lived in Zimbabwe, deputy minister of education, Senator Joseph Culverwell, did not sit well with some colored citizens because he spoke about his black ancestry and was proud of his African heritage.

Reflecting on this situation one morning, I left my apartment to take a walk under the jacarandas. *This is such a beautiful country to be so screwed up racially*, I thought fleetingly, knowing full well how it had come to be the way it was. I walked further along the tree-lined avenue toward the prime minister's residence but turned around when I saw a white man walking ahead of me with a double-barreled shotgun. He did not seem threatening or particularly secretive about the gun. He was just on his way, I guessed, from one place to another. He made me think of Georgia or Texas, where the whites used to drive pickup trucks with guns slung in the back windows. It was innocent but potentially destructive, stylish but primed for danger, obscene but only in the message. Yet too many times in my southern American heritage, the gun was used to threaten, to maim, to kill, and I would take no chances. When I got back to my apartment, I had not resolved the issue of the coloreds in my mind.

Charshee McIntyre, a professor from New York, had told me that she argued every day while she was in Zimbabwe because they wanted to call her colored when she was black. Her heritage was African and Native American, and she did not look like the Shona or Ndebele, but she was still black. I remembered what she said, "I told them that I was blacker than they were and that if they called me colored again I would go and complain to Robert Mugabe, who was prime minister but would become president later. Not that it would have done anything. I just wanted to let them know how much I disliked that term." Charshee was almost vanilla-complexioned with long black hair, a kind of high yellow African American with visible Native American features, but in her mind, like the majority of African Americans who look like she does, she was clearly not colored. There was no such race in her mind.

∽

When I had been in Harare only a short time, the *Herald* newspaper reported that Albert Mugabe, the prime minister's brother, was found upright in the deep end of his swimming pool in the early morning hours. Everyone scoffed at the report. How could a person be found drowned and standing upright in a swimming pool? What about his wife? Where was she? Didn't she notice her husband missing?

Wole Soyinka, whom I had first met in Washington at the Frederick Douglass Museum and then at Festac Town in Nigeria, came into town a few days after the murder. I met him near the old Meikles Hotel about noon one day, and our discussion quickly turned to politics, the society, and the African world; of course he then asked, "What's the story about Albert Mugabe?"

I did not know anymore than anyone else but offered the latest newspaper version:

> Well, Albert Mugabe's wife said that Mugabe told her he was going outside to clean the swimming pool at eight p.m. He did not return to the house, and she did not go looking for him. The servants slept through the whole thing. His five children did not discover the body in the morning, although they were playing around the pool. Then his wife noticed that Mugabe had not eaten his food, which she had prepared the night before. She did not go to the police. His body was found at noon, according to the newspaper, 'upright in the deep end of his swimming pool.' Was he killed and dumped in the swimming pool? Did the fact he had two wives complicate the matter?

Soyinka was just as puzzled as all the Zimbabweans. I told him that people were being killed left and right during those early days after the Chimurenga. He seemed perfectly comfortable with that, probably illustrating how little I knew of truly revolutionary situations. He had certainly seen enough of brutality, suffering, and murder in Africa, having been held in jail in his own country of Nigeria for his political beliefs.

There were still pockets of resistance in the white community and unstable elements among the ZANU and ZAPU forces. Anyone could have killed Albert Mugabe, we agreed. Some of the common people were saying that the god of water, Nguzo, had snatched his life from him. Others dissented, saying Nguzo operated in the lakes and rivers, not in swimming pools. The debate was philosophical, cultural, and given to much speculation.

Albert Mugabe's death brought sadness to a lot of people because he had been searching for a way to change the status of Zimbabwe's black workers. In fact, the day before his death he had issued a one-page leaflet (that disappeared from the streets after his death) supporting the Riddell Commission's recommendation that the minimum wage be raised from thirty dollars a month to fifty. He had admitted that it did not go far enough in eradicating the differential between whites and blacks.

After independence the average white worker in Zimbabwe still made thirty-nine times what the average black worker made. Albert Mugabe felt such a gap could not be tolerated. His implicit criticism of the government in the leaflet made the first week in December 1981 a week of potential political controversy and societal stress. So at forty years of age, Albert Mugabe, the first general secretary of the Zimbabwe Council of Trade Unions, was found dead in his own swimming pool.

Soyinka was interested in everything going on in Zimbabwe. My immediate aim while I had his attention was to tell him what was going on in the arts community, but there was a struggle going on in my heart about how much to tell him. What would he think of me if I revealed the extent of the control by Rhodesians in his entire program? Perhaps he would not mind at all—after all, he was a continental African and was used to white involvement in ways that I had not been while growing up in the segregated American South.

Finally, I simply spoke to him directly, honestly. I told him that there had been a real knock-down, drag-out battle between the former Rhodesian Arts Foundation, which had become the National Arts Foundation in name but still served the minority interests of the whites, and the Ministry of Education and Culture. The ministry declared that it wanted to see and intended to have an arts council or foundation that catered to the needs of the masses. The spark plug in its position and direction was the one-time impresario of foreign students and exiles in London, John Mapondera, a descendant of the mighty Chief Mapondera, who fought the white settlers in the First Chimurenga alongside the legendary spirit medium Nehanda.

The National Arts Foundation, seeing that change was inevitable, decided to hold a drama workshop for black playwrights. It quickly got the West German Embassy to pay for tickets for Wole Soyinka and three white playwrights, whose names escape me, largely because the men were not of Soyinka's class. Soyinka, who later received the Nobel Prize in Literature, could certainly have been the only master teacher of the workshop in African drama. And yet when the Nobel Committee honored Wole Soyinka and Africa by granting him the prize, I was happy but aware that Africa itself never did see fit to honor Soyinka, Chinua Achebe, Ngugi wa Thiong'o, Ama Ata Aidoo, Ayi Kwei Armah, or Atukwei Okai with its own award for stature. *Perhaps in time, perhaps in time,* I thought.

A couple of the white playwrights teaching the workshop came from South Africa, and the third was from Malawi. If this were not the most patronizing thing I had ever seen, I do not know what was. What could have been more blatantly political and self-serving than sending three whites to represent African people while whites were muffling the people's voices? Malawi should have sent a black writer, but President Banda's disorientation about Africa prevented it. He truly believed in the superiority of European culture and education and would have been dismayed had an African represented Malawi.

As astute as he had ever been, Soyinka understood the nature of the whole scene. Even though he was Nigerian, he had spent many years in England and the United States and could fathom the whole racial scenario. He spoke with great clarity, saying that the whole situation was an artificial creation because it did not involve the people's own culture. He told me he would say that when he discussed drama in the workshop. His own drama clearly reflected Yoruban motifs seen in the light of human experience.

Soyinka told me that Ogun, his powerful patron god, had delayed his arrival in Harare, and I believed him. That was a good thing for

the arts program because the workshops had lacked focus, meander-
ing from venue to venue and idea to idea. Everyone could see that
Soyinka's presence was missing. I told Soyinka, however, that those of
us, mainly authors and journalists, who met in the Quill Club at the
Ambassador Hotel, lacking any information from him, had thought
that he had deliberately avoided coming because of the controversy
between the government and the arts foundation. The arts foundation
had said it was because he did not get his tickets at the Lagos Murtala
Muhammad Airport—fairly likely for anyone traveling in Africa who
had to pass through there.

The day Soyinka arrived was to be the last day of the workshop.
His proved to be the best lecture of the series. Once he had finished his
talk, incorporating bits and pieces from our conversation, he begged
permission to leave to catch a plane.

Just before he departed we had a brief moment to talk. My wife,
Kariamu, and Glendora Johnson of the Buffalo, New York, Center for
Positive Thought were also present. I brought up the Zimbabwe Min-
istry of Culture and Education's hire of Peggy Harper to work with the
National Dance Company. Soyinka, never one to hold back his opinions
said, "It is a travesty."

"What do you mean?" I asked mischievously, because almost everyone in Africa knew that Peggy Harper made her living peddling
African culture to the dishonor of Africans themselves.

"She's obscene," Wole said.

"I've wondered how she has gotten over on Africans so well." Kariamu said.

Glendora said she knew, and we all listened. "Black people hate
themselves, even now, and Africans hate themselves more than black
Americans."

Wole spoke about our friend Abdias do Nascimento, a genius, visionary, perpetual radical, fighter, and intellectual from Brazil who had
trained his eyes to tell the false prophets from the decent ones. Nascimento was all those things and more. Notwithstanding his marriage
to a white woman, Elisa, who shared with him the disdain he held for
racists, he was ready to be seen fighting for the cause of Africa. Unlike
a lot of Africans married to whites, Nascimento did not refuse to fight
for his culture and his people's freedom.

Now Wole looked thinner, almost fragile, with his goatee flourishing on his angular iron head, a perfect living Ogun—creative, eager, and rushing to catch the plane back to Ife and the university battles against the Nigerian government. As he was leaving I said, "May Ogun continue to bless your work." He smiled, his eyes trying to penetrate the veil of Africa's lack of recognition of his work. I interjected in the silence, "You, above all, rightly deserve to be honored."

He spoke, "I hope to see you again before you go back to the States."

Reflecting on the state of culture in Zimbabwe, I thought about how Peggy Harper had been booted out of Nigeria only to land in Zimbabwe at the pleasure of the government and under the aegis of Senator Joseph Culverwell and John Mapondera from the Ministry of Culture. Mapondera had brought Harper to London to teach African drama when she was forced out of Nigeria. Many people viewed Mapondera as a social climber in the European world, often taking to the wrong causes much too fervently and destroying the good ideas and operations as a result.

One thing he did do well, however, is dissolve the National Arts Foundation in Zimbabwe, which had served the interests of Europeans under the Ian Smith regime and discriminated against Africans in the disbursement of its largesse. That action alone almost saved Mapondera from condemnation by the African intellectuals who discussed the future of culture in Zimbabwe in the bars around town. When I asked my friend Chenhamo Chimutengwende, who knew Mapondera from their days in London, if he could believe that Mapondera had done this, he said, "Yes, I can believe it. John can be tough and straight when he wants to."

Mapondera often appeared pompous, perhaps the result of an ego that had not been stroked enough. He was always agitated, never giving any one project the kind of attention it needed. Like an ant scurrying about for the next bundle of food or goods, he ran around Harare and cities overseas, making a name for himself in some of the fancy circles of Europe and Australia. There was so much promise in Mapondera, but he never really understood the full depth of African American influence on music and art in the African world. Not wanting, it seemed, to buckle down to make the traditional cultures respond to new and revolutionary times, Mapondera could not do what was needed to transform culture. This much Wole Soyinka observed—he came, he saw, he knew, and he flew away to Nigeria with his knowledge safely tucked in the folds of his cerebellum. As I watched the future Nobel Laureate leave for the airport, I thought how important it was for Africans to reclaim their culture from the colonialists, even the neocolonialists, who still appeared in Africa as maternalists and paternalists. Soyinka, I felt, understood this more than most other writers. Waving goodbye to him, I looked back to when I had met Wole Soyinka a year or so earlier in Washington DC, right after the publication of my book *Afrocentricity*. I rushed to give him a copy, which he took graciously, but I believe never got a chance to read. Just knowing what I now know about people and books, it is not possible for a person to read all of the books received from well wishers. I think Soyinka accepted my book out of his graciousness. Nonetheless, I felt that I had achieved something, I did not know what, by giving it to him.

Nevertheless, *Afrocentricity* became a favorite with many African people and has sold tens of thousands of copies all over the world. It turned on the simple idea that African people must work not to be beggars in anything, in neither materials nor ideas. It was fundamentally a book about changes, transformations, becoming. I could not have dreamed of a more powerful way to introduce the notion of Africans interrogating their own historical experiences first.

After independence Zimbabwe was full of excitement about the prospects for changing the racist histories, arts, and education system. Of all the people I was meeting in the country's political and literary circles, James Ravell and Thelma Ravell-Pinto, South African exiles who had lived for many years in Amsterdam, were the spirits most in tune with the intellectual and emotional currents of the entire African world.

Having been born into that dastardly system of racial stratification called apartheid, they had grown up as colored, only to reject such classification as adults and become Africans. They were Africans by both birth and political sentiment. They had been asked to come to Zimbabwe from Holland to run a retraining camp called Melfort Farms for women who had fought in the war against Rhodesia. Kariamu taught the same women dance and social graces; it was therapy and art, healing and beauty.

Thelma always had some interesting tidbit about some black writer. She knew many of them personally, particularly the South Africans. We knew the works of the poets because we had read them—Dennis Brutus, Wally Serote, Keoraptse Kgositsile, or Mtshali, among others. We examined, criticized, or exalted all of those writers in many of our four-hour conversations.

Of the South African writers, the only one who did not lose a step with Thelma and James was Alex Le Guma, who had witnessed their marriage as they had witnessed ours. His *A Walk in the Night* is the classic portrait of the young Africans' predicament in Cape Town. The perfection of his description, the detail and enlargement of life in the colored community in Cape Town, left him at the top of the Ravells' list of South African writers.

Of course, when we talked, Mphahlele came in for a full fifteen rounds of battering for his lack of heart. A disgrace to the literary profession in Africa, we all agreed. Yet we recognized his talents, as *Down Second Avenue* was a masterful work.

I met Mphahlele in Washington in April 1980. He looked older than the pictures I had seen of him—almost wizened, I thought to myself when he greeted me, wearing a dashiki. He was smaller than I had thought he would be, but energetic. I gave him a copy of *Afrocentricity,* and we sat down to chat about literature and politics.

I found him to be a greater person than his decision to return to apartheid-ridden South Africa might indicate. And when he explained to me his decision to return, I felt the pain of his exile. And I probably did not take into consideration the burden of family. His decision always intrigued me. Thus, in 2004, when the political and business community of South Africa invited me to give the keynote address at their annual dinner, I took the opportunity to fly up north to visit Mphahlele. After my visit, I was no longer dismayed at his return home; in fact, he had become one of the unfettered voices for truth in the Limpopo Valley.

There were so many Mphahleles in Zimbabwe. The Ravells were only two, and they believed that the time would soon come for a return to South Africa. The spirits of exiles, their minds were always attuned to Pan-African sentiments like birds in search of a proper landing place.

They resolved their dissonance—loving to be in struggle and living in freedom—but secretly supporting the guerilla war against the South African regime while maintaining a nonviolent support posture in an international assistance organization. James passed away in a Johannesburg hotel, struck down by a heart attack, and a few years later Thelma was stricken with a brain aneurism while in Cape Town. Both had always wanted to end up in South Africa; they vowed they would die in their own country, free people.

After spending time with the Ravells, I had a much more determined attitude about what Zimbabwe needed. As I said once to Naomi Nhiwatiwa of the Zimbabwean government, Zimbabwe needed some real-deal brothers and sisters from Brooklyn to teach the whites how to treat black folk. This was the practical Pan-Africanism that intellectuals had only philosophized about in classrooms and rallies, and there was a need to challenge the old Rhodesian history that was still being taught in schools.

I particularly wanted the people to learn to use their culture and other African cultures as a current resource. For example, they had numerous dZimbabwes, or stone cities such as Dhlo Dhlo and Khami scattered around the country, but had left it to Michael Gelfand, a Rhodesian, to write the story of these cities. I decided that I had to be engaged in the primary study of one of these, Great Zimbabwe. I enjoyed the privilege of researching and writing an article about it, but I first had to go to the Masvingo area where it was located to start my own research in the history of the builders of the great cities.

The day I arrived at Great Zimbabwe was like many other days in that beautiful country. The weather was perfect, the sky clear, a still blue, and you could see for several miles in either direction without obstruction from smoke, fog, or clouds. It was so clear that a person had to wonder if it was real; its clarity had magic in it, like I had seen at the top of Mount Baldy in California on a crystal clear spring day or Niagara Falls in July when it is cool and transparently clear. There are only a few places where you can see the earth as perfectly as I saw it that day.

I hastily climbed to the tallest point and looked down upon the silvery lake in the distance, trying to imagine what it must have been like for the great Mwene Mutapa kings who had occupied this seat in the heavens. The land and water below stretched out in a calligraphy of mystery as difficult to decipher historically as the reason why the Shona people had left Great Zimbabwe. Hills touched streams that ran into the lake as they had done for as long as the granite cairns have given them witness. Scores of caves boasted paintings dating back forty thousand years ago, which means the Khoisan people once occupied this area as well. *How many humans have climbed this hill? I thought. Who were they? What did they think about the serenity of this land?*

I felt myself getting in touch with *nyangas,* or spiritual forces, that I had not known were still hiding away in my soul. I felt a cluster of unusual happenings: déjà vus and imaginative conversations, signs and symbols. Perhaps as an African American I was reading too much into my solitude on the hill. I had felt the weight of too much rational history as I climbed here, step-by-step, and I wanted to abandon it for the clear word.

As the sun reached its zenith I became aware that I was spending too much time wishing that I could experience what those ancient Africans felt as they climbed this same hill, going to make sacrifices, to honor the dead, to pay homage to the Mwene Mutapa kings. What was left to me? Had I been robbed, stripped clean of my own memories of Africa? Wasn't my condition the same as most Africans who had been engaged in Western education? Had my own desire to learn everything I could insidiously entrapped me in some form of European knowledge that challenged Africa? It was not double consciousness but rather double trouble, and I would have to consciously reach out for some sense of this special place, which had not been in my schooling, had not been spoken of by my teachers, and had not been known by my parents. Zimbabwe, in all of its majesty, had remained tucked away in some rocky corner of Africa essentially lost to ordinary Africans.

There are over two hundred dZimbabwes throughout Zimbabwe, Mozambique, and South Africa. They affirm the ingenuity of Africans in a time when the continent reels like an inebriated man from the shackles of five hundred years of European control and domination. Regardless of whether Africa comes to its senses or stumbles and cracks its head on the steel railings of a powerful contemporary history, I will know the magnitude of what I saw that afternoon on the Zimbabwe hill. Like many other experiences I have had in the African world, this one inspired me to tell the truth with passion.

Standing on top of the promontory overlooking the remaining hongwe, the ancient stone bird, not yet looted by adventurers, I was exhausted by the climb but satisfied by the experience. I convinced myself that the ghosts of the past would return and restore the spirit that escaped Africa when Europe entered to pillage people and property. We kept soul, which is more sacred, but we lost spirit. We were a people beaten—a trampled will, weak and anemic, and unaware that Great Zimbabwe was first a vision in someone's head. Our memories were lost, amnesia set in, and we believed fantasy stories like space beings descending to the highlands to build the Great Zimbabwe.

As I reflected on the extent of the ruins of buildings said to have been built in the tenth to twelfth centuries, a guide approached me, and I told him that I wanted to return to the meadow by the ancient route. This was an alternate route down the hill, not the popular route most climbers used to ascend to the top. The alternate route down the hill was the secret one used when the ancient Zimbabweans wanted to escape enemies. They did not use the common route up or down but rather the concealed route. Although I had ascended by the popular and common route, I wanted to take the concealed route back to the floor of the valley. I surveyed every bit of the rocks, doorways, and grooves in the rocks, and I thought again what it must have been like to have lived the lives of the ancients.

I counted the stones within a space the width of a meter, the depth of a meter and ten meters high and came up with a total of 4,500 stones—stones that had to be cut, carved, and carted or carried to the construction site. I mean, there must have been millions of stones. Somebody did some work! And on top of the mountain too.

I walked over to the guide standing toward the sun, his hands folded behind his back in resignation, just waiting for me to make up my mind to go down. "May I help you?" he asked, unfolding his arms from his back and refolding them in the front.

"I want to know what you know about this place," I said joyfully.

"I just work here, do you understand?"

"Well, but you must know something."

"Don't know much. Nobody knows much."

"Hell, tell me what you know," I said with irritation.

"Are you a spy or something? Where you from anyway? You don't talk like a Zimbabwean."

"I'm an American, an African American, but I am working in Harare for the Zimbabwe Institute of Mass Communication," I said, trying to make sure he understood that Africans lived in America and that I couldn't speak Shona.

He understood all right. "Get some books down at the Souvenir Shop."

"That I'll do," I said, and cursed the minute I had spent in an inane conversation with an African who had been beaten by the system and probably never dreamed of building a Zimbabwe like the one he guided people through. A tourist official later told me that the guides were held over from the Ian Smith regime. The park employed blacks cheaply and provided little explanation or information for them. This guide had not been trained because apparently that was the way the whites wanted it. The whites coming up from South Africa as tourists did not ask the guides anything significant, and the guides did not expect black tourists coming from anywhere to ask them anything.

The next morning, just after seven, when the air was bubbling with joy, I visited the Great Zimbabwe again. This time I spent most of my time in the famous Great Enclosure at the top.

I gazed again on Great Zimbabwe's million or more stones of granite, smoothly cut by some ancient stonecutter. Between the numerous ruins there were aloes in full bloom, a Garden of Eden outside the house of history. What black deity willed these perfectly fitted walls? How did we descend so far from the genius of this Zimbabwe? The thought of the other two hundred dZimbabwes scattered over this region boggled my mind. This one was called Great Zimbabwe because it is the greatest in scope, plan, and articulation of the culture, but the architecture of the culture speaks from stones still undiscovered in the vast wilderness of Zimbabwe.

Like the pyramids in Egypt, the temples of Chichen Itza, Macchu Picchu, the Great Wall of China, the Nigerian Eredo, and Teotihuacan, Great Zimbabwe spoke from its shroud of mystery. I know that Great Zimbabwe speaks to us now, and it can capture your heart and mind simultaneously. I thought, *This is what it must be like to witness any of the great objects made by humans or nature.*

I fingered the stones with my own flesh, felt the wear of many years in them, and touched the permanence of their assertiveness. Tears flooded my eyes but did not run down my cheeks as I experienced the enormity of those ancient people's achievement. A chill like a cool shower came over me as I imagined what it was like when the city was full of people—blacksmiths, fullers, chandlers, turners, and musicians, all making iron, spreading ore, creating incense and candles, turning, and making music.

I was the first African American to write a research article on the Great Zimbabwe. When it was published, I received lots of congratulatories from Zimbabweans who had grown up on the skewed work of the Rhodesian historian Gelfand. Nothing had impressed me at the time any more than Zimbabwe, and although I had been in the archives reading and researching the white settlers' earliest documents, I had also questioned the local people about the stone cities. They did not know much about the ancient builders; all analysis had to come from deduction. Like a scrambling chameleon I found myself all over the site, from the anchorage of the tower to the crown of the hill, looking for something—some sign, some evidence of the meaning of the stone cities. I discovered that the elements in the museum—gold, silver, iron, ebony, ivory beads, and objects from China—told a lot about the trade between the empire and the rest of the world.

The massive walls and grandeur of Great Zimbabwe drew me to them several times, and each time I gained the same respect and felt the same powerful presence of the ancestors who did so much work on that land for so long. A land fought over is sacred by virtue of the ritual of war, though this was a land ritualized much beyond what was necessary.

I want to be clear that I did not live in the past. Although I was deeply affected by it, I could not nor did I ever forget the immediacy of the present. There were too many people walking around with too many experiences for me to forget. How could you forget anything while living in Bosnia, Liberia, Angola, Eritrea, Sierra Leone, East Timor, Palestine, Kosovo, or Darfur? When men and women fight, they don't just leave corpses; they leave memories.

One Monday afternoon, in the Zimbabwe Institute for Mass Communications, I heard a short young woman yelling urgently, "Comrade Freedom! Comrade Freedom!" as a tall, attractive woman of about twenty-three years of age came bounding through the door. She was literally a queen, with a carriage every bit as elegant as Hatshepsut's. Comrade Freedom had the chiseled look of a woman who had undergone strenuous physical training. Her skin was as smooth as finely polished ebony, and she had a smile on her face as she moved around the building.

To the delight of the few people still left in the corridors after the classes were over, "Pamberi Ne Chimurenga!" Comrade Freedom replied, meaning "forward with the revolution." The woman calling Freedom's name came to her and asked for an autograph. I would see this scene many times while in Zimbabwe. Freedom was special.

Watching with pride and joy, I stood next to Sekai Holland, who had returned from Australia to devote her life to the reconstruction of the country, and we greeted Freedom as she came into the main office. Sekai was a charming and pragmatic woman with a keen ability to analyze a situation. She had been Herbert Chitepo's private secretary until he was killed in Zambia. I was fortunate to know her, although she could exaggerate here and there. She knew the exploits of Comrade Freedom and admired her independence and confidence as a woman. Sekai saw in the younger woman, I believe, something of herself as a younger person.

"Freedom, meet Professor Molefi Kete Asante. He was a Patriotic Front supporter in Buffalo, New York, and aided ZANU support committees." Sekai smiled as she spoke.

"Molefi Asante, how are you?" Freedom's voice was feminine, tinged with the authority brought from the bush. She had high cheekbones, a well-built frame, a beautiful countenance, and a smile that showed the most perfectly straight teeth I had ever seen.

"Seeking to ensure the victory," I replied, in the revolutionary vein of the time. "I'm here as a consultant to the Institute, helping to train journalists."

She leaned over and whispered to me: "The revolution has failed," her words heard only by Sekai and myself.

"It is a matter of opinion," I said, challenging the heroine of the seven-year struggle. Of course, I did not yet know the full extent of Freedom's involvement.

"The opinion of the comrades is the only opinion I can really follow in such a matter," she said sternly. "It has failed."

Her intelligence was natural, easy, untrained in the formal circles of Western education, but instead raw, real, and experiential. I later found out why she had gone to war against the Rhodesians, and I discovered in that story something of her innate brilliance.

Four weeks after I met Freedom, Ezekiel Makunike, the director of the Institute, asked me to go with Freedom, who had been appointed as the Institute's registrar, to Mudzi, eight miles from the Mozambican border, to check on a group of student journalists developing a rural newspaper.

Mudzi was one of the country's least-developed and hardest-hit regions during the war. It was in the most hotly contested area and figured in the ZANLA force's strategies for liberation because it had been so badly neglected, was close to the rear bases in Mozambique, and had the most politically conscious population by virtue of the aggressive slave system imposed by the white farmers.

After the cease-fire Mudzi became very important because agencies and institutions sought to concentrate development projects in that region. The Zimbabwe Institute of Mass Communication was fortunate because Comrade Freedom had commanded a six thousand–man force in that region as a top commander in ZANLA. She was no armchair theorist about women leaders; she was the actual person in action. No one doubted her femininity, just as no one had doubted her commitment to the liberation of Zimbabwe. Hers is a name that lives on in the villages of the eastern region of Zimbabwe, as she knew every mountain, every hill, every stream, and every village, and she knew the deprivation of the people. Because of Freedom's familiarity with the region, our institute had chosen the hamlet of Mudzi for our rural newspaper project.

We drove northwest out of Harare toward the Tete Province of Mozambique, passing the huge irrigation schemes of the few white farmers who dared to remain, passing burned-out army vehicles from

ZANLA ambushes, passing "protected" villages that the Rhodesians had barbed-wired to enforce a six-to-six curfew, and passing nameless mountains and valleys where comrades had died.

Comrade Freedom, who could be especially quiet—perhaps by habit, maybe through training—said to me, "This is my land," as we drove around a hill that had been deforested by napalm the Rhodesians had used.

"It is beautiful country," I replied, taking in the panorama our altitude provided.

"One of my last missions occurred here when we ambushed a Rhodesian convoy." She pointed to a dirt road off to the right of the main highway.

"What happened?" I was eager to know something of the war, and out here I could see the scars of warfare that I never saw in Harare. *This is where people fought and died. This is where the poor were killed. This is Africa in pain.*

"The Rhodesians were bringing up reinforcement from Salisbury. We heard their trucks several miles away and decided that this was the moment we had waited for a long time. They had twelve trucks, some Humvees, and other armored vehicles. I told our men and women to wait until the convoy went between the mountains, and then we would blow up the road in the front and our soldiers would attack at the rear. When it was over, more than twenty Rhodesians were killed and the convoy completely destroyed," she concluded.

I drove silently, thinking that I was sitting beside someone who had killed many people. It was a thought that would return many times, but I believe it was the first time that I had been so close to someone who had killed, or at least it was the first time that I knew for certain that the person had killed. My Uncles DeBuddy and Moses had been in war in Europe and had both seen action, but they never recounted stories of killing anybody. They were just shooting their guns. Freedom was a living warrior who had put the enemy to sleep. She was beautiful, a queen of her people who did not mind telling about her exploits.

We passed the first sign to Mrewa. Freedom spoke softly, like her words would disturb the dead if she spoke louder. "I was born in Mrewa. It was a small town, and the people were peasants. They worked their own land and the land of the white farmers, making an average of fifteen dollars a month. No one really lived well; we were all poor. And we all depended on the land. I learned to fish—became pretty good at bringing in the evening meal.

"My mother was always a believer in the church, as long as I could remember. She prayed a lot. And since I loved my mother, I went to church with her. They had a missionary school started by some whites from America—now I know they must have been white southerners; they were racists. I went to their school, became their best student, and they told me I should prepare myself to attend their college in America. But one day in class I got into a discussion with the teacher about the oppressive condition in Rhodesia, how the whites mistreated the blacks, how the missionaries used our people as servants and slaves and paid them very little, as little as the white Rhodesians did."

As I strained to listen, occasionally shaking my head in agreement even if I missed a word or two because of her British accent, she continued, "The teacher told me to shut up because I did not understand that the Rhodesians were Christians and God's people. There was no division in the 'body of Christ'; we were all one. I told him that was a lie and he knew it. He then informed me that I would never get a scholarship to a Church of Christ college. I informed him that the Church of Christ could go to hell—and I meant it. After all, I could see how they believed that only members of their church, which did not have any black American missionaries, could go to heaven. It was a white church, a racist institution given to propagating spookism."

"That's quite an indictment," I said.

"Indictment? No, it is not an indictment, it is the truth," she said. Her allegations stung me because unbeknownst to her, the Church of Christ had been the church of my youth. I knew there was racism in the church, but I just expected there to be racism in all white institutions when it came to dealing with black people. The fact that she had experienced racism from whites in the Church of Christ was a surprise, though I tried not to show it.

"I stand corrected," I replied, as four or five monkeys crossed the road in front of the car. I often regret that I did not have the courage to tell her that the Church of Christ was the church I had been baptized into in Georgia. But I had the same impression about the church that she had. I felt that the church, like other fundamentalist churches, were institutions of white privilege. But I drove on, listening, saying nothing about my own past.

"Well, anyway, I left their school and started looking for a way to get to Mozambique. I knew the fighting was already going on in the eastern zone, and I just wanted to get my AK-47 and blast the hell out of the racists. As you can tell, my ideology was immature.

"At first I tried to recruit some girlfriends. They wouldn't go. So I talked one of my cousins into going—he was about eighteen—and then I talked several other young men into going for training. The momentum of the revolution had created its own recruiter in me even before I met any of the comrades."

"Weren't you scared, nervous?" I ventured to ask.

"No" was all Freedom would say, but at first I believed that was just a way of concealing her fear or that she did not remember what it must have been like for a young girl of her age to run away to the war.

In the course of our discussion and discussions with other female combatants, I found myself daydreaming about Maxine, Robbie, Jackie, and Martha in Valdosta as well as Barbara and Delores in Nashville—girls I had gone to elementary and secondary school with. Could they have handled the war that had matured Freedom? The question was always left unanswered. And then it would come, this flood of thoughts about what children were doing in Valdosta and Nashville, about the neighborhood kids who walked the dusky streets on summer evenings, dreaming of a better world. They thought they were tough, as we had thought we were tough. But could we handle real war like Freedom had handled hers at thirteen years old, in the hills and valleys of beautiful Zimbabwe?

And so I understood Freedom's answer when she said no, she had not been afraid, because in such situations, you grow into the scene, stepping unafraid to confront life head-on. She did as I had done, but I could not fool myself into thinking that the war between ZANLA and the Rhodesian Army was anything like the Nashville Christian Institute versus the Black Royals. So I learned to appreciate the sacrifice that the young people of Zimbabwe had made for their liberation and national emancipation. Our little street gang fights had no larger political purpose than what they were: fights for territorial respect. However,

I should explain that my preparation for "nonnegotiable demands" meetings not only came from the street gangs; I was also influenced by churches, community organizations, and my own father. No matter where you are, throughout your life lessons are being delivered in powerful ways, over and over again.

When Freedom and I entered the small village of Mudzi, passing monuments to the Portuguese who ventured into the interior of Africa during the sixteenth century and then crossing over roads that were nothing more than cattle trails, the people came out of their houses to see the car that was stubborn enough to take the muddy trail to the king's house. When we got there, to our amazement, some of the students from the Zimbabwe Institute of Mass Communication had already beat us to the site and had also collected a mimeograph machine.

We showed the locals how to use it, put the ink in, and run the thing like crazy to copy a sheet that had been prepared with the local and national news. Mudzi became an example of a national achievement that was repeated around the country. Rural newspapers sprang up because of our turning over local news to the chiefs or kings and allowing them to disseminate information. In Africa, this worked. There was no talk in these rural areas about the press taking an opposing view to the government; the paper was strictly about the news of development. Who was doing what to bring the local area resources and how those resources were being used were the two questions of interest. At that time Zimbabwe was expressing a socialist ethos, and the work we did in the countryside was consistent with an extraordinary commitment to political education and mass development.

When we drove away from Mudzi, I felt that I had begun to make a contribution to the general condition of the country. It was so minor, but it was important to the people to see me, to touch me, and to know that an African from the United States had come to their isolated hillside village to assist them. Those people in Mudzi would impact the way I lived the rest of my life. I knew something because of them that I had not known before: I could have easily lived in that isolated village forever.

Tichaona Freedom was pleased that the people of Mudzi had received me so easily. "Asante, the people like you here," she had said when I demonstrated the mimeograph machine. Of course, I had taken to them quite easily as well.

Now that we were leaving, driving down the crooked, muddy, hilly road toward the main highway, Freedom wanted to talk politics. "What do you think of socialism, Asante?" She had a habit of calling me by my surname. I thought it was a military thing; I had told her many times to call me Molefi.

"Well, I am a socialist, although I come from a capitalist country," I told her.

"Yeah, but what do you think of it?" she insisted. The western sun shimmered in our faces as it was about to set.

"It really depends on the people who are interpreting and implementing socialism. I do not believe in the Soviet Union's socialism; I think that it is a corrupt system." Little did we know how corrupt it was and how easy it would fall within a few years.

"We are agreed on that, but what about African socialism? You know, the socialism of Kenneth Kaunda, of Samora Machel, of Julius Nyerere?"

"Of Robert Mugabe," I intervened.

"No, not of Mugabe. I don't believe he is a socialist."

"He says he is a socialist," I reminded her.

"These African leaders can say anything for political reasons, but Mugabe is clearly not a socialist."

Freedom's statement brought to mind many talks I had with Manning Marable, Cornel West, Kwame Ture, Tony Monteiro, and Shakur Africanus, who love to make distinctions about who is socialist and who is not socialist. But I was struck by Freedom's denial of Mugabe's socialism; I wanted to believe that the person who had inspired me from the mountains and valleys of Mozambique had the highest ethical ideals for society. "How can you say that when he articulates his position on the television every evening?"

"You can say anything on television and for political purposes," she replied.

"But he claims to be a practitioner."

"Practice socialism, Asante, don't play dumb. Does the man believe in and practice socialism?" she persisted.

"Not in the way you think—that is, not in the sense that the people out in these parts can understand and see as affecting their own living conditions. I guess it takes time, huh?"

"Why do you want to make excuses for the man? He does not understand the necessity for changing the lives of the common people. We are in trouble in this country. I am seriously thinking about going to Namibia to fight against the South Africans or to Angola, where people still have a revolutionary spirit," Freedom said.

I could see the rub board of lines that had formed above her eyes and on her forehead. She was tense, angry, disappointed. I knew that there were hundreds, perhaps thousands, like her—she had given a big portion of her youth to fight for something that she thought would exist immediately after the whites were thrown out. It did not happen that way. Freedom had been a leader and a heroine, and so she was alright. She had a job, unlike most of the fighters who were uneducated, but even so, she worried about her colleagues, her comrades.

The French Peugeot sedan we were driving stuttered a bit as we entered Mrewa, and I hoped that we would not have to deal with any mechanical problems, as the evening was coming and I wanted to go on; we still had several hours to drive. But Freedom wanted me to meet her people, so we drove into the main square, stopped near a hardware store, and waited as she got out of the car and walked up the steps to the store.

People came from everywhere, almost instantaneously. The word was out that Freedom was in the town square. I got out of the car and followed her, observing the admiration the people had for her. One lady, who had served under Freedom on the Eastern Front during the war, brought her child to Freedom and thrust the little girl into her arms. A man, dragging himself on the ground because of some awful injury, beckoned to her, and she bent down, shook his hand, and said something in Shona that I did not understand. He smiled, turned, and dragged himself away. I figured it was a war injury and that he knew her from the days of the Second Chimurenga.

As others crowded around her, she introduced me as an African from America. The people seemed pleased that someone from so far away would visit their town. Little did they know that their favorite daughter had memorialized their town forever.

When we left Mrewa, it was dark. The people had treated us to drinks, conversation, laughter, and fellowship. I felt so proud for Freedom. At such a young age, I thought, she had become an old woman, not in physical age but in wisdom, grace, and humility. The bounty or the poverty of history is rarely planned, but one or the other is always available. Freedom had taken her chance and found the abundance of history in the treasure chest of her life.

∞

Harare, as beautiful as it was physically, was a city full of rumors and schemes. International intrigue and political plots abounded, and there were endless stories of this or that personality doing this or that act. Every word spoken in secret in the government was discussed in the streets; there were sieves running out of every door in Mugabe's administration. Every person who visited a minister or the prime minister was analyzed and assigned a place in the pantheon of activities taking place in Harare. Myths were created and heroes made and unmade. When the sun came up and blessed the fruit trees, it covered the workers moving hastily to their jobs—as it also bathed the tattlers, the busy-bodies, the negative talkers.

I met a group of American journalists in the bars and cafes of Harare, and occasionally in someone's home, who truly attempted to explain what was going on in Zimbabwe to the benefit of their Western audience. I also met some characters in Africa who tried to do the same—both writers from Zimbabwe and those who had crossed the border from South Africa.

Jay Ross, one of the best writers at the time and the *Washington Post* correspondent for Africa in the early 1980s, understood the political situation in Africa as much as any politician, having traveled and lived in and out of third-rate hotels all over the continent, feeling the pulse of the people. One night he invited a group of journalists and some local expatriates for dinner in his Harare home. Seated around his living room, sprawled on the floor with correspondents from *Reuters*, the *Guardian*, and other foreign presses, we discussed the situation in South Africa. For political reasons we only discussed Zimbabwe in more private settings, mostly one-to-one.

Georgia and Tennessee in the 1960s, where I had come to manhood, were just about like anything you could find in the old Rhodesia; the whites in Valdosta had used their power and domination much like the

Rhodesians did. Of course, in the South we technically had the federal law on our side, but it did not matter much. Local law was just another crook in our collective necks.

However, South African Boers were different than Georgians or Rhodesians. Everyone in Zimbabwe said so, even Africans. When I said, half-wishing, "It's going to blow any day," someone answered, "The Boers are a different breed than the Rhodesians. They will stick it out, and it will be tough," and a chorus of others backed them up. I knew then, as the only black invited to this social affair, that I was on the spot, where, of course, I never minded being.

"You remember Montgomery, don't you?" I asked.

"What about Montgomery is analogous to this situation?" asked Ross, being a good facilitator of discussion.

"Well, who expected Rosa Parks to sit down when she did and where she did?" I answered my own question: "No one. And what happened?" I answered again: "The whole fabric, design and all, of southern segregation came tumbling down, despite the social scientists' predictions."

"You may have a point," said Colin, of the Knight Ridder papers.

I figured I did, so I pressed it in a little more. "The South African situation is so ready to explode that almost anything could serve as a spark. One more person dying in detention, a bombing on a street in downtown Johannesburg, the killing of a black woman, the sassiness of a teenager in a store in Cape Town—anything, anytime, could cause it to blow."

Years later, though, I would see where we were all wrong because we did not anticipate F. W. de Klerk's release of Nelson Mandela from prison and the subsequent negotiations that brought about a democratically elected government. This was only the beginning of my many bouts with expatriates and the media in the newly independent Zimbabwe.

For instance, one sunny winter's morning I was waiting in the short line outside Harare's inoculation clinic for a yellow fever inoculation; I received my last exactly ten years earlier in Los Angeles. While standing there under the shade of a tree, waiting to go inside for the shot, I listened to the clattering chatter of the Indians and whites, talking about what it took to get into South Africa. They were well dressed; one of the Indian women had a silk blouse hung sari-like over her trousers—she was particularly eager to make sure she got the right shots. The other one was rather plump in the manner of those who have sat too much without any physical exercise. They were listening to two old wizened white women who felt a little closer to being out of black-ruled Zimbabwe.

I was amused. They probably took me for Shona-speaking, as they spoke perfect English right in front of me. The Indian women told me—that is, the back of my head understood—that they were going out of the country for the first time in their lives. I was eager to learn what they would do in South Africa, but all I could really tell was that they wanted out of Zimbabwe. I thought this was funny because the Indians had worked in Zimbabwe under white rule, but under black rule felt they would be discriminated against. They never gave the government a chance but instead fled to South Africa where whites still ruled, as if whites would rule there forever. I mused, *Life exacts its own price for prejudice, discrimination, and fear.*

As the cool winter breeze grew colder, I thought about the Indians in Uganda, under Idi Amin, who called himself "The Last King of Scotland" because the Queen of England said that she owned Uganda. Under his rule the Indians had to leave because they did not take Ugandan citizenship after remaining in the country for twenty years or more. They remained—and wanted to remain—British. "Well," Idi Amin said, "you have to go." What would happen to these Indians who were running to South Africa?

I have always believed racial peace is possible, but we all have to stretch ourselves in order to bring it about. So, at about the same time, late in 1981, there was a renewed effort to get a group of white nations together with a group of black nations and try to work out a sharing of resources and money. By that time I had received a Fulbright grant to maintain the work I had started with the Zimbabwe Institute of Mass Communications. The Zimbabweans had supported my efforts as I waited for my Zimbabwean work permit, so when the international effort to discuss resource sharing among wealthy and poor nations came into being, I was eager to know something about it, perhaps to participate.

When I showed up at the Mount Pleasant campus at the University of Zimbabwe, I found my way into the university crowd watching the dinhne dancers outside the student union. Two representatives, one white and the other black, watched the dancers, and I noted that there was a lot of dialogue going on between them. The white one, chin thrust forward, mouth tight, eyes sliding back and forth to the corners of his lids, whispered something to the black one, whose head was straight, lips smiling a little, and eyes dancing with the music. Listening, the black one smiled widely and motioned to the white to follow him inside the building.

Because I did not have a pass and I knew they were representatives, I thought I would follow them into the auditorium. "Where're you going?" said the security guard, halfheartedly, as one who discovers his authority in other people's responses.

"To the convention center, sir," I said with the arrogance and American English accent I had come to employ in situations such as this one.

"The program will start in about fifteen minutes," he quickly informed me, once he felt I had adequately indicated I was a representative. He didn't ask me any further questions. It was then that I saw the two men whom I had seen outside standing guard at the auditorium. They must have been secret service men.

I had really only wanted to hear Prime Minister Mugabe. He spoke with passion about the economic straitjacket the West had imposed on Africa. He challenged the white nations to give back some of what they had taken, sharing the wealth that had been stolen for almost four hundred years. He conceded nothing; his voice was firm and his manner serious.

A few days later I went to the Soviet film festival at the Seven Arts Cinema, hoping to hear something of the Soviets' intention toward the new country—but that was not to be the case. The whole thing was a flop. The Russians had merely brought two or three films to Zimbabwe to impress the Africans with their cinematography. I sat through something about gypsies—actually the Roma—and something else about horses or maybe Roma and horses, where they showed you how to ride, but quite frankly, I could see why Mr. Zhao and his wife, from the New China News Agency, Hsinhua, fell asleep. They were seated directly in front of me, and I tried not to look at them, hoping to avoid making them self-conscious.

Afterward the spectators asked what the Russians had expected to gain with these films. There were more people coming out of the adjacent theater where *Raiders of the Lost Ark* was playing than there were in our theater. I found myself thinking, *Certainly the Soviet Union makes better films than this.* Perhaps even if they had shown an old documentary of the Russian Revolution or a feature about their space program, they would have achieved a higher degree of praise. *So much for transformation of the culture of Zimbabwe,* I thought.

I chatted a little bit with Mr. Zhao and John Burns, the cultural attaché from the American Embassy, about the films. We spoke of nothing heavy but instead engaged in the usual public socializing of foreigners in a strange country—a sharing of opinions, gossip, and wine. These were experiences that were preparing me for a career in Black Studies that transcended the boundaries of the United States. I was participating in discursive small talk with worldly people when I had just begun to get my feet wet in political waters.

About eight days after the art show Glendora Johnson came from Buffalo, in the midst of sweltering heat, and told me that she had heard that a drought was in the making. This was bad news for the nation because already white farmers were saying they could not afford to pay their workers. The minimum wage had gone up to thirty dollars a month, and now people would be sleeping in the streets. Talk of political plots thickened in the streets.

The socialists could not organize things as fast as they wanted to, and the peasants, alongside their urban compatriots, would die of either heat or famine. The nation depended on its corn crop to alleviate hunger and enrich its coffers with export sales. With the looming drought, Africans turned to extraordinary explanations for the conditions of nature. Could it be that there were agents working against the nation? Was it possible that spies were in the government? Perhaps someone had placed a particular medicine on the economy or the prime minister? Many began to search out the cause for the distress.

December 10, 1981, was one of the most disappointing days in my life. On that date in Zimbabwe, a nation for whose liberation I had devoted considerable energies, Sekai Holland informed me that the director of the national broadcasting station was circulating a memo stating that I was not to be allowed to appear on the television, which I had done before, because of the suspicion that I was an agent of the Central Intelligence Agency. The entire conspiracy theory was suspect.

I never saw the memo and did not know why I was neither arrested nor officially informed of the matter. Initially, I was furious, ready to take on the whole Zimbabwean petty neo-settler establishment, but then, after reflecting on the tremendous lack of sophistication, the empty heads, the politically unread, and the stupid decisions made on the basis of nothing, I decided to begin to pack my bags and leave, even if it took seven months to do so. I was through with black self-hatred; through with blacks abusing blacks; through with being too bright and intelligent for a backward elite; through with being ready to save all black people, in both America and Africa; through with cheap, no-good rascals who saw every American, black or white, as being a spy; through with the notion that ethnicity did not matter in Africa, that only nationality and politics did; through with my naïveté about Africa; and, finally, I was through with the fact that every black from America had to bear the stigma of a white racist government that most of the world believed would stick its fingers in anybody's eyes. Yes, I was not dumb or blind. I knew what had happened in Ghana with the overthrow of Kwame Nkrumah and I knew what had happened in Congo with Patrice Lumumba. I was not ignorant of how the United States had manipulated the politics of several African nations. Yet I was angry that someone would spread false rumors about me.

I figured the CIA was in Africa, but I certainly had nothing to do with it. In fact, the CIA was probably following *me* around because I was the first American to be admitted to teach communication and journalism in Zimbabwe after the war. Who knows—the people I associated with from the American embassy may have been spies, but I was not. In fact, I had been told that the Americans had a file on me. After all, I associated with the Cubans, Chinese, and Soviets who congregated at ZIMCO alongside the Australians, English, and Canadians because we were all on the same path to usher into existence a new, proud, and liberated Zimbabwe. I was perhaps the most naïve of the people I met and socialized with, but in the end I was as I had always been—free and independent in my thinking and behavior.

A few days later I tried to fit together the patchwork of the heinous memo. I had been asked to appear on a program dealing with women's liberation and rights in Zimbabwe. The only reason I was asked to appear on the panel with three Zimbabwean women was because a few weeks earlier I had spoken about women's place in African society at a women feature writers' conference in Marandellas (now Mapondera), sponsored by the UN Educational, Scientific, and Cultural Organization (UNESCO). Ezekiel Makunike, my director at ZIMCO, had recommended me to the organizers, and I had gone with the idea that a liberated Zimbabwe had to adopt Samora Machel's notion that the liberation of women was not an act of charity but rather "a fundamental necessity of a true revolution."

I told the conferees that women were too often like beasts of burden, carrying children on their backs at the same time as they held hoes in their hands and boxes on their heads while men, I had seen in the countryside, walked casually empty-handed beside them. This made a hit with the women. This comment was reported in the papers, and I received many compliments for standing up for the rights of women. The women said I was the only African man with the courage to stand up for them. Thus, I was suggested as a participant on the television program on women.

The director apparently read the name Molefi Kete Asante and recalled a memo he had perhaps received from someone, somewhere—I do not know, it does not matter. The effect was that he informed the interviewer, a woman, that I was to be uninvited to appear on television because of my suspicious background. I believe this was a deliberate act to keep me from speaking on national television about women's rights. I did not speak on the program, and the issue of the CIA was dropped. My anger took a long time to abate, but I did get over it.

Looking back on the experience, my negativity arose not so much from the consternation with the situation but from my initial disappointment with Africans. I think that was the break, the knock on the head, the "hello" that was necessary for me to realize that the distance was not simply one of kilometers, the chasm was not merely an ocean, the differences were not only from different continents, but rather from different historical experiences.

Always, as an African American in Africa, I wanted to find deep understanding, new myths that I had no knowledge about but knew must exist, ancient mores and values, intimate secrets that were rarely revealed to others, and the people's intricate historical processes. When this did not occur, I felt let down by my own brothers and sisters, who were only my fellows in color, origin, general cultural responses to phenomena, and resistance to oppression. Anxious to establish contact with them, I extended the diasporan hand of unity, only to be told that I was an American, a citizen of a country that supported the enemies of the masses, which, unfortunately, was true. Protesting that all Americans are not racists and that indeed I had stripes for my gallantry in the cause of the Zimbabwean masses may not have been enough. A whole swarm of abuses because I was American finally forced me to accept the condition of my birth.

My eyes were opened, and it sharpened the image of myself, my history, my African American people, and my American citizenship in the face of Africa. I could no longer pretend to be African in one sense, yet I would always be African in another. It was this other sense, being African in the search for Maat—harmony, righteousness, justice, order, balance, truth, and reciprocity, the key values of the African soul—that inspired in me the faith that lasted for the rest of my time in Zimbabwe. My Pan-African zeal was not crushed, though I had been tested in my surface relationships with fellow Africans.

A week after I was denied the opportunity to appear on television, I was asked to serve as the chairperson for a week-long seminar on press responsibility at Ranche House College. After all, I had chaired the department of communication at SUNY Buffalo and was the senior communication scholar in the country, and the people in communication thought that I would lend credibility to their work. The Minister of Information, Dr. Nathan Shamuyarira, came to open the conference, and then I received another message, very casually, that the rumor was really a lie: I had never been suspected of anything and had never been under suspicion. According to the reports, Sekai Holland had confused me with someone else. Lots of small talk by low-level administrators and staff people, I was told. I said forget it.

Nevertheless, I went to see Shamu, as we called the minister, and voiced my concern about the situation. He was aware of it and wanted me to know that he fully supported me and thanked me for the efforts I had made on behalf of ZANU during the struggle for independence. He was friendly, charming, and intellectual; he had many stories to tell about the United States.

Shamu wanted me to know that his door was always open to me. "You haven't been by to see me since you have been here," he complained.

"Didn't want to impose myself," I offered. I had as much respect for the government leaders in Zimbabwe as in the United States and did not want to appear like a pushy outsider. Of course, every European white who came to the country felt that he or she had the right to go straight to the top with the smallest issue, but that was an arrogance that African Americans had not yet acquired and I hoped would never seek to acquire. Like the African leaders, I resented such an attitude in others; I would rather let my work speak for me.

"What do you mean, 'impose yourself'?" Dr. Shamuyarira asked.

"Well, I know you are very busy, and I did not want to make an appointment just to talk about small stuff with the minister."

"You have to understand that having a scholar of your significance around to discuss theories and philosophies is unusual. I know who you are and what you mean to the African world. Come in and see me anytime," Shamuyarira said.

"Yes, Chef, I will," I said using a Zimbabwean colloquial expression for the top person in an organization.

My objective, and certainly one that I share with many other people, is to reduce human pain and suffering and to always open channels for what the ancient Egyptians understood as khephri, or becoming. At the level of process and implementation, I have seen this objective in the works of many Africans on the continent as well. It was truly evident in the early days of the new regime in Zimbabwe.

In so many ways Nathan Shamuyarira, Naomi Nhiwatiwa, and Chen Chimutengwende tried to bridge the chasm between Africans and African Americans. I appreciated the fact that they made me feel comfortable, at home, and yet I knew that Dooly County or Valdosta,

Georgia, was more immediate in my own consciousness. I was an African American in Africa. My ethnic identification was African American. My citizenship was American. My cultural identification was with the larger African world. However, I experienced no double consciousness of the type Du Bois speaks about; I had no strivings in my soul about being African and American. The two categories were not contradictory, they were not in battle, and I certainly had no desire to be white. Yet like all of us, in many ways I was the product of numerous influences from our sojourn in the Americas.

Nearly two months after the CIA accusations I found myself deep into writing about Zimbabwean history and culture. You know how someone says that this or that 'drove them to drink'? Well, Zimbabwe drove me to the archives and historical museums. Originally I had no intention of writing a novel about Mzilikazi, the great Matabele king, but the endless clear skies and beautiful days convinced me that I should. This is where the idea for *Scattered to the Wind,* my novel, published by Sungai Books, came from, deep in the Zimbabwean archives. I wanted to write a book that symbolized the scattering of Africans throughout the world, and nothing captured me as much as the *mfecane* in southern Africa, which sent so many people to various parts of the continent. Plus, my wife at the time, Kariamu, was into Zulu mythology, Monomotapa expansion, the rise of the kings, and various cultural monographs from the Zimbabwe National Archives.

The documents were fascinating; they opened up a whole new historical and cultural field. I read voluminously—writing notes, rereading materials, and learning the most interesting things. Did you know that the Ndebele thought a man was a sissy if he did not have pierced ears? I wondered what the old Ndebele priest thought of me when I journeyed to see him my ears have always been unpierced.

The woman who ran the Zimbabwe Archives was Angelina Kamba, black but stiff. She came down to meet Kariamu and me at the entrance, and just stared. Finally, she said to a security officer, "Show them around," and quickly departed. I think that she was startled to see black people in the archives, though she was black herself.

The place contained all styles of Rhodesiana. I even found some ancient films of whites meeting Africans in the rural areas. After that first visit I went back repeatedly. As I looked through the card catalogs, I did my confessions to Mwari, the god of the Shona, and Nkulunkulu, the god of the Ndebele, and delved into research.

It struck me that Angelina's face was familiar; it was from my past in South Georgia. As I studied the archival records, I studied her face. Yes, it was the face of the stately old woman in calico whom I had seen walking down a lonesome road near Lakeland, Georgia, a few years earlier. Here I was in the national archives of Zimbabwe, feeling that I had seen the archivist before.

I found Africa in my past, I reconnected momentarily, right there in the reading room. It was awesome, this meaning of Africa, this wish for mother Africa. Whatever else I had found on the Lakeland road that afternoon, I now found a reflection in Zimbabwe. It was an odd psychological state, a repetitive experience, happening to me but outside of me in a phenomenal way.

When I left the archives and drove out to the countryside to purchase apples, I passed by another woman who must have been the incarnate image of the South Georgia woman—not in calico, but in an African print with Mugabe's face stamped on it. The woman walked slowly down the endless dusty road, carrying a large bundle of firewood atop her head. A baby slept serenely on her back, and the two suitcases in her hands were expertly balanced with each movement of her strong legs.

I was spiritually overcome by the serendipitous nature of these powerful images. I stopped my rental car and sat on top of a large granite boulder, looking and thinking. I then walked over to the side of the road to explore the fascinating cairns that jutted out of the Zimbabwean landscape.

Soon, the woman moving elegantly and magnificently disappeared in the tall grass alongside the road. I could see wildflowers shaking and vibrating from her passing, some giant presence disturbing the eerie peace of nature. She was off to her own home somewhere beyond the tall grass, in a clearing perhaps that could not be seen from the road.

"What rapturous elegance," I whispered to myself, picking up a few rocks and flinging them as far as I could away from the woman.

What strength, I thought, considering the weight she carried on her body. I almost wanted to follow her to see where she would end, but I thought better about it. I thought, another place and another time.

"What balance," I said to myself, scurrying down the boulder toward my car, only to find a family of baboons hurrying on their way on the opposite side of the road. I raced to my car—not being familiar with the predatory habits of baboons, I thought it would be safer inside the car, just in case. My fears were unfounded—I do not think they even saw me, so intent they seemed on getting to their destination.

Once in my car I reflected on my question of women in Africa being treated like beasts of burden. Immediately after independence intellectuals had been difficult to find in Zimbabwe. By the time most were working for the government, they were not discussing the same political and cultural issues that drove the war effort. So for discussion I turned to the young professionals: journalists, consultants, attorneys, entrepreneurs. When I tried to talk about women in Africa being treated like beasts of burden, I found them uniformly conservative regarding women's rights in the society. To compound my consternation, black women were legally classified as minors, and there had been no rush to change the legislation since Prime Minister Mugabe came to power. The men actually seemed to prefer to keep women in that status.

The condition of women in Zimbabwe was something just above that of servants as far as I could see. During the one hundred years of white rule, women had been reduced to the most inconsiderate inequality. The social system had neither supported women nor men in defining relationships; only whites had rights, and only whites could change the social and legal situations. Women had become carriers of burdens, who worked for others and gave all their money to men. Some men even paid for other wives with the money their first wife earned! I knew women had to be more vigilant or else they would lose the rights they had gained by demonstrating their valor in the war, as not even the revolution was prepared to guarantee their equality.

In the early days of the new government cabinet ministers married second and third wives while speaking for women's rights. The problem was the war legacy. They had married female combatants they met on the battlefield and in the camps, never expecting to be big party officials. Many of the war brides were not very educated;

consequently, when the "comrades" came into power positions and status jobs, they looked around and decided to marry other women. The situation became so serious that a series of television programs were devoted to it.

Sekai Holland became a regular on the programs. Despite the fact that she had a white Australian husband, she was the most outspoken woman in the country for women's rights. She seemed to recognize the controversial position she was in but kept insisting that the women in Zimbabwe were not free. Many men dismissed her as a "been to" who had lost all of her culture, but this was not the case. Sekai had always been a fighter and was one of the leading voices for women in the African world.

Meanwhile, life in the villages and even in the townships was hellish for women, who were often virtually slaves. So bitter was the cruelty whites imposed on blacks that black men often found their relief by choking the essence of humanity out of their women. In keeping with a tradition that has gone the way of the spear in most progressive societies, women did not have the legal rights that men had. I found the laws in Zimbabwe far more retrogressive than the ones in Ghana or Nigeria or Kenya. The Africans had not had a chance to correct the laws because, throughout Africa, the rights of women were far more respected, I think, than other parts of the world. Zimbabwe was an aberration.

One Zimbabwean man who had fought in the war of liberation cautioned, "A woman must always know her place."

"But isn't this what the whites said about Africans—'The African must always know his place'?" I said.

"That's different."

"How's it different, since both the black men and the whites defined the other person's place?"

"Our culture goes back hundreds of years."

"So do racism and sexism."

"But you don't seem to understand that the women wouldn't be happy any other way."

"I can hear the whites saying that Africans like to be dominated by whites. They wouldn't be happy being free."

"We Zimbabweans believe that women should be well treated but that tradition should not be tampered with."

"But you drive a Mercedes," I shot back. "You certainly don't follow tradition in transportation! You wear shoes! What's this talk about tampering with traditions? Some you can tamper with and some you cannot bother, is that it?"

"I just don't think the condition of women will change any time soon."

"As Ian Smith said about black liberation: 'Never in a thousand years,'" I mocked.

I did not make much progressive impression on the Zimbabwean men, but the women invited me to speak at conferences and on various panels. To the Zimbabwean women who seldom found men in their corner, I was an African American prince of sexual and gender understanding.

Now this woman trudging homeward off the Marandellas road and loaded down with goods underscored the role assigned to women in Zimbabwe. After the woman had disappeared, a bevy of six or seven young girls, all dressed in blue school uniforms, came along, singing and thrusting their books up and out in unison as they moved along. I knew then that the future was bright for the women of Zimbabwe. They had proved their abilities throughout the history of the nation, and the great Nehanda was the greatest national hero, although the men might claim Chaminuka was. These young girls were enough to ensure a better future in my mind.

After buying apples from a roadside vendor I went back to the Avenues where Kariamu and I packed the Peugeot and headed for the enchanting Inyanga Mountains not more than a couple of hours away near the Mozambican border. It took us longer than two hours to arrive at the hotel we had booked because we stopped for photos along the road. Huge rocks sitting atop each other appeared placed on the earth by some intelligent giant caught our attention. When we finally settled in an old hunting lodge that whites from Mozambique had used in the days of Portugal's rule, we felt that we had entered a new world, miles away from the bustle of Harare. It was nestled in a forest of pine trees with running streams and waterfalls in almost every direction—nature's preserve in a majestic setting, unspoiled by any of the modern conveniences one comes to expect in America.

People came here to rest and relax in the outdoors; golfing, hunting, shooting, and swimming went on incessantly. As the only blacks living in the hotel, we played it safe because most of the whites were old Rhodesian types who did not take too kindly to the fact that blacks were now allowed. We ate, walked the grounds, swam, and relaxed.

Two weeks later we drove to Mutare, which the British had called Umtali, the most perfectly situated city in all of Africa, between the Cape and the Mediterranean, a gorgeous village perched on the side of the mountains. If it were in the United States, it would be an inland village not too different in climate and vegetation from Santa Barbara. An eruption of blossoming flowers of every colorful variation stunned us with their straightforward projection of redness and orangeness. I remember recoiling in delight, saying, "This must have been what the ancestors saw who crossed the Zambezi, skirted the coast, and founded *musha* throughout this region." The musha, or towns, of this region are all picturesque villages that embrace the beautiful hillsides like parasites hugging giant trees.

The city of Mutare, home to about a hundred thousand people, was asplash with excitement. The Second Chimurenga War had taken its toll on the local young men, black and white alike, and now the people were out on the street trying to recover the time lost in the seven-year war. Yet they would never recover the condition of those days, so completely had the liberation forces freed the blacks from servility and the whites from their attitude of superiority. The many battlegrounds around this tranquil village bore loud testimony to a bygone era.

The vistas, rich with mountains reaching up to clear, unspoiled sky, the eucalyptuses standing sentinel around corners, and the people bouncing with gaiety because their wage had increased from fifteen a month to fifty a month, carried everyone away on rivers of the pleasant aromas, perfumes, and sounds of Africa. I walked the streets, looking, studying the interactions of people after the war, only to be disconcerted by the madness of the freedom. It was as if people had all been let out of jail at once. There were parties, dancing, singing—the endless singing of the national anthem, "Beautiful, Beautiful Zimbabwe"—and talk of reconciliation.

I have come to believe that no people believe in the possibility of human reconciliation more than Africans. Soon after his election as prime

minister Robert Mugabe announced that the first phase of his government's program would be called "the Year of Reconciliation," and the
people reacted positively. Years later this Mugabe would be forgotten
by political pundits and condemned for his assertion of the rights of
Africans to their own land. As an American national and having been
somewhat victimized by my own history, I was a little wary of all this
talk of reconciliation with an enemy whose aim had been to wipe out
Africans. The people of Mutare put me back in connection with my
African nature, and for this I found myself grateful, humbled. How
could I ever have thought it would be impossible to reconcile with white
racists when Africans on the continent clearly felt that it was possible?

Here in the eastern region, the Manyika capital, a major infiltra-
tion point for the ZANLA army, thousands of blacks and hundreds of
whites, mingling in their own little groups, danced the commerce and
window-shopping dance. They had each been freed from enslavement
to racism, and yet they hardly spoke to each other. I guessed that the
memory of the war still stood at the door of their hearts and refused to
hear the deafening roar of humanity, even with the sounds of reconciliation reverberating in the official air of politics.

Downtown, near a park, a small group of Indians—two men, three
women, and a bevy of girls between ten and seventeen years old—stood
watching an African load televisions into the back of a truck. I watched
them watch the African work, amused at their amusements.

The Indians had spread all over the country, occupying the merchant
shops and general stores, frequently replacing whites who went to fight
against the blacks. Few Indians had served in the Rhodesian army;
they were always able to buy their way out by giving money to white
officers or, if called to enter the army, paying young whites or coloreds
to take their place. Consequently, after the war they could support
Robert Mugabe's government without any recriminations. They even
donated large sums of money—nothing compared to what they had
raked out of the pockets of Africans—to the construction of a ZANU
party headquarters after the old one was blown up in 1981.

The African loaded about twelve televisions onto the truck and disappeared inside a decrepit repair shop, out of place on the most modern
street in Mutare. The Indian adults and their group of children—six
girls, I later counted—walked slowly toward the train depot. The women

wore saris, flowing in the stiff, dry wind, butterflies with thick rolls of uncovered fat shaking around their sides; the men were slim and soft—fragile, victims of too many vegetarian meals in a meat-eating society. They sauntered across the busy street, easily dodging the newly liberated drivers of Mutare.

ZAPU was mainly centered in Matabele territory and therefore did not command as many people as ZANU, the ruling party centered in Mashona territories. Because the Shona or Mashona people were the majority, ZANU was the dominant power in the nation.

Joseph Nkomo, a veteran freedom fighter whose history in the liberation struggle dated before Nelson Mandela's in South Africa, was the leader of ZAPU. He and Robert Mugabe briefly jostled for political power in the country, but the prize went to the leader of the larger party, and Nkomo was given several posts in the government. This was as it should have been, although his partisans in the Matabele area thought that he should have been the first prime minister of the newly freed nation.

Nkomo was a skilled politician and an astute revolutionary, and he used his influence with Mugabe to secure as many services and goods as he could for his people who had fought in the war.

The Mugabe government sacked Nkomo in 1982. Although it was not a permanent sacking, it did cut off much political access to Mugabe that Nkomo had generated for his Ndebele supporters. Attacks on Mugabe were intensified, and fugitive papers began to appear, accusing Mugabe of sabotaging the socialist revolution. But he maintained his position against Nkomo's presence in his government. Nkomo's major crime was being born on the other side of the ethnic line.

Most African leaders deny ethnic chauvinism's presence and get angry when it is discovered and pointed out. I found this to be the case in Nigeria, Zimbabwe, and Ghana. I suspect it is the same all over the continent.

"Why don't you admit tribalism exists?" I asked a Ghanaian accountant visiting Zimbabwe in a delegation of business leaders. As in other regions of the world, people are often tied to their ethnic communities by ancestral and linguistic bonds, and when they are confronted by different languages and customs, they often react negatively; sadly, this seemed to me to be the situation in Africa as well. I hated the word "tribalism" but found it useful in the conversation.

"That would be bad," he answered.

"Couldn't be as bad as tribalism itself, particularly when it produces nepotism, cronyism, and corruption," I said.

"What would the whites of the world think?" he offered.

"I don't know—actually I don't care, and neither should you."

"But we've been accusing them of racism."

"And so?" I asked.

"Brother Asante, we can't reveal our own tribalism just like that."

"The whites know that Africans are tribalistic. They encouraged it, used it. But we've got to admit it before we can change it," I said.

"You're right, but it's going to take a long time," he acknowledged.

"Let's be honest and start now."

In several cases the Zimbabwean Public Service Commission had kept African Americans from getting employment. Some blacks accused the whites on the commission until it was discovered that the whites usually favored the African Americans, but the Africans did not. This had a lot to do with the internal dynamics of racism, like when whites in the United States say to continental Africans that they find Africans from the continent easier to know than blacks in the United States. This was a form of "divide and conquer," or at least siding with one group against the other.

I found myself increasingly agitated by the residuals of colonialism. About two weeks after my encounter with the Ghanaian accountant I traveled to Bulawayo, once the capital of the Ndebele nation and now Zimbabwe's second largest city. It's a place where one could be lost in thought forever, so languid are the days and so sparsely populated some of the areas outside the city. I could drive for miles into the countryside and think of nothing but Africa without bitterness, without discrimination, or any other sickness brought by a doctrine of racial privilege or ethnic privilege. I loved those days and nights in the Ndebele region. When night comes in Africa, unlike any other continent, you get the feeling that nature wants everything and everyone to be quiet and have reverence. Africa wants you to sleep, but many nights I could not, as I pondered the plight of the continent, mired as it was in tribalism. My mind ran to the wars in Angola and Mozambique, to the fighting in South Africa, and to the instability throughout. Then, when daylight came, I often felt that I had been beaten with a stick.

During the daylight hours my discussions with friends took up the same topics I had struggled with in the nights. There were no flashes of lightning to quicken the pace of our thoughts as we considered the seriousness of South Africa's crisis; we simply spent our days discussing the latest political lessons, such as Moi's dismissal and arrest of six more University of Nairobi professors or the Kenyan government's threat of intervention in the university. I drank lots of beer and ate sadza with beef at the cafes. Soon I made my way back to Harare, the seat of all things political and cultural; it was the hub of international activity in southern Africa at the time. Every major European country had diplomats assigned to Harare, and the Cubans, Americans, and Chinese vied to be as important as the Soviets in the affairs of the country.

African intellectuals and activists made their way to the city to see for themselves the transformation from a white minority government to a black government. My friends Masizi and Matabu Kunene, South Africans who lived in Los Angeles and worked at UCLA, came by, and I was able to have the same conversations with them about Africa. Matabu, a strikingly beautiful Zulu woman, offered that "African leaders speak against tribalism, but they do not act on detribalism. These leaders are like the whites, who have spoken of the need for cooperation and fraternity while doing all within their power to undermine those virtues. Only when Africa throws off tribalism will we be able to advance the people."

"But isn't that like losing your skin?" I asked.

"Sometimes your have to lose skin in order to catch sense," she retorted.

I could see in Zimbabwe, as I had seen in Ghana, Senegal, Nigeria, Kenya, Ethiopia, Congo, Egypt, and other African nations, the abiding curse of tribalism—or ethnic chauvinism, as I preferred to call it. I know that some leaders in Africa, like Kenyatta and Moi, often used ethnic identification for political purposes. I had not seen the same level of ethnic chauvinism in Mugabe, who had made it a point to place some highly visible Matabele people in his government. Everyone hoped that Zimbabwe would be a better model for Africa because the record was not good since the independence of Egypt and Ghana in 1952 and 1957, respectively.

It did not matter how good you were at a position; if you did not have the right ethnic background, you would experience discrimination. In some places you were apt not to get into school, get a job, or even get a passport. Here I was, an African American, a totally distinct ethnic group of people sojourning in America, now present as an African in the heart of the continent and feeling that I was being treated better than other Africans, not out of goodwill but because I was also American. I was standing naked before the very tribalism I despised.

An African who had studied Jomo Kenyatta's brand of ethnocentrism told me that when President Kenyatta was called upon to give a graduation address for a Kenyan school, he was clearly tribalistic. He looked at the graduation list at the school and, upon seeing that no Gikuyu were on the list, refused to speak, saying, "Call me when you have a real graduation." Kenyatta, one of Africa's earliest revolutionary leaders against racism, may have played a role in trying to secure Gikuyu domination of other ethnic groups, and by doing this he increased the cascading ethnic chauvinism that was to beset the country long after his death.

It was true that an African's name gave away his or her identity as it used to in the West. Once, when you said your name was Chandler, Turner, Cobbler, or Fowler, people knew that you were a candle maker, an iron spreader, a leather beater, or a bird catcher. Certain European names also identified the wearer of the name as Welsh, Irish, Scottish, French, Italian, and so forth. But in Africa it was even more complex. Someone could tell your ethnic identity by your name. They also knew if you represented a ruling family, as Kulibaly was a ruling family name in Segu and Keita was the same among certain Mandinka peoples.

The intellectuals of Africa, perhaps more than anyone and certainly more than the politicians, know Africa is in deep crisis. To these Africans who think, write, and create, it is no abstract feeling, no ethereal happening, no ephemeral, passing condition. It is a deep crisis because it is a persistent crisis, one with roots not only in the European underdevelopment of Africa but also in the reasons why it was possible for the Europeans to do so in the first place. The intellectuals increasingly shout their beliefs that the problem is in Africa itself.

The best writers are saying that the contemporary African politicians, from Kabila to Museveni, from Jonathan to Zuma, regardless of their language, ethnicity, or ideology, are victims as much as they are creators and maintainers of the ethnic crisis. Some authors and intellectuals speak openly about one or the other ethnic group's shortcomings: the Asante are said to be stingy and thrifty, the Ibo are said to be hustlers and commercial geniuses, the Wolof are said to be judgmental and cautious, and the Hausa are said to be upright, straight, and dependable. These stereotypes are heard throughout the continent and certainly in the nations where these people originate.

During the time I lived in Zimbabwe I visited Bulawayo twice. Nothing could keep me away from Bulawayo and the southwest territories because this is where so much of the history of the country happened. This historic region in the center of what was called Matebele land in the old day was important to understand for anyone trying to make sense out of white minority rule in southern Africa. When the military genius and paramount commander Mzilikazi brought his people from South Africa in the nineteenth century, they settled around Bulawayo and spread out from there.

Bulawayo was also the headquarters of ZAPU, which had engaged in its own warfare against the white racist regime. Nkomo had been their leader, and his struggles with Mugabe caused some instability in the Matebele lands. However, no one had declared an outright break with Harare, and if Nkomo would not do it, no one else could.

This visit took place during the middle of April, as the Southern Hemisphere was transitioning to winter. More spectacularly, however, was the fact that Kariamu and M. Khumalo also traveled with me. He was barely six months old at the time but strong enough to make this trip. The drive south from Harare was monotonous, passing through low rolling countryside dotted with abandoned farms, occasional cotton fields, and grazing lands. After Gweru, the capital of Midlands, which separated the Shona-speaking area from the Ndebele speaking area, the landscape became stubby with small trees; dried grass cropped to the dust by large herds of cattle, many of whom were dying because of drought; and sandy riverbeds, which had tasted no water all year long.

We entered the area where political dissidents were still operating with AK-47s, the Russian automatic guns made famous by revolutionaries of the African and Asian continents. I had been warned about the dangers of traveling there, particularly on the side roads, but that is precisely what made the journey exciting. I had handled situations with robbers, police, and soldiers in Nigeria, Ghana, and the Republic of Congo, so I felt I could deal if necessary.

Fortunately, even when I drove off the main road to see small compounds and unusual hills and riverbeds, we saw none of the dissidents who were attacking local people and installations. In fact, we saw very few people at all. It was as if the entire area had been abandoned—and it had been. Everyone else knew what we found out later: because terrorists were seen in the vicinity, farmers and shepherds were staying out of the way for the most part.

About midday we drove into a park-like setting that seemed like it was out of a storybook, complete with fountains, flowers, couples holding hands, children playing, and music in the air. We felt like we had come through the most dangerous stretch of highway in Zimbabwe to the safest place. There was an air of serenity about Bulawayo.

Bulawayo was dazzling. We spent hours exploring its historical sites, the most interesting of which were the memorials to Mzilikazi, son of Chief Mashobane, and Cecil John Rhodes, who had appeared, it seemed, in African history with neither father nor son, mother nor siblings. His father was apparently a preacher back in England, and the young Rhodes decided to journey to the warm climate of Africa for health reasons.

These two memorials, one to Mzilikazi and the other to Rhodes, both dead, attested to the turbulent history of the region surrounding Bulawayo. Mzilikazi, leader of a proud, disciplined Matabele nation, an offshoot of the Zulu nation, had entered the area in 1838 and conquered the indigenous people, establishing the kingdom of Matabele. Nearly fifty years later Rhodes, through emissaries Rudd, Thompson, and Maguire, had managed to swindle Mzilikazi's son, Lobengula, out of the territory. The Rudd Concession formed the basis for the kingdom of Rhodes, Rhodesia, though it has never been firmly established that

Lobengula signed the concession giving the British South African Company exclusive rights to the gold and other minerals in the land. In fact, later, Lobengula gave a German named Lippert a similar concession, which Lippert sold to Rhodes.

The memorial to Mzilikazi is on a dusty country road, fifteen miles south of Bulawayo. On the way we met a lone Ndebele hiker about ten miles from the memorial. Trudging along in a world only he knew, he was the epitome of self-possession.

"Brother!" I cried out, using my African American Ebonics equivalent of "Say man," "Hello," and "Mister." The startled man stopped as I pulled up alongside him.

"Mzilikazi's memorial?" I asked, trying not to use too much English, as it was rare to find a person in the so-called communal lands who understood it well.

He pointed in the direction from which we had just come.

"Sibongo," I said, knowing that he must have misunderstood my pronunciation or not understood the English word "memorial." We had not passed the place, and according to the map, *he* had passed it.

So we drove a few miles, and there was a marker pointing to the memorial. We felt good making this pilgrimage to the memorial of a once-powerful African king. We remembered our trips to Jamestown, Virginia, in honor of the twenty Africans who came ashore in 1619; to Great Barrington, the hometown and site of a future memorial to W. E. B. Du Bois; to Atlanta and the Martin Luther King Jr. memorial; and to Auburn and Lake Placid in New York to visit Harriet Tubman's memorial and to honor John Brown.

Mzilikazi's memorial is a stone monument shepherded by a mopane tree whose bark has been stripped by traditional hunters seeking communion with the spirit of the great conquering king. We parked our car and walked to the lonesome site of the memorial, wondering aloud why the monument wasn't placed in a more auspicious setting, but we answered ourselves by remembering the history of the region.

The white regime had built the memorial to Mzilikazi, as it built the one to Rhodes that we visited later. The difference in the quality, location, and monumentality of the memorials was evidence of the difference the whites thought existed between them and Africans.

A small gate gave access to the memorial, which was surrounded by an iron and cement fence. Considerable amounts of cow dung littered the ground inside the fence, like so many mountains of irony—bull manure on the sacred monument of the Great Bull himself. Some peasant rancher had obviously been using the ready-made enclosure as a cattle corral at night, easily possible because it did not appear that the monument was regularly visited by either the locals or tourists, and there were no signs or sounds of human life for at least five miles.

To reach the Rhodes memorial, you have to drive through the Matopos Hills, a huge reserve of fantastic rock formations. At the summit of a massive granite rock, called the "View of the World," lies Rhodes's grave, honoring Rhodes's own wish to sit at the pinnacle of the earth and survey the world all draped in the Union Jack. A few feet from Rhodes and on a slight declivity is the grave of Leander Starr Jameson, the leader of the pioneer column that entered the Matabele kingdom in 1890. Near the northern edge of the granite rock is a monument to fifty white soldiers that a Matabele force killed in a battle at the Shangani River in 1893, one of the few white memorials to a defeat. Perhaps in the future the Zimbabweans will properly commemorate the victors who slowed the European occupation of the country by their daring ambush at the Shangani. In a properly written history the victory would be celebrated because it delayed the coming onslaught.

Bulawayo had a decidedly different character than Harare; somehow it seemed more authentically African. The women of the city walked like magnificent pelicans dancing on water. The men still had their martial character, their dignity, and their respect. I admired the way the Matabele carried their history in their manner, their propriety, their customs. Perhaps because the whites had made Salisbury (later Harare) their city, they had left Bulawayo's flavor intact, although under the white regime it too was primarily a city for whites.

After independence the Africans in Bulawayo took the city over more completely than they did in Harare. As a government center, the capital city, Harare found its black professionals, neosettler elites, abandoning the city for the suburbs in the evening and remaining behind their closed office doors during the day, whereas in Bulawayo, the black professionals used the city as much or more than the whites did.

Driving back to Harare, I could not stop thinking how wonderful this firsthand experience of Africa was. Through the years many times I would feel the same emotion, this sense of astonishment that I had come from Georgia to see the land of my people's origin. And yet the excited monkeys that swung from the trees on the side of the road were not nearly as happy as I was to be headed back to Harare, where I could write in my journal and hold discussions with my friends about what we had seen on my trip. Both Kariamu and M. Khumalo were eager to get back to the comforts of city life as well, though I must say that they seemed to enjoy the sites along the road as much as I did.

I have never understood why Africans whose national dress was obliterated by the colonial experience did not accept some of the West African designs as their universal dress. After all, the various white nations of the world adopted French dress as the standard for their suits without becoming French. When the Dutch gave up their wooden shoes for Italian-style ones, it did not mean that the Dutch had become Italian. It seems Europeans became less ethnic about certain things, whereas the Africans retained their ethnic exclusivity in the matter of dress, even though some people had very little to argue about.

A few days after returning to Harare I donned my elegant maroon and yellow Yoruba agbada, the one I bought from a Nigerian vendor in Ibadan, and strolled down Samora Machel Boulevard toward Julius Nyerere Avenue and my favorite gift shop, intending to purchase ivory pendants for my friends. The day was bright, the sky clear, and the air fresh, clean, crisp.

"Professor Asante," a man's voice called out from behind me.

"Yes?" I turned to see a large African man dressed in a well-tailored European suit. With a smile on his face, he approached me, and I recognized him as the lecturer I had seen in the Social Sciences Building at the University a few weeks earlier during a lecture by A. J. Ayer, the British philosopher.

He examined my agbada, his dark eyes darting up and down my fabric. "You're not Nigerian, are you?" he asked, his tone knowledgeable. I thought he may have known that my name was Ghanaian, but then I thought that he might be insulting me by claiming I should not be wearing a Nigerian cloth.

"No, and you're not British either," my sharp tongue twisted the blade on the "either." We both laughed.

"I understand your point," he said sheepishly.

"Do you really understand my point?"

"Well, it does seem that Nigerian or Ghanaian dress is as beautiful on black people as European dress."

"If you choose, just know *why* you are choosing and *what* you are choosing. Don't condemn me for wearing Asante kente when you are wearing Scottish plaid; understand that they are both cultural, ethnic, and are derived from a given environment." I felt I had made my point, but by then I was hot under the agbada. He had brought up all of my heated African American emotion.

Perhaps what came across in my voice was the anguish I was experiencing in seeing so many blacks still trying to be whites, when in the United States we had begun to look back to Africa. I reluctantly reminded myself what Elsie Smith, a professor at SUNY Buffalo, had tried to tell me when I decided to go to Africa to live for a while—that African Americans could probably teach Africans a lot about Africa. It was no longer a mystery to me; the fact was stark, standing right in front of me in the ninety-degree heat in a black pin-striped three-piece suit with a button-down Van Heusen shirt. Whatever it was I had been going to buy at the gift shop had to wait; I crossed the street and went into the lounge at the Monomotapa Hotel, that citadel of opulence in the heart of Harare, to have a Castle beer.

I left after an hour or so and walked toward the Avenues. The sun was hot, and people walked slowly. At a large intersection I watched and waited for the Easter Sunday crowd of strollers to pass, more numerous than I'd seen in the city before, but on closer inspection, I realized it was not a crowd but a parade, with a young black man holding a giant cross in front of him, moving solemnly as if he were walking into a long, dark chamber.

I leaped out into the street to snap some pictures with the camera I always carried with me since someone blew up the airport arch and the ZANU headquarters. Just to record anything that might be of interest to the history of the country, I thought I should always have the camera—but I never took pictures of people up close without asking their permission because I hated the way Americans did that as if the locals were curios or something.

"What the hell is going on?" I asked a group of people.

"It's an Easter march," someone replied. I could see the parade was a church group because I noticed a bearded, collared, white man coming from the opposite direction with a cross.

"This is excellent irony," I said to no one in particular.

"It means the revolution has failed," a tall, dark woman said.

"It may mean there never was a revolution in the first place," I said, snapping shot after shot.

"There could have been. There was supposed to be, but without political education, the people cannot change." I noted the woman speaking—it was Comrade Freedom. A group of people stood listening to her as the two parades of Christian marchers converged on Fifth and Rhodes (they had not yet changed these streets' names). Comrade Freedom was a war heroine, and everyone seemed to know her. She told the women and men listening that I was the proponent of Afrocentricity, and I nodded my head and waved my hand.

"Me, I'm a Marxist," she told the group. "I believe that the Marxist-Leninist doctrine is the only scheme for our liberation."

"Liberate your mind first, even before you go to Marx," I said, half looking toward her.

"Marxism is the only cleanser for petty bourgeois ideas."

"Nationalism would defeat racism," I said.

"But socialism will defeat class oppression," she retorted.

"Class and race are one down here in Africa, it seems to me. The white people are the class and race oppressors. Look around," I insisted.

The church parades were now right in front of me, the stragglers having caught up just as the crosses were being erected in the median across from the Earl Grey Building.

"Lenin was clear on that question."

"What question?" I didn't understand her.

"Race is a secondary contradiction."

"In Europe," I retorted, tired of hearing the same old Marxist analyses of the African problem.

"You won't listen," she said.

"It is clear to me that Africans need a strong shot of pride, maybe even national fervor—that would help break down interethnic problems. Then, if you still need a socialist solution, go to it."

Nearly a full year of studying socialism in Africa colored my reaction. Socialism was working nowhere. Tanzania was on the brink of mass starvation; Mozambique had asked all the capitalists who left the country to return; Angola had never started being a nation; and Zimbabwe was floundering because of the damper it placed on entrepreneurs. And outside Africa the Afro-Latin nation of Cuba was calling for multinational investment.

"Perhaps one day we will have our African solutions for African problems," Comrade Freedom said to me.

The people standing around heard us, but no one said anything. It was my impression that they did not know what we were talking about, nor did they care. They just watched the interracial group pray and sing. I finally waved goodbye to Comrade Freedom and went to my home in the Avenues.

I became more aware that Africa needed Afrocentricity as much as the United States did. They had Africanity—that is, African culture, styles, and traditions—but they did not have a self-conscious understanding of Africans as subjects in human history.

An oppressed people, victimized by psychological attacks, often accept the images and gods of the oppressor. Here in Zimbabwe I was seeing the extent of the struggle for the minds of the people—and ideas had to be at the center of any struggle. As Mark Christian, my friend and colleague, later said, the trauma of racism and discrimination was so great that it would take more than a tune-up to change black people's attitudes. He insisted that we needed an overhaul.

I ran into Stanlake Samkange, the famous novelist and historian, a few days after the parade. He spotted me because of my clothes, because for many years I have made a practice of wearing something made by the hands of Africans.

A man approached me on the street in front of the Meikles Hotel, saying, "You're not from here."

"No, I am not, but how do you know?" I asked, puzzled.

"Because of your clothes. You don't see Zimbabweans in that type of clothing," he said.

"I am Molefi Asante from the United States."

"I am Stan Samkange," he offered.

"*The* Samkange, the novelist and historian who taught at Tufts and Northeastern universities in Boston?" I had heard his name, and now I remembered that he lived in Zimbabwe.

"Yes, I left Northeastern University a few years ago to return home. My wife, Tommie, is from Mississippi, you know?"

Stanlake and Tommie Samkange, who taught at Tufts, had been very active in African Studies while he was in exile from Rhodesia in the United States. Now back in Africa, they had settled into new positions in politics, education, and bookselling.

I eventually got to know him fairly well. Samkange understood my talk about an Afrocentric Zimbabwe and encouraged me to talk to the young Zimbabweans. I did, and I found them receptive. I would later come to believe that Afrocentricity impacted Samkange's Ubuntu movement, which gained popularity during the Mandela and Mbeki regimes in South Africa. Stanley, as we called Stanlake, was a smart man, a critical thinker, and a quick learner; although retired, he was still creating ideas. Government officials, college professors, and students took to my ideas rather easily and invited me to their homes and institutions to give lectures on African history.

You could go into Stanley Samkange's Little Professor bookstore downtown in Harare any day and have a conversation about Marcus Garvey, Malcolm X, Nkrumah, or Martin Luther King Jr. Samkange had pictures of Garvey hung around the store, and the classic *Philosophy and Opinions of Marcus Garvey* was displayed on the shelf. Samkange loved Garvey and spoke so highly of him because he wanted the Zimbabweans to take on his spirit of self-determination and independence.

I liked Samkange, and he liked me. He invited Kariamu and me to his Castle for dinner. He and Tommie had saved enough money in America to be able to buy the Castle, the most prominent residential structure in Harare, for little or nothing because whites were fleeing the country for South Africa after independence. He had also kept his Rolls Royce; it was always prominently parked downtown near his book and gift shop.

In the old Rhodesia Stanlake Samkange had been one of the first Zimbabweans to qualify for a liquor license, considered under the old regime to be the most important license a black person could hold. Stanlake was from a royal family, and even though he did not often pull rank with his African brothers and sisters, he was fond of letting the whites know who he was. He was nobility itself. No one talked or walked with greater dignity; it was as if he floated over the earth that he had return to inherit. His ancestors had ruled over the land before the whites came, and no white person in the country came from a better background than he did.

He loved Zimbabwe, even with all of the faults he saw in her political situation. In his own way, until he died, Samkange was a lover of Zimbabwe, conquering with his quick wit and his sharp insights the Europeans' stubborn arrogance. I used his example, to the extent that I could, as the best ideal for the new Zimbabwe.

That night Samkange's wife, Tommie, and I got along fine because we were both from the southern United States and spoke the same language. I told her that the Mississippi River was the most compelling physical symbol of our suffering in the United States, and she agreed. We sat out on the Castle's veranda and spoke of rivers.

The rivers of Africa somehow kept pumping life into the yesterday-done-gones and what-about-tomorrows. Later, whenever I felt a little depressed about the hell blacks had to put up with from their white fellow citizens in Zimbabwe, I dreamed of African rivers—yes, the Mississippi was one, the Ohio another, and the Withlacoochee. These American rivers were intricately interwoven with African history. But also the Nile, the Congo, the Limpopo, the Zambezi, and the Niger were African rivers. I'd seen them all, so Langston Hughes's words kept coming back: "I've known rivers: Ancient, dusky rivers." You could not look upon the Nile or Mississippi without wondering about the thousands of Africans who had passed that way before. Cruising up the Zambezi, away from Victoria Falls, I had the feeling that the rivers of Africa were always somewhere close to the black person's consciousness.

Water   so much to cross in our minds, in our hearts, in our adventure. *Why do you suppose baptism holds such attraction for black people?* I had frequently asked myself. *Is it because of the crossing itself?* Africans are not generally known as lovers of water, yet in West Africa, the Wolof and the Akan peoples are among the only deep sea fishermen who fish in canoes, fifty or a hundred miles out to sea. Along the Congo, Nile,

Niger, and Zambezi, some of the best fishermen in the world regularly haul in large catches. Perhaps it was that Africans did not use the waters simply for pleasure. Swimming and motor boating and skiing on the waters—these activities were left to whites.

Sure is the disease bilharzia in most of the rivers and streams in Zimbabwe, but even so, I saw white people waterskiing on Lake Mc-Ilwaine. When they fell into the water, bilharzia and all surrounding them, they just treaded water until the boat picked them up. The parasite that infected their bodies was no respecter of persons.

A few months after we had dinner at the Samkanges' we went to visit one of the resorts that had been reserved for whites during colonialism. It was up in the mountains north of Harare, one of the most beautiful spots in Zimbabwe.

When we had checked in, I went outside to walk around and saw a short, stocky African man standing near a colorful jacaranda. "White people got no sense," he said to no one in particular, or maybe it was to me, as I was the only non-Zimbabwean around, but he sure didn't look at me.

"Yeah, I know," I answered, probably on another level than he was thinking of at the moment.

In my mind the American Babylon had created a living maze for the brothers and sisters in the United States, and I would read in the newspapers about the Wild Bill Hickok types of stunts being pulled in the name of politics. Ronald Reagan had teamed with a Johnny Mack Brown, Gene Autry, or Roy Rogers to turn the tables on the masses. Yes, it was true—whites had no sense. *Wolves in sheep's clothing*, I thought to myself. *A kaleidoscope of what could be and what was happening.*

The man said nothing more to me; I believe he wanted to, but could not find the right words. We looked at each other, and I left. I was determined that nothing would disturb my quietude, not even the hell of an American Babylon. I spent my time at the resort reading and relaxing with books on southern African history in preparation to write *Scattered to the Wind.*

∞

Inside our flat in the Avenues, when we were bundling up against the Zimbabwean winter in July or August, I found myself reflecting on the danger of living in southern Africa so near white people who did not want Africans to ever have equal opportunities. They would use any form of organized violence to maintain the Africans' second-class status. Clearly one could run to Africa and sometimes find in Africa what one was running from in America.

I questioned a lot of things. One was the fact that whites seemed to dominate the African National Congress, or ANC, in Zimbabwe. The fact that the ANC in Zimbabwe had a preponderance of whites from South Africa as members caused considerable apprehension about its ability to wage a guerilla war, and we were even afraid that agents of the South African government had infiltrated the ANC. It would be necessary to separate the military wing, the Umkhonto we Sizwe, from the ANC's propaganda wing to ensure secrecy in military operations. When Joe Gqabi, the ANC leader in Zimbabwe, was killed, many of the white hangers-on went scurrying for cover; Umkhonto we Sizwe's twenty-six attacks in 1981 inside South Africa had sent panic through the white settler population. And now the whites who were members of the ANC in Zimbabwe feared that the killing of Gqabi might cast suspicion on them as agents of the South African government.

That same year Nadine Gordimer's *July's People* had anticipated the fall of South Africa and the dependence of whites on their former black servants. It was too much to take, too much fear—and so the whites who fled from Rhodesia to South Africa joined the various right-wing violence groups, going after any black or white who supported majority rule. The Umkhonto we Sizwe took advantage of this fear and struck the Sasol plant, a military base, and other key installations, all to demonstrate its capability to reach into the heartland of the country.

The ANC in Zimbabwe was virtually under the control of a Mozambique-born, naturalized South African Portuguese couple who regularly held South African parties at their university home. These gatherings, usually attended by a large number of white South Africans, were meant to introduce ANC supporters to newcomers in the South

African community. Allegedly the BOSS (Bureau of State Security), South Africa's dreaded octopus-like secret service, had agents present at each of these meetings. The rumor in Harare was that the Portuguese couple had the backing of the South African government.

A number of young blacks refused to join ANC because of the overwhelming number of whites, many claiming a dual membership in the Communist Party of South Africa and the African National Congress. All of the whites at ANC meetings frightened the blacks. As one young African from Soweto who had managed to escape South Africa and enroll in school in Zimbabwe told me, "The ANC has too many white spies. It's a dangerous organization."

"Do you think it will be effective in the armed campaign against South Africa?"

"Only if the military wing is all black."

"Isn't that against ANC policy?" I asked, knowing the truth.

"Yes, but that's the problem. They do not have enough security with whites in the organization."

"So you won't join?"

"No, never." He supported the liberation struggle but chose Steve Biko's organization, the Black Consciousness Movement, over the ANC. He was so full of energy that I knew that his days in Zimbabwe would be numbered, because he would end up sneaking across the Limpopo into South Africa to fight against the regime. It was true—he did.

Listening to young bloods such as him speak about the African National Congress in Zimbabwe, I never forgot what David Gweshe, the master dinhne teacher, had said about the English woman who wanted to control Zimbabwe's culture. Peggy Harper, the famous British would-be maternalist of African musicians and dancers, once asked Gweshe to take her to see the medium of Nehanda.

Gweshe was visibly struck by her arrogance. Her utter disregard for tradition had colored her tenure in African countries before, but this was just too much. How could a white person even form her mouth to ask to see Nehanda's medium, when Nehanda had fought to rid the country of whites, and Peggy Harper's ancestors had hung him by the neck until dead? What did she want to know that the master teachers of Shona culture could not tell her? What business did she have with the medium of Nehanda? Did she not know it was dangerous to play with the spirits? Was she only a child dabbling in places she did not understand?

No, Gweshe said, he could not take a white person to see the spirit medium of Nehanda. Did Peggy Harper know what she was asking? Did she know that she would be putting Gweshe's life in danger as well as her own? Everyone should have known the history of the event that led to the First Chimurenga.

On April 27, 1898, white settlers hanged the leaders, Mbuya Chahwe, the spirit medium of Nehanda, and Sekuru Gomboreshumba, the spirit medium of Kaguvi. Three others—Hwata, Gutsa, and Zindoga—had been accused and murdered as well because they fought against the policies of Henry Hawkins Pollard and his terrorist actions against the people.

Hearing the story, many people said, "Reconciliation was a policy for the living, not a policy which the spirit of Nehanda would have understood."

There were obviously too many uncultured whites looking for ways to influence the future of Zimbabwe, but the natural observations and the common sense of the regular African people made it impossible for them to find support in their attempts to meddle. Like the young South African fighter who followed Steve Biko, David Gweshe reached back to the 1890s to claim his natural hero, Nehanda, and to protect her image and medium from the contemporary invasion.

From the beginning I liked his intelligence and easy familiarity with his traditions, something that escaped too many African Americans. Direct, bright, and confident, Gweshe led a dinhne dance group that had received national acclaim. Descended from a line of Kore Kore kings, he had a strong attachment to his culture and would list the kings for you if you even looked interested.

"You know, Asante, the whites tried to take our culture, to say we had no culture, but the people carry the culture in their hearts," he said, motioning with his hand to his chest.

"I know," I said sympathetically, remembering how the ballet dancers at the Rhodesian Ballet Company spoke with disdain of the "native" dances.

Kariamu and I drove out to Dzivaresekwa to see his group in rehearsal one day. At the soccer stadium where the Boderekwa Performing

Group was to rehearse, three young boys chewing blades of sweet grass spoke in animated voices to each other; all around them, young boys kicked a soccer ball over the close-cropped grass of the field. This was Dzivaresekwa, the pool that one laughs at, but of course no one laughs at Dzivaresekwa now because it is the home of David Gweshe, the master Shona dance teacher, the embodiment of traditions.

The master went to a house in the town and asked several young girls to assemble the dancers and singers. Within thirty minutes forty young children had gathered at the stadium with their drums, mbiras, and ngomas. Gweshe came out in his Shona priest uniform of black and white, the traditional colors of the Shona people. He was astounding, impressive, and when he began the moves of the powerful dances, the assembled masses that had gathered in the stadium applauded gratefully at the master's brilliance.

As I was seated on the grass in front of the dancers, taking pictures with my Canon AE-1, three local ZANU officials came over to me. They wanted to know who I was, what I was doing with my camera, and why I had chosen to come to Dzivaresekwa to do my research. I told them that I was from the United States and that I was not doing research but instead watching and recording the performance of Gweshe's group at his permission and request. We then struck up a conversation about the Chimurenga and the challenge Kariamu had taken on in creating a national dance company for the prime minister, a conversation occasionally interrupted by applause for the dancers. They left, satisfied that I was who I said I was.

But I kept thinking about how suspicious Zimbabweans were of me. It seemed that they should have been less suspicious of me and more suspicious of the whites among them because the whites were the ones who had created the institutions of oppression in their country. But colonial oppression was no less thorough in whitening the Africans' minds than were segregation and racism in the Americas. Also, you did not normally see black people walking around with cameras, and the government was extremely sensitive to people with binoculars and cameras. Here I was, loaded down with all this equipment, so I must be somebody meaning to take some secret photographs. Of course, there was also the possibility that the former white Rhodesian intelligence people had been tracking the African Americans and trying to poison the minds of the Zimbabweans against us. At this stage in the country, anything was possible.

Gweshe had begun prancing around, blowing his whistle, while two of his dancers engaged in mock battle. They waved their battle axes, stomped the earth, and rhythmically bounced over the grass. Others appeared with hoes, making digging motions and dancing with complete control over their young bodies to the music of the mbiras and ngomas. When it was over, with great pride Gweshe accepted the applause of the people who had assembled.

It was a good free show, but he wanted to make it better, and that is why he had asked me, Kariamu, and Glendora Johnson, who was visiting from the States, to attend his rehearsals. He hoped to get Kariamu to provide him with aesthetic details based on her Umfundalai technique. She was pleased with the prospect of giving him some tips; he was already the best professional she had seen in Zimbabwe.

We drove out of Dzivaresekwa, and I remembered the three young Shona boys chewing grass beforehand. *They might be leaders of the government in twenty-five years,* I thought. That was something that they could aspire to, and perhaps, I thought, the same thing could happen in the United States, where there were beginning to be a few signs that things were different from my youthful days in Georgia. Yes, it could be possible that an African would rise to the level of the presidency. Two years later Jesse Jackson ran for the Democratic nomination. Then, in the winter of 2008, the election of Barack Obama stunned all the doubters about human possibilities. Obama had become the embodiment of the dreams of many young African Americans. The three Shona boys leading their government do not seem so long distant now as it had seemed then. Like President Obama, the youth of Zimbabwe stretched their frames up toward new vistas.

One clear spring night, after a wonderful dinner of beef cooked several ways enjoyed with Thelma and James Ravell as well as South African poet Masizi Kunene, during which time Kariamu and I revealed that we were expecting a child. After dinner I stayed up late, writing in my journal about the prospect of being a father. I wrote,

On the eve of the birth of my second child, I dream of what could be if the world was perfect, but since it is not and will never be, the challenge of having a child has become increasingly difficult. Yet I wanted to father this child. In some ways, many ways, this is a joyous culmination, a beginning, a consolidation of aims, and yet it is also a firm basis for a mission. The relationship must be for order, harmony, community, society, as well as for each other—this it must be, even for the child, if relationship is to be an inspiration.

I knew in my heart that this child would be an achievement of love, a stamp of love, but neither the achievement nor the stamp was love itself. It should never be. *It was not so with Eka, whom I love dearly as my first-begotten, and it will not be with the promised child, whom I shall love equally and as richly*, I thought.

I was forty-two and nervous about being a father at that age. Although I knew I could do a good job, I wondered if I had the energy to keep up with a child so young.

And when MK Jr. was born on November 3, 1981, at Mbuya Nehanda Maternity Hospital, he was the most beautiful baby I had ever seen. He was the first child with US citizenship born in the new Zimbabwe. Years later he pointed out that he was the only one in the family actually born in Africa.

Joy was everywhere. Even amid the occasional bombings that still peppered the nights, joy came. Our friends gathered around us and praised our names for having such a fine nine-pound baby. We were happy parents.

Kariamu named him Molefi after me. Khumalo was after the Zulu royal clan, and his middle name would be one way of differentiating between two Molefis. I said to his mother, "He's a 'the third,' you know."

"How so?"

"My mother named me 'Arthur' after my father, but since I changed my name in 1973 with my father's permission and encouragement, I believe that in spirit, Molefi Khumalo is actually Molefi the third." I would have named my son "Arthur" out of respect for my father had I not believed so strongly that African people should have African names, and even now I refer to my father as 'senior.'

That night, while I was awaiting his birth, I thanked the African and whatever other ancestors came back to earth in this child. And then I wrote this in my journal: "Life is constant; the earth is forever within the universe, and we are but the twigs on the great tree of humanity."

Not long thereafter we met Ibrahim Jassat, an intense, wiry apologist for Marxism, who had just returned home from London. His brother, Ish, brought him to see me, explaining that I was the resident African American ideologue of Afrocentricity. Looking back, I understood that Ish knew his brother would pick an argument and I would engage him. Ibrahim Jassat was a slight, peach-colored man; he and his brother were Zimbabwean Arab-Indian coloreds, a mixed family with several African relatives. In America they would have been classified as blacks.

Ibrahim had been in exile in Britain for years, studying orthodox Marxism from books. He was bright. The flash of his eyes told me he was a thinker, though I came to discover that he was slow on action. He was convinced that Marxism was the answer to the economic problems of Zimbabwe.

"What do you think of our country?" he asked. People always ask foreigners that question, even if they have been in the country for years. Anyway, I answered, saying that the orthodox Marxism he proposed wouldn't work on an economic or cultural level. Ibrahim leaped at that statement, explaining to me the precise Marxist-Leninist position on the transformation to socialism from capitalism, a position I knew backward after debating it with several colleagues.

To deflate the issue, as we had promised to see each other at another time, I spoke on the question of culture as crucial. "You see, my friend, an economic revolution leaves the people in chains. In a few years they will be as impoverished or more so than they were before the economic revolution, and it will be an impoverishment of the spirit.

"Marxists misunderstand the nature of racism and have performed no scientific analysis of the clash of races in modern societies. The reason for this is clear: their original analysis of society and most others were developed in Europe, not in multiracial societies. Class emerged as the chief contradiction in those societies where the conflict was between competing economic forces. This was true in most of Europe and in Asia. That is not to say that the question of nationalities did not arise but rather that nationalities as understood by Lenin and expanded by Mao had certain language and geographic criteria and were not racial per se. Only in the struggle against European and capitalist racism in the Americas have we seen the sharpening of the race contradiction."

Ibrahim replied with a detailed discussion of what Lenin said about black Americans, and then he stated that my position was petit bourgeois. He had a Lenin goatee, which he periodically fiddled like a stringed instrument as he sat in my house talking about the prosecution of the revolution.

"Have you read the African American cultural nationalists?" I asked him, knowing that this would stop his intellectual tripping right in the middle of his prolonged leap into Marxist analysis.

He gave me a you-are-not-serious look and smiled out of the corner of his Afro-Asian mouth. "Who?"

"Karenga, Malcolm X, Garvey, Farrakhan, Muhammed, the early Baraka." I saw he had never even heard of most of the names, so I continued to lead him.

Ibraham shook his head in silence and I continued, "It is rich literature if you want to be considered intellectual."

"But you must read in order to know what is and what is not revolutionary." I kept him pinned to the theme. "African Americans have written some of the most positive literature around, don't you know that?" I stared at him.

Ibrahim was a Marxist seasoned by books by C. L. R. James, Lenin, and even the writings of Trotsky. He had run away from the Zimbabwean struggle in the countryside only to take up revolutionary reading in London. Although he professed to be more and more fed up with half-assed steps to revolution, he had escaped the authentic praxis by reading.

As he went on to describe being a Muslim and a Marxist, he sounded more and more like a schizoid. "I'm a practicing Marxist, but my religious beliefs are Islam," he would sometimes say, or, "There is no contradiction between Marxism and Islam unless one is clear on both." I fully admitted my confusion.

He had read everything Marx, Engels, and Lenin had ever written, but he did not know black Americans or their literature at all. He didn't even care to read it. One day later on our way to the Monomotapa Hotel for a beer, he said, "Molefi, you have an admirable flexibility. Your problem is that you read everything—capitalist bourgeois literature as well as socialist literature."

"What's wrong with flexibility?" I asked.

"What's wrong?" he asked incredulously.

"Yes, I'll read anything."

"Precisely—that's your problem," he retorted as we strolled across Julius Nyerere Avenue.

I gave him a severe glance, a combat technique I learned in college to counteract condescension. We passed the brown-and-gold-clad doormen and entered the hotel lobby.

"The cultural nationalists would have been good for Zimbabwe. After all, while war may be a significant cultural act, it is not necessarily a transforming act," I said.

"That's nonsense," he answered as we sat down. We ordered two Castle beers, the kind the poor people called Samkanges, after Stanlake Samkange, the famous writer who had bought a big stone castle.

"Maybe nonsense to you," I responded, "but I suspect it would have been valuable for your revolutionaries to have understood nationalism before socialism."

"I see we cannot agree on political questions. There is no need for us to continue the discussion," Ibrahim concluded.

The neo-Babylonian sunken lounge had begun to fill with Scottish rugby players on their way to play the South African team. Voices rumbled through the heavy smoke; singing and laughter drowned out the music being piped throughout the lobby.

Ibrahim started talking about jobs in the new Zimbabwe. With a PhD in political sociology, he had encountered difficulty securing a position. I knew he would have a hard time with ZANU's Central Committee, with people on it like Chenhamo Chimutengwende and Nathan Shamuyarira, stalwarts of political ethics and ideas as well as intellectual theories.

So while we sat there amid the inanities the Scottish jocks spewed out, Ibrahim tried to convince me that the party would soon get him a job. I didn't believe him. I thought he had become a votarist for ZANU in Zimbabwe *now,* after the liberation war, rather than when the fighting was going on and he was a student in London; after all, few of the Zimbabweans who had lived in London seemed to know him.

Our swivel chairs faced the large window, and reflections from the park lights outside danced on the aluminum and brass light fixtures. I felt pleased and rather combative. Maybe I would challenge Ibrahim's perceptions of ZANU's commitment to the likes of him, I thought.

The scene in Soyinka's *Death and the King's Horseman* in which the son of the horseman decided to cast away his Western training and accept tradition came to my mind. Would Ibrahim be able to find himself in this new order where black men were no longer on the bottom? How had he prepared himself for this new era in Zimbabwe's history? Could he accept the fact that blacks now wielded political power?

I said something to him about the lousy record of coloreds and mixed-race people in the liberation struggle. I expected a sharp rebuttal; it was not forthcoming. Instead, he gave me his standard lecture on Marxism: "Marxism does not recognize race and region. The economic imperatives of blacks in America are not different from those of the people of Bulgaria, Albania, or Zimbabwe. You can't think regionally. It is reactionary." He said this with an intense disregard for the noise around us, so I hardly heard him.

"I'm not a regionalist. My thinking is holistic. We ought to read everything—that is, if we are to be truly free," I said.

"Freedom is indivisible."

"We have no argument with each other on that."

Two weeks later I met one of the ANC's operatives in Zimbabwe, a South African named Chibedi. This was one of the exciting aspects of life in Zimbabwe the discussions with revolutionaries and freedom fighters from Africa and Asia.

Chibedi explained to me how the apartheid police would choose African police: "'Go arrest your mama and daddy' is the first order given to Africans who want to be South African police." His voice rose with indignation.

"Do they do it?" I asked.

"You bet they do. The Boers have learned how to use us against each other," he said dejectedly.

"How will the war be fought and won in South Africa in that case?" I asked, confused.

"Because mothers will shoot their sons who are traitors. It happened in Zimbabwe and Mozambique, and it will happen in South Africa." Chibedi seemed stern, rigid as he spoke, and I knew he was telling the truth.

"I see."

"I don't know if you really understand our situation. It is desperate, and blowing up the Sasol and other plants means that we can put the country's lights out. We can cripple the economy—that's the gut of the society."

"No, I can only know what I read. I have not lived that experience, although I know what racism is and have felt the sting of it enough in America to consider it irrational and stupid."

"Brother, it is the most vulgar system in the world. I do not think any government system is as arbitrary. White people in the West are upset over communism, but apartheid evaluates everything on color. No Marxist society is based on such an irrational principle." He was growing extremely agitated.

"Yeah," I said, hoping to bring the interaction back under control. "The apartheid system is like stale puke—the taste is everywhere and the smell infiltrates every human thought."

A couple of months later I heard that one of my former students from SUNY Buffalo was now a professor at the University of Zimbabwe. When Vimbai Chideya Chivaura discovered that I was in the city, he felt that I should certainly participate in the Carnegie Conference on the future of the university. After all, my credentials were stronger than any of the speakers already scheduled, and he, along with others, believed that it would be a historical mistake not to have me speak, as I was in Zimbabwe anyway. However, he wanted me to prepare a paper for presentation within the next week.

I labored under several difficulties—at the time Kariamu was getting into her final weeks of pregnancy, and I didn't have any of my books with me, as they were delayed in the mails somewhere between Buffalo and Harare. Also, my electric typewriter wouldn't work on the transformers I had brought with me. Yet in two days I had the paper written using local typewriters. Chideya graciously consented to having his secretary type it and asked me to pick the paper up the following week.

When I went to proofread the paper the next week, I was informed that Chideya had left the university for government service and that Mr. Tsicherayi was handling the conference. I went to see him after proofreading the paper and making the necessary corrections, but when I went, he was away from his desk. After contacting him two days later, I was informed that the executive committee had to meet and decide whether my paper was acceptable to the conference. Tsicherayi was a pleasant fellow—short, jovial, and in his late twenties or early thirties. He confessed to me that he didn't think I would have any trouble getting the paper approved.

However, a few days later, as the ancestors would have it—or the executive committee—Tsicherayi had to inform me that my paper on an Afrocentric university was not deemed to fit with the other papers. He had no other explanation except to say that the committee felt my paper would not be in keeping with those already selected.

The secretary who had made copies of the paper had it distributed anyway because, as she later told me, she believed it was a provocative contribution to the discussion of education in the country. I did not discourage its broadcast, and throughout the next several months I heard from individuals on the streets that they had seen the paper, which pleased me. It could never have gotten into the white-controlled magazines such as *Moto* or the *Journal of Social Change.* These journals were paternalistic attempts to direct the course of Zimbabwe's socialist and people revolution. But as the condition of Zimbabwe's economy has since shown, the attempts failed, despite the sanctions, threats, and intrigues of the West.

My paper questioned the idea of an African university that Europeans who held to the belief of the inferiority of Africans still dominated in thought and practice. I questioned the colonial motifs on the campus that did not reflect the revolutionary spirit of the people.

Why didn't the university, with its titular black leadership, dismantle the structure of racism that the Rhodesians had built into the curriculum? Why didn't the government ask all professors to turn in their resignations and then, after investigation, sort out the proper intellectual direction? Why did they still use the old racist textbooks? Why didn't the students have any information about other African people on the continent? Why did they know so little about the African Americans who had supported the revolution? These were the concerns I raised in the essay I had hoped to give at the conference, but alas, it was not to be.

My Afrocentric ideas would have to be delivered in small, informal settings, such as the meetings held in the homes of the African Americans in Harare. We had the first Kwanzaa in the country at the home of James Harris, who had come from Washington DC as a representative of the AFL-CIO in an effort to discover himself as an African. He was very successful in organizing unions and, indeed, in creating union—the man could organize. And the workers in Zimbabwe had been exploited so long; they needed what he was able to do.

The white liberals in Zimbabwe, working from the same basis as the white racists—a belief in the inferiority of blacks and the progressiveness of whites—created an enormous stumbling block to the revolutionary movements. They did this in Zimbabwe as well as in Angola and Mozambique and again in Namibia and South Africa. The journals they created reflected their paternalistic attitudes; they refused to allow Africans to speak for themselves, and a foreigner such as I, with a radical perspective on the need for nationalism to combat white racism and socialism to combat class oppression, could not be allowed a public platform.

The white liberals argued that the black entrepreneurs had to be attacked first, and once socialism was established then justice would prevail. It was the same lie they had told in Angola, and Jonas Savimbi's brutal National Union for the Total Independence of Angola, or UNITA, was being attacked roundly because of its insistence on majority rule, which the Angolan Marxists saw as racism. The government of President dos Santos, like that of Agostinho Neto before him, was mainly mulatto and white, and Savimbi knew that the masses of people would soon reject the Popular Movement for the Liberation of Angola (MPLA) in Luanda because it did not represent the black masses. (Although I believe that Savimbi was a reactionary, it goes without saying that MPLA made many mistakes.)

The principal failure of the Angolan Marxists was their failure to see that nationalism must precede socialism and that the war should have been a nationally transforming act, which it was not, and therefore, the nation had never found its own solidarity as a people.

Neither Zimbabwe nor Mozambique nor Namibia had nationalizing experiences in their years of struggle. While I lived in Zimbabwe this issue burned in the hearts of those who had fought in the struggle but found themselves wondering what it all had been for when white consultants were being employed for ten times the salary of the average civil servants. No black consultants were employed at those rates, and in fact, in the first three years of independence, only one black, an epidemiologist, out of the hundreds who came to Zimbabwe, was employed as a consultant at all.

In free, independent Zimbabwe, like in cruel, oppressive Rhodesia, white was too often right. But now the whites were liberal South Africans and Europeans, not Rhodesians, and somehow the blacks who seemed eager to drink their morning tea with the whites managed to give their independence to the Rhodesians' cousins.

One dusty afternoon I stood in Harare, near Remembrance Drive, and heard a man whom some assumed to be crazy, shouting in Shona the names of villages that the Rhodesian Front government razed from the earth. He then recited over and over, to the percussive rhythms of automobiles and buses making the turn off of Beatrice Road, the word "Chimoio." In that fated place in Mozambique, the Rhodesians had massacred nearly five thousand women and children living in a refugee camp. Even now, there are those who cry when they remember the scene.

This poor man who soon went on his way into the evening crowd had not given the benediction to the liturgy of revolution but had only opened the book for another look at the hurt, a hurt I thought would only be cured by raising the people's dignity and cultural awareness. Achievement and success—even entrepreneurial accomplishment—can be a rewarding bonus for pride. That day will come in Africa, perhaps in Zimbabwe before other places, but it will come because it has to if the continent is to survive as a viable social, political, and economic region.

I have had many visions of the demise of the universities in Africa. Outstanding schools like the University of Nairobi are in trouble, and their fate may be much like Makerere University in Uganda under presidents Obote and Amin.

"It is a terrible calamity," Matabu Kunene, Masizi's wife, told me when she visited Harare.

"Will the university in Nairobi survive?" I asked.

"Universities in Africa always survive. That's a part of the prestige thing, but the university will be a shell without substance. The best professors are leaving the country, foreigners are being attacked, and only Gikuyus seem to be able to survive. It is so awful, so brutal, so unfortunate." Matabu's eyes showed real sadness.

Masizi, her husband, one of Africa's truly remarkable poets, had been mistreated by the university during his sabbatical from UCLA. They denied him access into the closed community of university academics, humiliated him by refusing to honor portions of their contracts with him, and showed actual disinterest in his academic works. Africa screamed at him from its dirty, one-way side street of abuse and ignorance. And there was ignorance everywhere.

The ignorance that stalks you with clan chauvinism and ethnic animosities is the cruelest type of ignorance because it has no objective but the stifling of other people. In Africa it takes the form of outright prejudice based on language or totem discrimination. The politicians often preach against ethnic hatred while at the same time engaging in the worst forms of the crime.

CHAPTER 5

CREATIONS

I LOOKED UP INTO THE SKY outside of Domboshawa, where a pregnant Kariamu had climbed the rock to see the cave of the early humans on our first drive to the South, and I saw at the pinnacle of the sky the shimmering stars like dancing pebbles in a massive lake, and I realized the overwhelming strength of the mystic presence of nature in Africa. This presence constitutes the source of so much mystery, the curse and richness of Africa, as it has been for other continents.

If you could stand out in the open meadow of some African land in the heart of night, away from the glare of urban lights, and look into the vast sky, you would wonder how such a beautiful continent gathered so much misery. What have been the responses to the natural mysteries? How many innocents have died because they were compelled to drink poison? How many children have been eaten by crocodiles to save their villages? How many women have been skewered because of some jealous wife? It is true that the Catholics had their "proofs" in the medieval period that saw men burned to death with hot coals because they did not float when weighted with irons. But in contemporary Africa, the overpowering belief in the mysterious conquers the imagination of the educated as well as the unlettered.

I hold no romantic notions of the African continent because I have traveled its length and lived in its bosom—what I saw in Africa on numerous occasions sobered me. Afrocentricity remains one of the best ways to understand and deal with the historical cleavage between Africa and Europe.

It remains, however, impossible for me to jump to the Jesuitical arguments I developed during my years at UCLA. There was no need to be aggressive or clever in my arguments; in fact, it was just the opposite for me: I had to be sincere, and I was. Africa was different avenue from the one I grew up in, and the haints of Georgia could not conquer the overpowering political, social, and economic troubles. Yet I could see, living in Africa, that the conditions of Africans would not change until the people abandoned the ways, habits, and school curricula inherited from the colonial era. I could make a case for an Afrocentric revolution, and I did so everywhere I could.

The rise of one-party states followed by the suppression of dissent led to the inevitable rise of dissidents who, despite their small numbers in some states, created enough havoc to be considered threats. Immediately after the opening of the Zimbabwe Parliament session in Mugabe's first years, Mugabe's enemies began to scheme about his overthrow. All of their efforts failed, and he remained in office. Nevertheless, his enemies, white and black, continually sought to unseat him, despite the fact that the populace had freely elected him. In 1982, when Ian Smith collapsed in parliament, men wearing army uniforms attacked Mugabe's house. More tough rhetoric emanated from the chambers of power, and more resistance emerged.

This is always the pattern in Africa, and Zimbabwe was not the last nation to experience the seesaw of repression and expression, which are counterparts. This much the leaders who fought so often for their own independence must know, even if they use the rhetoric of their own blackness.

Black people do not want to be oppressed by blacks anymore than they want to be by whites. Cheikh Anta Diop, the late Senegalese author, argued this from his small office on the edge of the University of Dakar campus as much as Ngugi wa Thiong'o has from his rural village in Kenya. They both knew the same thing Molara Ogundipe-Leslie once told me at the University of Ibadan in her rich, resonant, feminine voice: "The continent is basically reactionary against intellectuals."

"But can there be any salvation?" I asked her.

She answered the question but not the problem, saying something like, "Why should salvation be sought in the first place?"

Almost every African intellectual I know is committed to the transformation of the continent, and yet as a group they remain among the most pessimistic people in Africa. Jailed, abused, ridiculed, and tortured by numerous guardians of the state, the intellectual class has been victimized by politics. Because of this, the governments stagnate, the arts are stillborn, the sciences are stifled, and politicians who no longer remember their vows—if they ever made them—monsterize the political will of the people.

Years later I saw Wole Soyinka, Chinua Achebe, Ayi Kwei Armah, Ama Ata Aidoo, Molara Ogundipe-Leslie, Isidore Okpewho, and Ngugi wa Thiong'o in the United States and wondered why they could not find peace in their own countries. However, the answer was always right in front of me: the political machinery of some governments is actively against intellectuals. They were the brightest, most intelligent writers of a generation, and they were rejected from their countries.

I found this very distasteful, and I once mentioned it to Atukwei Okai, the Ghanaian national poet and longtime president of the Pan-African Writers Association (PAWA), when he was traveling in the United States in the 1980s. He argued that a writer's first responsibility was to his society. He wanted to be in Ghana when things happened. If Jerry Rawlings took over the country (which he did), then Okai believed he would have to be there to provide some direction.

Atukwei Okai was tall, lanky for a Ghanaian, and expressive, outgoing, and jovial, with lots of high energy. When he took to the stage to read his poetry before a crowd in Buffalo, we were all "shimmering like sun-kissed seashells," as Atukwei said. We had experienced the performance of poetry like we never had before. Yes, we had Haki Madhubuti, Amiri Baraka, Ted Joans, Sonia Sanchez, but here was a brother from the continent as full of fire as any person we had seen. All the influences of his youth the fontonfrom drums in Ghana, the grand eloquence of the Russian poet Yevtushenko when he had studied at Lumumba University in Moscow and fell under Yevtushenko's influence, and the refinement of the University of Iowa writers' program—conspired to make him a remarkable poet. He was the best poet of Africa when he was at his prime, and even now, after serving as mayor of Accra and president of PAWA, Okai must be considered in the top ranks of the poets of the continent.

Okai introduced me to Winnie Mandela. When Winnie Mandela got up to speak at the Pan-African writers' conference in Accra in 1995, she captivated the audience with her charm, emotion, and smile. "I want to give a prize of a million dollars to the best writer in the interest of Africa," she declared in her best populist style, and the audience leaped up in applause. It was as if she had unlocked emotions penned up in the writers and ordinary Ghanaians for many years. I talked with her, cajoled her, listened carefully to her words of praise, and felt her positive energy. Up close, she was much softer than the image the press had created; in fact, she was sisterly, in love with her country and people.

A parade of poets has peopled the continent's history. As Winnie Mandela spoke about the creative powers of Léopold Senghor at the writers' meeting, I thought of President Senghor's place in African history. His passion for art and culture would be unsurpassed by any other leader of contemporary Africa, although challenged by Agostinho Neto of Angola; Senghor was the poet-president, the champion of the proper respect and usage of language. But he was also, like all of us, complicated, complex, and contradictory. I remember him as the president in whose presence I was as a student in the late 1960s and then as a professor in 1985 at the Negritude conference in Miami. He gladly received me in his presence for general discussions about African culture.

Senghor came to UCLA when I was a student, and as a campus leader, I was invited to have dinner with him and the chancellor of the university. Over dinner he claimed that America would teach Senegal how to do business, and France would teach it how to be cultured. I remember not liking this statement; it struck me later that I had a deep belief that Africans did not need Europeans to assume the role of teachers like they had in the past. I did not upset the dinner; I remained silent or asked some marginal question that masked my real concern. I was not proud of my performance and vowed to never conceal my real thinking again.

Léopold Sédar Senghor became exceptional not only because of his poetry and literature but also because he gave Senegal a commitment to change, however delayed it was and however flawed his rule of that nation. As the first African leader of a nation that had won its independence peacefully, he established himself in the annals of African history. Thus, an intellectual who became a politician may have achieved the place in history other African leaders sought by extending their rule until their deaths. Other presidents would also follow his precedent.

One part of the reascension of Africa will have to be the commemoration of the continent's history. This would include the memory of leaders like Léopold Senghor, Kwame Nkrumah, Sékou Touré, Jomo Kenyatta, Nelson Mandela, and Julius Nyerere as well as the recent heroic past on the battlefield. However, one must be clear that the authentic resurgence of Africa will be sparked by the intellectuals—not merely those who have been schooled but the Afrocentric thinkers and doers who will roll up their sleeves, take up their purses, and actively bring into existence the new Africa. Alas, the memorials to fighters and warriors will reinforce the fundamental goal, and the memorials, sibongo, of the national figures will strengthen the relationship with the ancestors. This, then, is the precociousness of a true victory.

I went to Chinoyi one cold day in July in search for the Chirarodziva Pools and the Chinoyi Caves, but I discovered the history of the Africans' fight for freedom from the white minority regime of Ian Smith. The first battle of the Second Chimurenga was fought on April 28, 1966, in Chinoyi, making that city famous. The liberation forces had sent six men into Rhodesia to attack the military; the Rhodesian whites had killed all six of the fighters. Their deaths while climbing up the steep walls of the Limpopo River banks sent the signal that the war had started. And here I was in Chinoyi, the city named for Chief Chinoyi of the Shona people.

Two things stood out in my mind from the visit: the Chinoyi caves and the feeling of white hatred of blacks. The whites knew I was not from those parts, and like the inhabitants of the small white towns in the Midwest, they looked straight through me. But I knew, as they must have known, that their time as African masters was limited. They simply had not had time to learn the new rules of social conduct. Riding on empty, they gave the bluff their best shot—but Harare's reality, which was so much different from theirs, would soon come to the people of Chinoyi.

Chinoyi, like most Rhodesian towns in Zimbabwe, is a single street lined with stores and a small park off to the side. It was a quiet town, but it had seen so much trouble and violence in the past. The Rhodesians had built these little one-horse towns throughout the region, distinct from the teeming natural villages of the African people.

Chinoyi is the symbol of courage. It is in many ways like the monument the whites built to those defeated by the Matabele at the Shangani River in 1893. Here in Chinoyi the six courageous revolutionaries were gunned down, but they were the initial expression of African willingness to rid itself of oppression in Zimbabwe.

While I was in Chinoyi something happened that was so important that I still have to pinch myself to believe it was real. One night, at midnight, I stood at the edge of Musi wa Tunya, the Smoke that Thunders, and I heard a million lions roaring as the water hurtled over the cliffs. Of course, I got soaked. The falls create a constant rain forest, an incessant Congo of water pouring down on everything within half a mile. Outside of the rain forest, aridity forms a perfect circle around the falls.

I slept in the small hotel nearest to this divine creation, but when the dawn broke, I went again through the outer fringes of the rain forest, feeling the light mist from the mighty falls before actually seeing the cataracts of Musi wa Tunya.

And then I came upon the statue of Robert Livingstone bearing the insignia "Liberator," a dubious caption to be sure. It was Livingstone who called the falls after Queen Victoria, as if one man could change Africa's history at will.

I heard a hundred ominous thunders and saw the rushing waters of Devil's Cataract pouring over the rocks like one giant flood compressed into the narrowest canyon. My heart pounded with excitement, awe, and humility as I moved nearer the natural lookout point, with nothing but a row of thorn bushes separating me from the sheer drop into the Zambezi River Gorge. I looked to my right and saw the Rainbow Falls, beautiful beyond description and larger than the Devil's Cataract, which had so thoroughly impressed me. I walked along the water-soaked edge of the gorge for a full mile, watching the waters pour over the rocks with such tremendous force that I swore it must have been like ten Niagaras.

And finally I saw Main Falls—everlasting, constant, a mighty torrent of brownish Zambezi water garlanded by an appropriate rainbow. Through the haze I could see that this was the most delightful natural sight in Africa.

Yet I remained aware of what almost everyone knew: that naming this magnificent falls Victoria Falls was a sign of arrogance and a statement of white dominance in the heart of Africa. Like a slice of sunlight, I saw clearly the crisis in our own understanding of our African selves. Whites believed truly that the earth belonged to them, and whatever they wanted to name a thing, they could, regardless of its local name. This was an act of godlikeness that assumed the forefront in all white supremacist ventures. To name a thing is to claim it for your own history, your own story. Embedded in this situation is the crisis of national identity that confronts most African nations. Only in a great reconstruction of agency, creating the will to act, can Africa recreate itself and restore the memories of the ancestors as resources for transformation.

This was not simply a Zimbabwean or Zambian issue. I did not find it and leave it at the border of these two countries. The mighty Musi wa Tunya would live forever, but Africa could only live as long as its people understood the nature of what we faced. Repeatedly I had set my face toward an African redemption, only to be told that it was not yet time. Everything I saw indicated that our dislocation as a people was due to the lack of memory, the loss of direction, and the disorientation that comes with reading too many European authors whose disregard of Africa was clear in their writings. I also knew the depth of intellectual confusion that colonialism and enslavement had planted inside the African mind. The cultural crisis has a weight beyond the present capacity of the African states or people to manage. It is both a cultural-economic crisis and a crisis of the spirit.

On my fourteenth visit to Nigeria, this time to be an external examiner for the language arts department at the University of Ibadan, I sat with the novelist and critic Isidore Okpewho, and our discussion led to his 3 a.m. cry of anguish, an honest attempt to deal with the agony of the present: "But Molefi, when will Africans be able to grasp the enormity of the situation facing the continent?" We were at the faculty club, sitting outside under the moonlit sky because the drinking bar had closed but we were not finished with our discussion.

My answer, I confess, was lame, and has only sounded more so to me since: "When Africa comes to grip with its past."

Isidore listened, but the frustrated shaking of his head implied that coming to terms with the past would take too long, given the immediacy of the problem. Anyway, most Africans and their leaders were unaware of history as far as we could determine. As Isidore said, "We know colonial history, but remember little of Africa before the coming of the Europeans."

You did not have to be a Marxist to understand the significance of history as a revolutionary material condition for the rise of a people. Both in diachronic and synchronic aspects, history is vital to the solution of the African crisis. When I left Africa for America, I had developed a profound vision of the continent. I knew what was in store for South Africa, and I knew what would be necessary to rid the continent of its own sense of inferiority.

I got back to America convinced that a cadre of twenty-five thousand conscious African Americans, or a similar number of Ghanaians and Nigerians, would make a major contribution to the transformation of the country of Zimbabwe. This had to do with my belief that West Africans had undergone deeper transformations than those in the east and south. Time would soon tell me otherwise, but at that time I was deeply committed to African revolution. I did not know how to bring about that transformation without an organization, so I had to postpone the vision.

The same dreadful vision haunted me in 1990, when Mandela walked out of prison in South Africa. I knew that before long the Russians would occupy the seats of advice and government council and that the African masses would still see white as right. This was the awful legacy of apartheid and racism in southern Africa—it was one of the major lessons I learned, a provocative lesson.

It has not been long since the independence of South Africa, but like the independence of Zimbabwe that first attracted me to southern Africa, it has become ensnared in the five hundred–year web of treating white as the standard of what is right. South Africa will have a hell of a time unlocking the consciousness of an African population that still believes in white superiority. African Americans have yet to overcome the trauma of our own enslavement in this country after nearly one hundred fifty years this side of emancipation.

Somehow reading a story in the *International Herald Tribune* in 1982 about the African American playwright Charles Fuller laid bare my own ethnicity in a way that rocked my orientation. Actually, Fuller's interview made me homesick for the chaos I knew in the United States. Charles Fuller, the screenwriter, great playwright, and winner of the 1982 Pulitzer Prize, was an important influence on my decision to return to the States. He stood above and outside of the mainstream. He created his own rivulet, and those who wanted to know found a refreshing pattern to his logic. The *Herald Tribune* quoted Fuller as saying that he was "a black writer." I remember liking the fact that he accepted his essential Africanness as being the center of his work; it had been the same for me. If I had been an Armenian writer or a Ukrainian writer, I would have had to accept the truth of my historical reality. As a black person living in the United States, Fuller's blackness was inescapable, but even more, he did not seek to escape it. Thus, the author of the powerful drama *A Soldier's Play* had once again defied those who wanted to say that he was merely a writer "who happened to be black." At such moments many African Americans believed that they had really made it and so did not have to be black anymore: they would just be humans. Fuller understood that our humanity was not at question; what was at issue and was always at issue in a racist society was whether or not a black person identifies with African American or white history.

In white history—what passes in a hegemonic society as mainstream history—the black person, even if he or she denies this blackness, is nothing more than a marginal figure. Universality is in the black experience equally as much as it is in the white experience, as Fuller knew when he gave his quote to the journalist.

It may have been the first time that I truly understood that African Americans constituted a legitimate African ethnic group. We were African but we were not Zulu, Mashona, Matebele, although, like them, our roots were on the African continent and we shared in so many of the same responses to history, culture, and art. I resonated with everything that Fuller said in his interview. I understood him without ever having to guess the context, imagine a new world, or ask someone for an explanation. He was talking pure African American common sense. Fuller had won the Pulitzer Prize for drama and was prominently mentioned as one of the great writers of his era for *A Soldier's Story*. I could sense that it was time for me to re-enter the fray of the United States.

I went back to the State University of New York at Buffalo where I had been teaching before I went to Zimbabwe. After a year at Buffalo I knew that it was time for me to move on from that institution. The battles I had with the administration were often public, and I believe that with a circle of friends like Arthur Lee, Sidney Wilhelm, Abdias do Nascimento, and Leslie Fiedler becoming smaller, I had to find new opportunities. My African American vision had been encapsulated in a frail vessel of inauthentic interest. Few administrators seemed eager to champion the cause of freedom and fairness. Of course, I knew that this was often the case with other institutions, so I had to seek a move.

I welcomed the invitation to come to Temple University. I had interviewed for the position and was accepted, and immediately I knew that I had chosen a huge responsibility. Chairing the communication and African American departments at Buffalo made me aware of the challenges that Temple would present. When I took the position at Temple University, I immediately started looking for Charles Fuller, the man who had made me proud by refusing to deny his heritage although he won the Pulitzer.

Boldness is often the ticket to openness. One must try before others are requested to go out on a limb for you. It is like swimming to the waterfalls in the Damasaguas River in Dominican Republic. When the leader of the group jumps from the cliff into the swirling waters, it gives you a sense that it is possible. I took that attitude to Temple and jumped into developing a graduate program in African American Studies. President Peter Liacouras, who had interviewed me, told me that an urban university in the United States had to have African American Studies. He said, "I want you to build the best department in the nation." He meant it, and I believed him.

However, when I proposed the creation of the doctoral program in African American Studies at Temple University, I knew full well that there would be opposition, although I did not know how strong or from what corners. Like any attempt to recover the African vision on one continent or another, it would be a fight. Luckily, Temple was equipping itself with some outstanding scholars and creative people.

I was hired during the heyday of Liacouras's progressive administration. Peter Liacouras, a second-generation Greek immigrant who had been the law school dean, sought to improve the profile of what had been mainly a commuter university. The fact that the president wanted the best department was an amazingly brilliant symbol of boldness. This was just what I needed to hear.

Patrick Swygert, the executive vice president, became a major ally in the push to create the first PhD in African American Studies, but Provost Barbara Brownstein, an intellectual who wanted to ensure that the university did all it needed to do to create the best academic department, had fears about Afrocentricity, as many white people do. Yet in the end she acquiesced, accepted my arguments, heard the voices of a generation of African American scholars, and supported the proposal.

Not only was it the right thing for Temple to do; it was also the politic thing to do for the African American community given the strength of the Yorktown Community Association under the dynamic leadership of Lillian Safisha Green. In several meetings with the group, something Samuel Evans, the de facto leader of the African American community, and Reverend Father Paul Washington, who ordained the first female priest in the Episcopal Church in 1974, approved, I had made the case for the doctoral degree in African American Studies as a distinctive enterprise in building for the future. Green's executives met with Temple officials to voice their support for the PhD proposal. Lillian Green, a veteran school administrator, eventually received her doctorate through the PhD program in African American Studies.

Although the top administrators were supportive of my initiatives, the work was more difficult at the level of the College of Arts and Sciences. This was the locus of power for academic programs, and there were individuals in traditional departments who were intent on putting hurdles in the way of the doctoral degree in African American Studies. For instance, assistant dean in the College of Arts and Sciences, a black history professor, Emma Lapsansky, wrote a two-page, single-spaced letter attacking the idea of a graduate program in African American

Studies. The dean, Carolyn Adams, had given it to her to read, and Lapsansky had essentially dismissed the idea. This shocked me because I had expected (and received) resistance from some whites but had not anticipated that a black woman would write such a cruel piece about creating a "ghetto" in the university. My response to her objections cut right to the core of her problem with her own blackness and had the impact that I intended. She never voiced her objections to me again and soon left the University for Haverford College to the delight of African Americans and whites who knew that Temple had to overcome its provincial perspective on African American knowledge. Black Studies is not history; it is a separate, different discipline based on assumptions that do not necessarily undergird historical research in America. Historical information is fundamental, but Black Studies, as Maulana Karenga had shown by this time, included many other interests: communication, arts, politics, economics, and culture. Furthermore, as I had taught Black Studies, it is not merely the study of black people or black culture but rather the study of African people from the standpoint of their own agency. Emma Lapsansky was neither the only nor the most adamant hostile voice. Others would throw stones and then hide their hands.

I could easily handle some questions, but I did not think that the sociology chair, Magali Sarfatti-Larson, would say to my face, "You'll get this PhD program over my dead body!" She had not even thoroughly read about the program; she had just heard about it and believed that it would take students away from sociology. Furthermore, she had a reputation as a white liberal who was born in Italy and grew up in Uruguay and Argentina and was supportive of hiring blacks into the sociology department. So I thought that her questioning of us taking students away from sociology was way off the mark. How could that be possible, when they hardly had any black students in the department? African American scholars had already decried the lack of black students in various departments at large universities.

Perseverance was something I had learned on hot Georgia days, riding the rows of cotton tucked in the corners of the woods. I had to make it to the end. I would not let the heat, the hard work, or the sweat get me before I had done what I was supposed to do. This had to be the only path. Joy and rewards always came at the end of determined work.

With the support of Reverend Henry Nichols, one of the black members of the Temple's Board of Trustees, the proposal was finally ushered safely to approval. In the fall of 1988 Temple became the first university to have a doctoral program in African American studies, admitting thirty-five graduate students out of nearly five hundred applicants to the doctoral program. Although I had considered it a battle, in some cases even a war, I never felt compelled to quit. By 2010 I had directed more than one hundred dissertations in my career at UCLA, SUNY Buffalo, and Temple.

Two colleagues remained true to the vision that I had articulated at Temple. One was a South African, C. Tsehloane Keto, and the other was a Guadeloupian, Ama Mazama. Both proved to be outstanding intellectuals, scholars, activists, and friends in their own right. They were champions who took seriously their commitments to students and the African world. Keto had been a professor in the history department at Temple, and I lured him to the department with the idea that he could train more students, do more good for Africa, and distinguish himself forever with his work. He came over to the department, giving up his line in history, and worked with me at breakfast meetings to strategize ways to defeat our opposition. We took the South African war for freedom and paralleled our activities for academic advancement with that of the brothers and sisters on the ground in southern Africa who fought for liberation. Keto would say, "Molefi, they will have a problem with that," meaning that the whites on campus would not be in favor of this or that program or project. I would tell him, "Tsehloane, the struggle has just begun." He would laugh and say, "Let's do it, then." My name, "Molefi," was adopted from the Sotho people, his own ethnic group, and he liked using that name when he referred to me. The fact that we were successful in establishing a fine doctoral program and recruiting faculty meant that we had seen the vision in effect.

Keto went home to South Africa after Mandela was released from Robben Island. Because he was quite skilled, he found moving into the academic circles in South Africa quite easy. He was eventually made the head of Vista University in Pretoria, but soon after that university was merged with another, he passed away while on an official trip to Atlanta. His loss was tremendous on both sides of the ocean, and the

National Council of Black Studies, the leading professional group of Africana Studies scholars named a fellowship program after him.

Ama Mazama entered the struggle for Afrocentric studies with a doctorate from La Sorbonne with the highest distinction in linguistics. Her work on the languages of the Congo and their relationship to the languages of the African diaspora had already brought her academic accolades when she arrived at Temple from Penn State and the University of Texas. Immediately she could tell that the road that I had trod had not been easy and that, with Keto no longer active, the department would need strong support from the remaining faculty to push through a progressive agenda. Of course, the enemies of Afrocentricity were also busy, and the university pushed through a couple of bad leaders for the department. In the end I was left with one colleague, Professor Mazama, who had the courage, integrity, and ingenuity to maneuver through the potholes of disappointment and betrayal of the academic scene. People with limited capability or at least with limited productivity have nothing to fall back on but their willingness to sell their souls for the favors of the administrators. Mazama and I found that out and soon discovered that although we were the most active scholars and the best-known faculty members in the department, the jealousy, mean-spirited nature of the anti-Afrocentrists and the white administrators who seemed to enjoy seeing blacks fight against blacks, encouraging back-stabbing and undermining, caused us to spend too much time defending the paradigm. We vowed to up the work production and make it so that any student who wanted to declare competence in the field had to read our works. We wrote every day—discussing our findings, debating our conclusions, and refreshing our vision. In addition, we knew that by out-producing the nay-sayers we would make them obsolete in the profession. That is precisely what happened.

Sage Publications, the venerable academic publisher, liked our work and published two monumental encyclopedias that advanced the field tremendously. Of course, we had some administrators question the reputation of Sage itself. This was ludicrous, but it was the business of academic politics. Nevertheless, our first encyclopedia was the *Encyclopedia of Black Studies*, which gave the field its major reference work written entirely by scores of scholars in Africana Studies. The second, an idea proposed by Ama Mazama, who had in the time of her tenure at Temple University also become a mambo in the Vodun religion, was for an *Encyclopedia of African Religion.* It met with immediate success and was hailed in the journals and the field as a major achievement.

Earlier in 1990, when Adeniyi Coker, a Nigerian, became the first person in the world to receive a doctorate in African American Studies, I remember being delighted that I had fought for the doctorate program. Soon the first white students, Cynthia Lehman and Sandra Van Dyke, established that whites could learn from the perspective of African people as the subjects of their own history. Afrocentricity was a legitimate perspective on facts, and its impact on critical race theory and the so-called standpoint theory would be that those fields would bite off of Afrocentricity without admitting their inheritance. This was alright with the early Afrocentrists because we knew that the ideas of centrality, agency, and perspective were firmly locked into the advancement of our discipline. Our students would become our greatest promoters. Soon after we admitted the first white students we admitted several Asian students. Two of them succeeded in graduating, one dropped out. This left Japanese student, Suzuko Morikawa, and the Chinese student, Yuan Ji, as the first from their countries to complete the doctorate in African American Studies. Temple was on the map, and its history could never be supplanted.

Ama Mazama often asked me, "Molefi, what did you feel when you were seeking to create the doctorate in African American Studies?" It took me a long time to understand the question, but one day I said to her, "As I struggled to create the program, I could feel something sacred, a bond, a sense of working to make life better—indeed, a social and political mission to create something that would transform human reality and add to the edifice of justice. This is what motivated me to write and argue for the PhD program." I remembered she smiled and said, "I could have told you that."

Debating Afrocentricity with many scholars, preachers, and commentators brought me lots of attention in the nineties. The legendary African American poet, Mari Evans, became an adviser and friend during this time. I had known her before; she was our queen in the 1970s, the fiercest among the poets, neither Giovanni nor Sanchez had as much African fire in their bones for some of us. Mari is the kind of person you would feel you had met before somewhere at some time. I loved her honesty, commitment, and grace. She was like one of my aunts, maybe like my paternal Aunt Georgia. She had the same grace and elegance of carriage and seemed in charge of all situations, though she never overtalked. This takes a special degree of confidence if you are as gifted as Mari Evans.

When I was in Indianapolis, training teachers in the use of an Afrocentric curriculum, Mari Evans heard I was in town and summoned me to her place for dinner. I could not resist because I had promised her that I would come to see her the next time I was in the city. I also wanted to talk to her about my new book project. Mari was known for her frank views on everything, and I knew she would give me her opinion. I also knew that she wanted to talk to me about her newest book, *Clarity,* that was going to be published by Third World Press.

We sat in the kitchen, and that is where the story really begins. She is an excellent cook, a gourmet chef in the African American Southern tradition. We talked about politics but kept coming back to food. We argued about the future of the African race in America but ultimately agreed on the genius of the African American cooks who made something out of nothing. She said that erasing racism would probably not happen soon and that maybe Derrick Bell was right, that it would always exist so long as we had a white hegemony. She kept cooking. I did not see anyone else and wondered if she intended for me to eat all the foods she was preparing.

I relaxed and we ate corn on the cob, collard greens, fried chicken, and sweet potato pie as we talked. She was my elder sister, giving me the benefit of her judgment and opinions about everything and everybody, telling me what to watch out for and who to trust, and what to write and how to publish. It was a marathon of intellect and wisdom.

I left Mari Evans's house pressed into the mortar of the African world, and I had been reminded that I could not forget the trauma of my ancestors' American sojourn, although I wished for some type of cultural therapy to wipe away the deep emotional scar. However, I did gain an exceptional understanding of the meaning of Africa to me, an understanding that would wrench me from any form of self-delusion, pity, and negativity. I was fully African, in the sense that as a citizen of the United States, I was in touch with my origins and my cultural ancestors, and they were always reaching out to me. If the truth be spoken, I was always in the care of cultural keepers, magicians of words, and dramatists of ordinary lives.

Although Charles Fuller may have been at the time the brightest luminary in our intellectual sky, those at Temple represented one of the most impressive groups of scholars and creators in the nation. I invited Fuller to help create the dynamic community at Temple, and I had also reached out to bring others into the mix. At one point our fourteen full-time faculty members had the possibility of making even more academic history as the only fully articulated Afrocentric department. We were not Marxists, not Socialists, not system theorists—we were Afrocentrists first. We took seriously the mandate to build a department that would reflect the integrity of the African experience in the United States and the diaspora. But soon the jealousies that can never be underestimated in universities produced rumors that we were seeking to have a department of superstars. Word came back to us that the dean was unhappy with superstars, but we insisted and persisted that because we had the only Pulitzer Prize winner at Temple University, we should have been shown more respect for our recruiting.

I published *The Afrocentric Idea* in 1996 with Temple University Press, and it got rave reviews, with the exception of Melvin Dixon's lukewarm praise in the *New York Times Book Review*—and yet the fact that it was reviewed in the *New York Times Book Review* was in itself a sign of the book's impact. I held seminars, and school districts started in earnest to invite me to assist them in creating Afrocentric curricula. I worked to create community projects for school children as well as training programs for teachers. Of course, I also debated Arthur Schlesinger, Cornel West, Mary Lefkowitz, Dinesh D'Souza, and others on the importance of looking at African people not as objects or marginal beings but as central to our own history, as agents of history. These debates, especially the four times I debated Mary Lefkowitz, sharpened the ideological position of the Afrocentric movement and demonstrated that the work we had begun was powerful, magnetic, and, yes, controversial to some people. For a brief moment Lefkowitz, a classics scholar at Wellesley, became the darling of the intellectual right because she challenged some of the tenets Afrocentrists held. Of course, she created some tenets that Afrocentrists never held, like saying

Afrocentrists believe that Aristotle was black. By the time we had our last debate at the Smithsonian, Lefkowitz was willing to admit "Molefi, everyone knows now that the ancient Egyptians were black." When I had a chance to speak I said, "Mary, I wish you had read the accounts *before* you wrote your book."

Schlesinger and D'Souza were eager to say that they engaged an Afrocentrist. I respected Schlesinger for his contribution to the political debates about the future of the American democracy. His reputation was large; he had been one of John Kennedy's most important voices. Of course, I disagreed vehemently with him that "black Americans" had to accept the dominance of "the Anglo-Germanic project" as the only route to genuine acceptance in the society. He once told me that if I could learn to identify with the Anglo-Germanic project and master its nuances I could be anything I wanted to be in America. I remember sitting at dinner at East Stroudsburg University telling him, "Dr. Schlesinger, I am all I want to be in America."

I had no respect for D'Souza simply because he had little respect for himself and paraded, as many reactionaries tend to do, as all knowledgeable on issues that were way above his experiences, training, or understanding. An Indian who had grown up in the Portuguese-influenced environment of India, converted to Christianity, used a Portuguese surname, and claimed to be a new representative of the "minority" people in the United States, D'Souza was a fake, an inauthentic symbol of intelligence among whites who admired his Ivy League education at Dartmouth and essentially used him to say what many of them could no longer say about African American people. He married a white American and took on positions that were identified with the extreme wing of the conservative element among the Republicans. Like other Indians and some new "minorities," D'Souza had no understanding of the struggles against slavery and segregation, and for Civil Rights. In fact, at our debate at Vanderbilt University, where Ray Winbush had invited us to appear before hundreds of onlookers, D'Souza claimed that the so-called Untouchables or Dalits should remain discriminated in Indian society. He refused to support the Indian government's quest for affirmative action for the oppressed Dalits. This revealed more about D'Souza than it did about the Indian people. I found numerous avenues to demonstrate that he had no knowledge of the African American situation in this country. We tangled a couple of times on *Nightline,* but I soon tired of correcting D'Souza's errors of fact and judgment.

Conversely, my dialogues with Kwame Ture and Cornel West have taken on a life of their own because we have always been in search of the same goals. We believed that given the rich and textured history of African Americans, our people were most qualified to assist in determining the future of the country. Our disagreements have been about tactics and strategies to achieve the objectives of liberation. Ture articulated a finely tuned theory of African socialism and believed that it was essential for us to organize in order to bring into existence on the African continent a political dispensation that would care for all international interests of African people.

Cornel West and I have shared the desire for truth, justice, mercy, and all the values that are at the heart of a decent society. Where we have differed has been on issues of culture. I run toward Africa in all of my thoughts, actions, and interests, and I have often believed that he runs, as fast as he can, away from Africa. Perhaps it is that he knows so much more about European thought than he knows about African ideas and thoughts, but in the end our dialogues have turned to my emphasizing the Afrocentric idea of African agency and he has pointed out the broad base of nihilism in the African community. West also preaches the Christian doctrine as if it were salvation for black people. I think, however, that religion, especially Christianity, is an imperative death for black culture. Nevertheless, we have remained friends who share many of the same battles against institutional racism.

These debates and dialogues strengthened my resolve to advance the theory of Afrocentricity. Of course, not all of the people who watched me do this work meant anything good for me or my cause. There were times I believed that several weak, mediocre, politically infantile individuals' only ambition was to frustrate the implementation of an Afrocentric transformation, but I was determined to do everything within my power to create space for African agency. The plantation was gone; we were on our own in theories and practice.

Many days I felt all alone, abandoned by those who had declared their commitment to an Afrocentric interpretation, only to be too willing to succumb to the material rewards and temptations of a system that would use them and throw them away. The intellectual battles wore them out, and they felt that association with any idea that challenged the established order was futile. But my strong sense of ancestral reverence always redirected my feelings. I could not let Harriet Tubman down, or Nat Turner, Martin Delany, Plenty Smith, or Hattie Shine. I was supposed to be the one who stood when others fell. As far as I could remember my daddy, Uncle DeBuddy, and Aunt Georgia had drilled discipline and honor into me. I remembered that Anna Julia Cooper had said, "When and where I enter, my people enter with me," and this kept me always fighting for what was correct and ethical.

In 2004 Paul G. Vallas, the then Philadelphia Schools superintendent who went on to become the school chief in New Orleans, took the recommendation of a community group to hire me to write the first mandatory course in African American Studies for high schools in the nation. Sandra Dungee Glenn, a leading member of the school reform commission, became one the most outspoken advocates on the commission for this project. We met with loud opposition.

I wrote three courses—African American History, African History, and the African Diaspora—because I believed that one of these courses should be taught in the ninth grade, one in the tenth grade, and one in the eleventh grade. I was hired to train the future teachers of the course. The School Reform Commission accepted and approved the teaching of African American History as a mandatory course, and it was first taught as a pilot in the spring of 2005.

The controversy over the course did not subside with the commission's approval. Starting in September 2005 the mandate called for all ninth graders to take the African American History course. Vallas was a strong supporter of my idea that African Americans are sewn into the fabric of American history and no one could understand the full meaning of America without African American history. In a city with more than 185,000 students, two-thirds of whom were African Americans, offering this course was a no-brainer. The School Reform Commission that set policy voted five to zero to establish the policy. Three of the members of the panel were whites.

My book *African American History: A Journey of Liberation* was the first history book written expressly for high schools. This fact alone should have provided the book a prime position in the school district's adoption of a text for the course that I had written. But in the meantime the district had moved Dana King, a teacher with limited knowledge and understanding of African American Studies, into the post of African American Studies affairs. King told me that she felt my book would have given me too much influence in the district, although my book was used in four hundred districts throughout the country. Nevertheless, she took the lessons that I used for the workshops for future teachers of the course and attempted to write a supplement to my work. Something so visionary, so forward-thinking became a corrupted element of modern education in Philadelphia. King knew neither how to monitor the course nor what to do about teacher development. And although the course remained on the books, I am not certain that it fulfilled either the objectives of my original course proposal or the aims of the community groups that had fought for it for forty years.

In April 2005 I gave a speech at the African Heritage Studies Association Conference in Ithaca, New York, in the same hotel where I first heard the indefatigable Professor Yosef ben-Jochannon speak. He was a lion, roaring words of fire at the falsifiers of African history. No one had done as much as Dr. Ben, as he is affectionately called by those who know him, in bringing the ancient civilization of Egypt to the African American lay audience. The more he was attacked by white academics who wanted to debate him on the issue of Egypt—a debate he seems to have always won—the more he became an icon in the black community. As a retired professor from Cornell University's Africana Studies and Research Center, he was one of the conference's guests of honor.

Abdul Nanji, the president of the association, had asked me to give the luncheon talk on African culture. The audience was studded with luminaries of the African world, including some of the founders of the black studies movement—James Turner, Ron Daniels, and Abdul Alkalimat, among others. As I left the podium to a standing ovation and made my way toward the exit door, I heard someone say, "Dr. Ben wants to see you. Dr. Ben is calling for you!" I went to the front of the room where he was standing and embraced him.

He reached into his pocket and whispered, "I want to give you something. I want you to have this." He was giving me a one hundred dollar bill.

I could not contain my tears; like a broken pipe, the water would not stop, and I left the auditorium broken with the memory of this aged warrior, who had fought so many battles and whose very existence was the death of docility. As I was going downstairs in the hotel I met Leonard Jeffries, the legendary dean of Harlem academics and professor at City College, and told him, "The old man offered me money. He claimed that he was so proud of me, he wanted to give me something, and the only thing he had was a few dollars." Seeing tears still flowing down my face, Leonard tried to humor me by saying, "I wish he would offer me some money, since I know that he is living on a fixed income, and from time to time struggles to pay his own bills. He did that, Molefi, to clear up any issues he may have had with you." I was puzzled but thanked him for trying to comfort me, and I left the building.

Later, as I reflected on Dr. Ben's public demonstration of appreciation, it occurred to me that because of my friendship with Maulana Karenga, Dr. Ben had often seemed distant, as he followed John Henrik Clarke. As I reminded Dr. Ben on several occasions, Karenga never treated them with disrespect and third-party commentaries on Karenga never influenced me, and yet among some of the elders, there persisted some irrational disdain for him. Nevertheless, I treated them all with respect. Even when Karenga held the first meeting that led to the creation of the Association for the Study of Classical African Civilizations, Dr. Ben, venerable and respected, had been one of the people most honored. I admired Karenga for his strength of character, his straightness in support of good, and his deliberate attempt to forge solidarity with those who had often criticized him. His main problem with colleagues may have been the power of his personal logic, his magical charisma, and his sense of cultural confidence. Nevertheless, we shared the same objective of making the world better by making our people better, by not allowing circumstance or history to dictate to us what we could do for ourselves. This is the Karenga that the masses respected and love, and in some ways Karenga and Dr. Ben were tied together in the grand march to recover African history.

I had met Dr. Ben several times in the tombs of Egypt, we had held joint meetings at the various hotels in Egypt, and student leader Pamela Yaa Reed had brought him to Temple University to speak on my behalf when I was under siege by some reactionaries at Temple. I realized that Dr. Ben had heard me speak at Ithaca, and it brought to mind some of his more direct and forceful speeches on African history. In Egypt he would teach the trained guides about the history of Egypt, and in doing this he instructed scores of African American historians on the issues of Egypt. Furthermore, he knew that I had often been criticized because I was unafraid to speak the unsanctioned word. My appreciation for his courage, given the way Temple University had treated him and Lawrence Redding when they were teaching at Temple, was without question. Dr. Ben's history was written in sharp words, unadorned language, and direct confrontation with Western scholars. I admired his comprehensive knowledge and his willingness to challenge reactionaries in religion and science. Not since the days of J. A. Rogers had an African person created such a dynamic community of talk about Africa.

In 1993 the elders of the Akyem came knocking on my door, bearing a message. The great clan families of the Akyem at Tafo in Ghana wanted to put my name forward to the Queen Mother and Paramount King for enstoolment. I agreed, and a ceremony was held at the Memorial Hall in Philadelphia that attracted hundreds of people. I was given a course of instructions by Akan elders and told that I would have to eventually go to Tafo to perform the ritual in Africa.

Enstoolment is the process of making a person a king. In the West a king sits upon a throne, but in the enstoolment ritual a king's power is activated when he or she sits three times on the ancestors' stool. In Ghana there are women who serve as kings as well. The term "hene" is often translated "king," and a woman can be Tafohene—that is, "king of Tafo"—as well as a man. During enstoolment the individual in question then inherits the divine qualities of the first ancestor who sat on the stool.

It is not correct to say that I expected this; it would be better to say I have spent my life seeking to understand the world as an African on the basis of tradition and the artistic and moral values that define the good and the beautiful. Therefore, when the elders approached me, I was ready, but I was unsure what it all meant.

When my plane landed at the Kotoko International Airport in Accra on July 3, 1996, three years after the initial meeting with the elders in Philadelphia, Gladys Brobbey, senior manager of Ghana Commercial Bank, was waiting with her driver. I was impressed that my Akyem elders in Philadelphia, Nana Okwae Asare and his wife, Adjua, Kwame Botwe-Asamoah, and Kofi Yemoa, had made such good arrangements. After I checked into the Hotel Wangara, Mrs. Brobbey said I was to go to Old Tafo the very next day to informally meet King Nana Adusei Peasah IV, who had agreed I should be enstooled, and receive instructions about when I should return to Tafo to swear the Great Oath.

The next day my driver, Mensah, and my guide, Attah, both extremely knowledgeable about the culture, collaborated to bring me from Accra, the capital of Ghana, to the small, ancient town of Tafo, in search of the Tafohene, the Paramount King of Tafo. Once we turned off the main Accra-Kumasi road at Asafo, we went down a dirt road that reminded me of the one I took when I went to find the childhood home and burial place of the great Senegalese scholar, Cheikh Anta Diop. These roads were common in Africa, as they had been common in the Georgia of my childhood.

We passed Effiduase, Dwaben, Koforidua, Asokore, and other, smaller villages, all familiar from my reading of Akan history and my interest in my newly adopted ancestral homeland of Akyem. When we reached the palace, Attah got out of the car and went in, only to find that the Tafohene had traveled to Accra that very same morning, probably passing us on the highway—he had hoped to greet me in person while there. Nevertheless, the Gyasahene and the Okyeame, two court officials, asked Attah to bring me into the palace—customarily, visitors do not enter until they are sent for by the king or the Gyasahene, the administrator of the royal house.

I entered the palace and the master drummer announced my presence to the elders—thus, behind the ancient walls of the palace, in the courtyard where Nana Okru Banning and Nana Adusei Peasah walked,

I heard my name for the first time on the mighty drums of Tafo. Then the Okyeame presented me to the palace attendants and greeted me formally in the name of the king. They ushered me into a large room, with seats arranged around the wall.

I had the odd feeling that I had found my place, or that this place had found me. I am not sure how to describe the feeling of belonging that came over me, even though I had never been in that town before. After nearly four hundred years in exile from my place of cultural origin, I was returning to Akyem, the ancient seat of power in the Akan States, the most stubborn defender of African sovereignty, and the Ghanaian state that refused, under the leadership of the queen, to sign the British Bond of 1844.

I was given a seat to the left of the Gyasahene, who welcomed me home, told me that they had been waiting for me, and explained again the absence of the Tafohene. As he spoke in Twi, Attah explained the expressions that I did not understand, and he translated for me when I told the royal officials in English that I was happy to return after my ancestors had left in chains many years ago. Several of the elders representing abusua, or clans, spoke up to receive me as one of their own who had returned.

They took me to the center of the courtyard, to a small shrine erected in honor of the ancestors, and poured libations thanking the ancestral spirits for my presence and return. The mighty atumpan drums sounded again, and then we returned to the great room.

When we sat again, the Okyeame had each of us drink from the same cup. I feared the cup held water, and wondered, "Should I dare drink water so far away from the capital city?" Of course, I did not hesitate to take the cup, and when I sipped from it, I was pleasantly surprised to discover that it held gin. I believed in the ancestors, though I did not know what the drink was, and when I felt the burning sensation of gin, I knew I had done the right thing.

The Gyasahene decided that they should find me a place to stay for the night; they insisted that I had to stay to meet the king. I agreed, but I had neither clothes nor the proper shoes with me. At last Attah rescued me, suggesting that I meet the king in Accra at the home of the Kyebihene, the titular head of Akyem kings, also called the Okyehene. Attah said, "We will bring Molefi back tomorrow to meet the king officially at the palace, but let me take him now to see the king in Accra." He gave his word that I would be back very early for the official visit.

We made preparations to leave for Accra. The pleasant drive through the Aburi hills brought us to the bustling city of three million. You could see it from the hills, sprawling out toward the Atlantic Ocean like some African Los Angeles with neither head nor tail. Mensah was a good driver and soon found the walled villa of the Okyehene.

The Tafohene, who had been contacted by telephone, met us outside the villa. He was dressed informally, in trousers and a bowling shirt. I was surprised, but he soon put me at ease with his receptive manner, intelligence, and humor. He was an affable man with a winning smile and penetrating eyes.

He quickly explained to me why he was in Accra: "The Queen Mother of the State of Akyem, who is not the wife of the king but the chooser of the king, has crossed over to her village. Queen Sekyiraa II's passing prevented me from carrying out any other duties, and as second in command to Kyebihene, I must take care of all funeral arrangements. Nevertheless, since you have come from America, I must work out the details of your visit as well."

The Tafohene then led me to the top deck of the villa, where we had a panoramic view of Accra, and he told me a lot about the customs and traditions of Tafo. The king was impressive, and I felt that we liked each other. I appreciated his graciousness, although this was a time of much pressure and protocol for him. After about an hour of discussion, he told me that I should come to Tafo the next day, not in the morning but around 5 p.m.

The next day, as we drove, after Attah and I had thoroughly discussed all aspects of the enstoolment, he said that he wanted me to call him Michael Daniel instead of Attah, because it was biblical. Here I was, an African from America getting ready to be enstooled in the African ritual, happy to finally secure a place in African tradition, and my guide was insisting that he be called Michael Daniel.

I refused. Straight-out refused. I thought I would try to teach this brother that there was nothing wrong with his name and began the process of educating him about African history, colonialism, imposed religion, self-hatred, and African dislocation based on not knowing or not respecting cultures and traditions. I said, "Attah, you know you are not white and you are not Jewish, don't you?"

"Of course, you are right. I am neither Jewish nor white."

"But you still want to deify somebody else's culture instead of your own," I said.

"I don't understand 'deify,'" he claimed.

"Okay, let me put it this way. Why make someone else's culture or religion more sacred than your own?"

After that question and his mumbled answer about liking Michael Daniel, I decided to think about my own sense of Africanity. Here I was in Africa, in Ghana, about to be adopted into a culture that in a strict sense had not been mine within the last two hundred years. I wondered, *Wasn't this somewhat like wanting to be called Michael Daniel?* I told myself my adoption was African, and his was European; there was a big difference. *In fact, the Akan culture may have been my original culture, but it is not possible for him to be European.*

Mensah Akuffo, the driver, remained happy with his name. Strangely, the less educated man had a greater appreciation for his culture than the more educated man, who wanted to be Michael Daniel; in fact, it was probably Attah's education that made him think that Michael was a better name than Attah. This is the African condition around the globe. I liked them both, however, and we had a lot of fun.

When our Toyota Corolla pulled up to the royal palace in Tafo, it was only 4 p.m. As was the custom, Attah went inside to see if I should enter. He discovered that all of the senior elders had gone to the funeral of Queen Sekyiraa II. He came outside with about five or six palace attendants, and an extended conversation ensued behind the car about my lodging. I sat impassively, as my lodging, I had learned, was not my business.

Eventually, Attah got back in the car, sitting next to me in the backseat, and one of the elders got into the front. Attah explained to me that the wife of the king had told them to take me to the Cocoa Research Institute of Ghana (CRIG); the king had already made arrangements for me to stay there.

The CRIG, once the world's foremost research center for cocoa, is set amid a lush garden, landscaped and kept beautiful by constant attention. It has housed some of the most important people in the world, even serving as a hideaway for British royalty from time to time. There were about a dozen bungalows scattered around the main buildings.

On occasion I almost forgot the sacredness to which I was being called and wanted (perhaps an American impulse) to do too many things for myself. The elders had to examine everything before they would let me out of the car. They went into the bungalow and looked around, checking the bed, under the bed, the refrigerator, and the bathroom, and then they asked me to enter.

Soon the entourage—Attah, Mensah Akuffo, and Krodua Asare, the elder—left. They told me that I would see the king the next day. I was alone and, as far as I knew, the only person in the bungalows in the middle of this huge estate. It was the weekend, so I couldn't see any workers around. I had no phone, radio, Internet access, or television.

To my surprise the king drove up ten minutes after the entourage had left; he had been held up by the funeral. Tafohene came with his own attendants, including the Okyeame, the king's linguist. Tafohene was imposing in his black cloth, the funeral dress of the Akan.

Nana Adusei Peasah IV was a relatively young king—forty-two years old—and progressive by the standards of most traditional societies. As we talked, sitting around the table at the bungalow, I realized how much he was interested in the advancement of his people.

We spoke for barely thirty minutes. I could tell he was exhausted, and yet he was sensitive about my having had to wait. He said that he would see me the next day, and he would take me to the funeral. When he took his leave with the Okyeame, master drummer, and several elders, I prepared to retire for the evening.

With the lights off, the bungalow was the darkest house I had ever been in. I lay in bed, thinking about the swearing-in ceremony that would take place the next day. I had been led to believe that I would have been sworn in as a king by now. Yet because of the passing of the Queen Mother, it was impossible to go on with any other ceremony. The Ghanaians did not seem concerned that I was paying my own way and that I would eventually have to leave the country or change tickets to catch another flight. At any rate, I had not anticipated the delay, though the king had not anticipated the death either when he invited me to come.

It had been nearly fifty years since a Queen Mother had died; the redoubtable Queen Sekyiraa II had ruled Akyem with a strong hand for exactly forty-seven years, and at one hundred three years of age, she had gone on like she would go on forever—debating, chastising, making kings and deals, and generally laying down the law of Akyem. Sekyiraa was the epitome of the Okyehemaa, royal head of the Akyem. Never refusing to fight for her people or criticize a king when she saw him straying from the traditions, the Queen Mother was a remarkably strong character even in her old age. Now, the great mountain had fallen.

I found that the several-day postponement of my enstoolment was fortuitous in many respects. The Tafohene found the opportunity to introduce me to the many kings, queens, princes, and princesses attending the funeral, and I had the chance of a lifetime to observe the full power of Akyem culture—nothing had prepared me for what I was to behold during the funeral.

In the morning, when the king came to get me to take me to the funeral, I was already up, having woken at the break of dawn, prepared for whatever would happen. I had already given thanks to the ancestors, Nana Okru Banning and Nana Adusei Peasah I, and eaten the food that some of the ladies at CRIG delivered to my doorstep.

As a member of Tafohene's court, I entered the royal palace with him to the sound of the mighty Akyem State horn, said to have been decorated with the jawbones of enemies slain in battle two centuries earlier. As it announced the arrival of the mighty kings of Akyem, the horn's long, powerful blasts, like the roars of a lion, were enough to strike fear into the heart of any enemy.

Outside of the Okyehene's private sitting room was a waiting room full of kings and queens. The Tafohene found a seat for me and then entered the private chamber of the Okyehene ahead of any other king, as was his right.

Tafohene was, because of the colonial dispensation, the second in command to the Okyehene, although traditionally he was the first king of Akyem. Each of the Akan groups has its own titular head. The most famous, of course, is the Asantehene, the head of the Asante Nation, who is at the same level as the Okyehene among rulers of the Akyem Nation.

Whatever the colonial situation had been, there was an easy relationship between the two kings. Soon Tafohene opened the door and beckoned me to come into the chamber. Krodua Asare, the elder son of a former king but not a king because the Akan trace kinship through the mother, spoke to me: "Fix your cloth; you will be in the presence of a great king." I redraped the cloth over my left shoulder, leaving exposed my right shoulder and arm according to Akan custom, and entered the room.

Okyehene greeted me warmly as the Tafohene explained to him that I would be the new Kyidomhene of Tafo. The Okyehene was friendly, not very talkative, but sharp, intelligent, and a good listener. Occasionally he interrupted the Tafohene to ask me a question. I felt he wished me well in Tafo, and I told him that I would serve Akyem with dignity and pride.

I was in awe. Here I was, a person from the Deep American South, a long way from my ancestral roots, standing in the presence of two of the most powerful traditional leaders in Africa and soon to be made a king myself at the funeral of the mighty queen, the Okyehemaa. Little did I know what I would experience at the funeral, but in that room with the Kyebihene, who was the Okyehene, and the Tafohene, the owner of the land, I was in a surreal state, transported out of my physical body into a world of spiritual beings. I was not yet one, but I could see everything else around me that was, as if I were on the outside looking in.

The funeral procession toward the body of Queen Sekyiraa II was growing longer and longer when I came out of the king's chamber. The Okyeame Yaw Duah, the principal linguist who spoke for the king, and the court elder, Krodua Asare, asked me to follow them to the viewing. We enjoyed special viewing rights because of being royalty and did not have to stand in the longer line.

When we entered a large room with all of the windows opened, I noticed that some people were taking off their shoes. I did not have to remove mine because I was also a royal—technically, I was already the Kyidomhene of Tafo, having been enstooled with the permission of the court in a large public ceremony in Fairmount Park in Philadelphia three years earlier in 1993. Nanas, kings, do not have to remove their shoes when in the presence of other nanas or at the funeral of a nana.

Queen Sekyiraa II was lying in a massive mahogany bed that was decorated tastefully with numerous adinkra symbols and flowers. She was dressed in regalia befitting her age and status as the head of Akyem. An elder was seated beside the bed, keeping guard as thousands of people passed by to get one more glimpse at the queen who had ruled for a half-century.

Once we passed through the room I was led to one of the palace courtyards with other royals, where I was told to rest, listen to the music of the ntintin drums, and drink palm wine, a traditional ceremonial drink, as the weather was very hot. I did it all, except play the drums, impressing the drummers with my coordination, or so I thought, although I knew I had to work on getting the rhythm right. They were patient with my inexperience, as Ghanaians tend to be.

I found the palm wine strong but refreshing. You could grow to love it too much. The court elders from Tafo seemed pleased that I drank palm wine from the same gourd as everyone else, but I did find myself hoping, as I drank after the sixth or seventh person, that the wine would destroy the bacteria. Though worried, I had never heard of anyone tracing any sickness to a similar practice, such as when churches in America took communion from the same cup. Drinking the palm wine from the same bottle was an act of solidarity as much as it was an attempt to replenish my fluids.

Not very long after we had finished the palm wine, the Tafohene, the funeral's chief organizer, came into the courtyard and said to me, "Nana Okru, I want to outdoor you for the other kings." No one had ever told me about "outdooring"; although Kwame Botwe-Asamoah, my principal teacher and trainer in all things royal, had taught me how to walk, how to speak, how to gesture, he had missed outdooring. I was dumbfounded. I whispered to Krodua Asare, "What is the meaning of outdooring?" He told me that the king wanted to show me to the assembled kings in the great courtyard.

Before I could follow the Tafohene to the courtyard, however, it was imperative that I change clothes. I had dressed for the funeral in the usual Akan manner, with a black cloth and black and red sandals. For the outdooring I had to wear a Batakari shirt, which is a traditional military shirt, to signify my new office as Kyidomhene—this was absolutely necessary because the defense of the Tafohene and the state depended on a general who was willing to be the rearguard. The shirt I would wear was a talisman itself and represented ancient tradition. It was decorated with about twenty amulets, all sewn into the fabric, front and back, indicating my invincibility as a king under the Tafohene.

Once I was dressed the Tafohene directed me to walk behind him, ahead of the drummers playing both royal and military rhythms. As I walked counterclockwise, greeting the assembled royal families, I noticed that an entire entourage from the Tafohene's palace in addition to other kings and their attendants and drummers were following us around the massive courtyard.

The panoramic vista of so many colors and the music of so many drums transported me to a state of deep bliss like that when I was chanting in the stool house, or at the Akyem shrine, or in a lively black Baptist church in Georgia, or at a good jam session of outstanding jazz musicians. I had seldom felt so deeply spiritual, one with humanity and the universe, as I did seeing hundreds of musicians and dancers celebrating the life and death of Queen Sekyiraa II—to the Akyem people an event more important than the death of anyone but the Okyehene. To be outdoored on such an occasion was the height of blessing because so many other royal houses from all over the Akan world had assembled for the funeral. The Tafohene said he considered it fortuitous that the death of the queen and the presenting of a new king converged in that one moment, as hundreds of people watched the outdooring.

Instead of taking a seat with the Tafohene to be greeted in turn by each king's entourage and musicians as I would normally, because of the funeral situation, I was returned to the palace as I had left, with the drummers singing my praise and Tafohene expressing his pleasure with us, his people, who had made a great showing of style, tradition, elegance, and propriety.

After about an hour of relaxing I was told to change back into the funeral cloth and was ushered back to the courtyard to a seat near the Tafohene. Now was our time to be greeted by others. I sat there for three hours, greeting other kings who were making their rounds. The sun got hotter, and the umbrellas did not protect us from the heat. The longer I sat in the black cloth, the more I struggled to keep it on, but I could not adequately adjust the cloth while sitting, and it would look quite common to have to get up to throw the cloth again so as to get it right. I didn't want to look like an amateur and embarrass the Paramount King. At length, I was rescued when the energetic Okyeame Yaw Duah came to lead the Tafohene and me to a private place for food. After a short while the Tafohene left the courtyard where Yaw Duah had brought us. I remained until I had finished eating.

The food was delicately prepared, but the pepper sauce served on the side was a veritable fire in my mouth. I ate and drank and sat back, listening to the royal family members of the Okyehene's court.

Around 7 p.m., when I was dog-tired as we used to say in Georgia, Tafohene, who had been gone for hours on official business, reentered the courtyard to inform me that his driver would take me back to Tafo. I did not show that I was eager to leave, but I relented easily. The funeral would have to go on until 2 a.m., and Queen Sekyiraa II would be buried near other ancestors in the secret royal mausoleum of Akyem in the sacred forest somewhere outside Tafo and Kyebi. The Okyehene and the Tafohene and a select group would take her in the middle of the night while most people were asleep. Only this group and the keepers of the royal mausoleum would know where she was buried. Of course, the next morning Nana Krodua Asare told me that the queen had not been buried in the early morning but that she would be buried that very evening, to further confound those who might try to do something to disturb the universe. This meant that I would have to wait yet another day before I could be enstooled.

The following day, when Nana Krodua Asare came to my cottage to talk with me, I politely asked, not knowing if I should ask, "Has the queen been buried yet?"

He answered, "Yes, the universe is at rest now, and we can continue with your enstoolment, but I came to talk with you about the ceremony and the history of Akyem." He was unaware that Kwame Botwe-Asamoah and Kofi Yemoa had given me a fairly thorough orientation prior to my Philadelphia acceptance as Kyidomhene.

We sat out under a large tree not far from my cottage. He began talking and I listened. I felt his consciousness lock onto mine, and I saw the seriousness in his eyes. He said, "Tafo is an old place; it was old when Asante was young."

I asked, "But aren't the Abuakwas part of the Asante nation?"

He replied, "When the Asantes were being attacked by Arab slave hunters, a portion of their people came to Akyem and asked our king for protection. We have protected the Abuakwas since that time. They were given land for farming and have lived among us in peace." He went on to tell me that there had been terrible wars between the Asante and Akyem, brother against brother, and sister against sister. He described the several clans and different nations that make up the Akan-speaking people.

I asked, "Do the schoolchildren learn this information?"

"No, the schools have not integrated this information into their curricula."

"They need to know," I insisted, thinking about what happened to African Americans who did not know history.

My adviser and attendant stayed with me for hours, talking about history, Africa, culture, tradition, rituals, and then about the ceremony. He was a master of detail. By the time he had finished talking I knew all that I needed to know. He asked if I knew the Great Oath. When I told him I knew it in Twi and could speak it on my own, he was pleased. Before leaving he told me the next day they would come for me early, and I must be prepared to spend all day at the palace.

The sky was the bluest I had ever seen in Ghana when dawn broke the next morning. I had slept well, but I felt nervous. I had taken time in the cottage in the forest to purify my thoughts, to ask the ancestors for guidance and wisdom, and to remember the oath.

When we reached the palace courtyard, the drummers were already making the place throb with the heavy sounds of the atumpan and fontonfrom drums as well as the kete. People had assembled inside and outside of the courtyard; it was like a festival.

I had brought my cloths with me, several of them, and the Batakari that was necessary for the enstoolment. You could not be enstooled in kente or any royal cloth; it had to be a farmer's or a hunter's cloth. The Tafohene said I should stay put until the gyasahene came to bring me downstairs to the courtyard. He then went to change into royal regalia and then led a group of clan elders and court officials out into the courtyard.

When a court page came to tell us it was time, I walked behind the gyasahene, stepping to his rhythm. When we entered the courtyard,

I saw the scores of people lining both sides. As I walked I tried to re-member my training—what to do and what not to do—and yet I think I must have had a smile on my face, because when I passed Professor Addo-Fenig, one of the first Ghanaians I had ever met, he whispered, "You must be solemn. You must be solemn." I appreciated what he said, and I immediately changed my countenance. I think I may have smiled several more times as people smiled at me, but I had become conscious of every action.

When I entered the canopy where the royals were seated in state, I was led to a lion's skin and told to sit on it. Dancers appeared and danced for long stretches, one or two at a time, until finally two African Americans took the dance floor and followed the rhythm of the Akan drums. They were dazzling dancers. Next, master danc-ers, some nearly ninety years old, got up to perform intricate moves expressing Akan traditions and history. Most of the dances seemed to represent the defeat of enemies; each depicted feigning and strik-ing, feigning and striking, while complex foot movements suggested running in battle to catch enemies and to disarm or kill them. After all, this was the dance of the general who would protect the people. I watched intently to catch the moves because I knew that I would have to dance soon.

When this was finished, the drumming stopped and the gyasahene spoke to the Tafohene and the people on my behalf, explaining who I was, my lineage, and the reason the elders had chosen me. As soon as he ended his speech, the okyeame repeated it to the Tafohene. After consultation between the king and okyeame, the okyeame spoke on behalf of the Tafohene, accepting me as a candidate for the kingship and the role of kyidomhene. I was asked to come before the Tafohene; several attendants, young men with bulging muscles, took me by both arms and led me to a spot in front of the king.

Nana Adusei Peasah IV, dressed in a beautiful blue cloth, golden shoes, and his most decorative crown, smiled, and I thought, *I am half-way through this ceremony, and so far, so good, if the king approves.* I did not know whether to smile or not; I think I assumed a neutral expression. The gyasahene said I was prepared to swear the Great Oath. Tafohene passed me the Tafo sword, giving me the blade, and I took it in my right hand. I took a deep breath, and got ready to pledge myself to the king and my people in Tafo. Nana Krodua Asare said, "Go on, and swear with the sword."

I held the sword high so that the people could see it, and then I began the Great Oath:

> Me Kofi Asante,
> Me kyeri makyi ko Tafo Akyem Abuakwa
> Nana Okru Banin, nana na me
> Nana Adusei Peasah, nana na me
> Me ka ntam se
> Se, Nana Peasah ne Okyeman
> Fre me awopa
> Osuo mu oh
> Awia mu oh
> Anadwo
> Meba
> Gye se yadee
> Se me maama
> Meto ntam kesee.

My swearing the oath in Twi, even bad Twi, had a powerful effect on the crowd. However, I felt annoyed because, as I spoke, Nana Krodua Asare was behind me speaking the words. His voice and mine collided in the oath, and I was frustrated that he did not trust me. He did not want me to fail, but I had learned the oath in Twi as a part of my responsibilities. At the end of the oath the Paramount King, Osabarima, the great Tafohene, Nana Adusei Peasah IV, took the blade from me and swore the Great Oath to me.

We had shared our faith in each other and our respect for each other; Tafo's destiny had become one with my own. A link had been formed between the soul and body, between the earth and heaven, between the profane and divine. We now shared a sacred bond.

Then they led me out to dance for the people. I looked back toward the Tafohene and bowed. An expert dancer, one of the older men, went out before me and danced the kyidomhene dance while I acknowledged the drummers. Next, I tried to follow the complex movements of the elder dancer, but I was shown to be merely an amateur. The ubiquitous

Nana Krodua Asare whispered, "Dance like him; dance like him," and the audience applauded, probably more out of fun than anything else. Yet, when I saw the new Queen Mother wave her hand and make the Akan victory sign, I felt some boldness while trying to listen and move to the subtle cowbells tightly woven into the fabric of a multiplicity of drum rhythms. I would have to learn many things before I mastered the Akan dances.

When I took my seat again on the lion's skin, the Tafohene, a superb dancer, took center court and danced, to the delight of the crowd and the drummers. He spent less than a minute in front of the drummers, but it was enough to let the elders know that the king was virile, alive, awake, and physically strong.

Then, two strong men took around Old Tafo so that the townspeople could see the new king. They did not have a palanquin for me, so I rode the shoulders of the young men, both trusted court attendants. I was nervous about the mile-long ride because I had been told that my feet should not touch the earth and my sandals had been removed.

When we returned to the courtyard, I was exhausted from the sun and the physical ordeal of being transferred to other men's shoulders as those who carried me grew tired. I paid my homage to the shrine of Tafo, located in the middle of the courtyard, and then followed the Tafohene out of the courtyard into the palace. One day was over.

The next day the Tafohene and his driver came earlier, and we went to the sacred stool house, where we met some of the lower kings and the keeper of the stool house. In the small courtyard we poured libations and drank some of the gin as a sign of sharing with the ancestors.

I did not know what to expect or how to act; the elders in Philadelphia had not given me instructions on this. Although Nana Krodua had tried to prepare me, he was a practical man and often just said, "Do what everyone else does," so when the king took off his shoes to enter the stool house, I took off my shoes.

Ten or twelve of us entered the stool house behind him, including Gyasahene Kwame Osei, Okyeame Yaw Duah, Okyeame Awia, Nana Amoako, Abusuapanin Nkomsah Yeboah, the Amancredohene, and other stool elders, such as Nana Krodua Asare, Nana Osei and Nana Yeboah.

We stood in front of the assembled stools representing the mightiest names in Akyem, the greatest kings and queens, and observed their presence and chanted their names and deeds in Twi. The nation had been founded around 1500, and the stools of all the kings and queens since were represented. One day the elders would honor the stool of Adusei Peasah IV, the current king who was leading us in remembrances of the ancestors.

When I left Africa the next day, leaving the continent of my origin and the land of my ancestors to return to America, the continent of my birth and the land of my citizenship, I had not only become a king but also a more keenly aware human being. I knew what many did not—that Africa was real and that its people were nobler than I had ever imagined. My feelings for the land of my origin and the land of my birth had matured to the point at which I fully appreciated the long chain of events that had brought me so far along the way.

Epilogue

I T IS POSSIBLE THAT, after all the struggles at universities and in various other venues, that events in different parts of the African world can ensure for us that an unsanctioned word would always find its voice: watching my son, M. K. Asante Jr., graduate with an MFA from UCLA's famous School of Film and Theatre Arts; the two hundredth–anniversary celebration of the Haitian Revolution; visiting the grave of anti-apartheid activist Steve Biko in South Africa; and the massive community agency and activism in New York that pushed my name forward for the directorship of the Schomburg against formidable conservative odds. Connected like linked Egyptian *feluccas,* for me these events made one grand oration that cannot be defeated, speaking the truth about African identity, people's agency, and the need to overcome ideological poverty.

There is a real serene sense of tradition to see one's child graduate from the same university as you did. I could not hold back the tears, though I tried because I remembered that when I had graduated from the same university years earlier, there were no family members present to see me get my paper. My parents were unable to come from Georgia to California just to see my graduation, and here on this beautiful day on UCLA's mall, my son, M. K., had a wonderful group of family watching him walk across the stage for his degree.

There was no other place for me to be on January 1, 2004, but in Haiti (*Ayiti* to the local people) during the bicentennial celebration of the first African republic in the world. Although the great earthquake that destroyed Port-au-Prince in January 2010 changed the face of Haiti forever, one must never forget that Haiti's legacy is one of humanity's most enduring victories over circumstances.

When the Africans of Ayiti revolted against the French government and defeated Napoleon's Grand Army in 1804, a new revolutionary chapter was written in the history of liberation. New names emerged in history: Papa Boukman, Cecile Fadiman, Mackendal, Mariesaint Dede Bazile, Toussaint L'Ouverture, Jean-Jacques Dessalines, Henri Christophe, and Alexandre Pétion. Haiti is an incredibly dynamic nation that has been robbed of so much of its potential, but the people remain close to their history even without the clothes, property, and food that they often need.

There I was, in such a historic country on one of the most significant commemorations in the history of the African world—and yet as we were beginning our celebration, other forces aimed to disrupt the festivities. A full year earlier it was reported that four Western powers—the United States, Canada, France, and Britain—met to discuss strategies for destabilizing Haiti. The social reconstruction efforts of President Jean-Bertrand Aristide, the national hero, disturbed them, and they did not like his overtures to Cuba. Aristide, as president, was a genius who knew the soul of his people better than anyone, and he wanted the Haitians to overthrow the foreign ideologies in their minds, to raise themselves from dependence. Neither the corporate lords nor the political puppets wanted him to succeed. American officials supported thugs, led by Guy Phillipe, who came across the border from the Dominican Republic and used their American weapons to wreak havoc in small Haitian villages. The reports and information about the rag-tag group ran rampant in the black community in the United States, and I worried that the democracy the Haitian people enjoyed under their elected president would be stolen from them. They seemed so happy, excited, and free.

The people lost their president and their freedom, and when the earthquake struck the nation, there was no one of Aristide's charisma and personality who could direct the reconstruction of the country.

Did René Préval, who took the president's seat after the kidnapping of Aristide, ask the president to return to the country after the disaster? No, and his disappearing act during the earthquake had further marginalized him and laid upon his people the burden of trying to sort out its problems without its natural leaders.

Haiti, a nation that occupies about a third of the island of Hispaniola, which it shares with the Dominican Republic, was once the richest European colony. At one time it produced nearly one-half of the wealth of France. The Africans who entered Ayiti, imported by the Spanish, entered early; after all, this was the first land that Columbus saw when he sailed across the Atlantic toward America. For Africans it was the land where our ancestors had first felt the whiplash on their backs, the land where they first planted and harvested sugar for the white man.

What is Ayiti to us now? It remains one of the most potent symbols of black revolution against injustice in the annals of history. Ayiti showed other oppressed people that oppression does not last forever if the people have the will to fight to overthrow their oppressors. Blacks in other colonies in the Caribbean and in the southern United States found an example in the Haitian people.

The Africans of Ayiti whipped, defeated, and humiliated the greatest white army of their day, giving the lie to the invincibility of the white army. Napoleon had sent two of his favorite generals to subdue the rebellion in France's wealthiest colony, but when the battles were over, the enslaved had thrown off their shackles and sent the French back to their homeland.

On August 14, 1791, Papa Boukman, Cecile Fadiman, and Mariesaint Dede Bazile, in a ritual of defiance, declared the enslaved Africans in revolt against the brutal French slave masters. The holy area, marked only by a tree more than 250 years old, is called Bois-Caiman. In that isolated region of the country, under a huge stand of trees, they carried out the African ceremony that committed the black people of Ayiti to revolution.

The Battle of Vertières will live in history as the proudest moment of the revolution. I stood at Vertières before the statues of the glorious giants of the revolution and wept because we have not retained an understanding of what our ancestors did at that sacred place. It is told that in today's Ayiti, after Aristide's removal, French and American soldiers regularly urinate on the statues. In 2010 UN soldiers were said to have brought cholera from Asia. How quickly we lose our dignity in history when the oppressors believe that it is still possible to humiliate black people. Fortunately, we can say that at the end of his presidential term René Préval, after permitting Baby Doc Duvalier to re-enter Haiti from self-imposed exile in France, had to open the doors of the country to Aristide, who has seriously dedicated himself to the mission of educating the Haitian population. Although Parti Lavalas, the political party founded by Aristide and others, was banned from the recent election in Haiti, the fact that the nation now has its most unifying personality is a win for the future. Only a lost people forget how to count their own victories; Haiti has begun the task of healing, and with that process will come a renewed energy for sustainability of political and social institutions.

We must remember that when the Haitians had defeated the French Army, the Haitian people had every intention of remaining free, although they were the only free African nation in the American hemisphere—so another leader with vision rose. The name he had from slavery was Henri Christophe. He built seventeen fortresses along the coast of Ayiti to protect the liberty of the first black republic, but none of these fortresses came close to the magnificence of La Citadel, with 365 windows, each armed with a cannon, massive walls built of stones, rocks, and the blood of animals as well as impregnable mountain fastness that earned its name Invincibility. Napoleon never tried to recapture Ayiti, and La Citadel was never attacked; it remains to this day the soul of Ayiti.

On January 1, 2004, at 5 a.m., I was swept along with a great flow of Ayitian people, led by Ama Mazama and Garvey Lundy, to the Presidential Palace's plaza for the ritual "eating of soup with the peasants" that President Jean-Bertrand Aristide hosted. During the French enslavement of Africans, it was against the law and custom for blacks to eat soup, so the Ayitians turned the eating of pumpkin soup into a national symbol of resistance. President Aristide announced two centuries of freedom and a millennium of peace.

An Afrocentric philosophy, in which the people always work in their best interest, will place contemporary Ayiti on the same page as historic and heroic Ayiti. This country, ostracized by Europe, invaded twice by the United States, bankrupted by France's threat and demand that it pay for its freedom an amount now estimated at $21 billion, and isolated from other Caribbean islands by white racist colonialists, has maintained African courage, dignity, and heroism despite the political, economic, and cultural daggers stuck in its back.

President Jean-Bertrand Aristide, who sought dignity for his country, will certainly be seen as one of Ayiti's most enlightened leaders. What was his crime but the audacity to throw off oppression? This little nation set the model for courage and determination, and I am convinced that it will discover and use its legendary historical strength of will to restructure and reclaim the Haitian nation. The election of his once-ally turned opposition leader after the kidnapping of President Aristide, René Préval, as president of Ayiti, created a constitutional crisis because there was already an elected president of the country. The earthquake of 2010 then created a platform for international intervention, diplomatic posturing, grave meddling into the affairs of Haitian government and corporate activities. However, all of the money pledged in public has not been granted in the rebuilding efforts. Meanwhile, cholera, dysentery, and other diseases and ills of the society are laid at the feet of the mismanaged reconstruction of the country.

I saw President Aristide in South Africa, the country where he was exiled, on two occasions. The first was a courtesy visit to him and his brilliant wife, a lawyer, Mildred Trouillot, and the second after the giant earthquake of January 12, 2010, in Haiti. I spoke at length to the Aristides on February 24–25, 2010, during the course of an appearance as a speaker at the University of South Africa's Symposium on Africa and Haiti. It was on this occasion that I learned that he was willing, as is his humility and philosophy of service, to give up the idea of being reinstituted as the elected president in order to be able to serve his nation as an educator. He was first a teacher, then a priest, then a president, and he is now willing, despite the calls for him to resume his presidency, to work with the establishment of a world-class university in his native home.

Jean-Bertrand Aristide is an incredible linguist, being able to speak in French, Creole, Spanish, and now in Zulu since his exile in South Africa. He studies the languages for comparative structures and etymologies.

I could see him creating an institution that would value excellence and knowledge above all other abilities.

In 2004 I had visited South Africa at the invitation of Mafube Publishing to give the main speech in celebration of the tenth anniversary of independence. My work in shaping the curricula in schools and affecting the courses in colleges had impressed the South African leaders. In 1998 Thabo Mbeki, as deputy president, had given a big speech on African Renaissance that sounded very much like Afrocentricity. American universities had changed their language and approach to African people and had begun to see the value of agency. Antiracists like Tim Wise, Joe Feagin, Ellen Schwartz, and Peggy McIntosh had done so much to educate the white populations that Afrocentricity was receiving a positive response in many places outside the United States. I would be asked to travel to China, Japan, India, France, Germany, and Norway with the Afrocentric message, but here I was in 2004 in Johannesburg.

I had landed once before in Johannesburg's airport during the days of apartheid and did not want to visit the racist regime at all during that time. But because the business and political community had invited me, I took the opportunity to go and see what had been accomplished since the release of Nelson Mandela.

Ana and I traveled at the expense of the organizers to South Africa. Upon our arrival we were received by a delegation at our Sandton hotel, and before we could settle in we had other callers, including some African Americans living in Johannesburg. I cannot recall ever being received with such honor and dignity as we were among the South Africans; delegation after delegation came wanting to discuss Afrocentricity, Kwanzaa, African politics, and other subjects. It is true that I was a leading supporter of the movement for liberation in that country, including choosing the name "Molefi" in solidarity with the struggle, but nothing I did could have merited the praise and respect I received.

Xolela Mangcu had been asked to accompany us throughout the country, and he was an expert at ensuring that we saw everything and met everyone. He was a nervous type, always working, drinking Red Bull, driving fast, talking fast, and thinking he had missed something, but he always made sure that we were on time for appointments. Once we had taken tours of Soweto, Jo'burg, and Tshwane, I expressed my desire to see where Steve Biko was born and where he was buried. This request was granted, and we flew to East London, rented a car, and drove to King William's Town.

Biko was the first South African to have had a visceral effect on me. I read the classic critiques, reviewed the liberation magazines, kept up with the Pan-Africanist Congress and the African National Congress, and considered myself knowledgeable about all aspects of South Africa until I began to read a few of the words, unsanctioned and courageous, of Steve Biko. I found myself lifted to a level of antiracism sentiment that had not been tapped before. I think this was because Biko's words echoed not only the South African story but also my own Georgian story as well.

In King Williams Town I made two discoveries: that Biko was born in a small township named Ginsberg and that his wife, Ntsike, still lived there. We were invited to lunch at her home, and in the spirit of Africa, could not refuse.

After a very tasty lunch we purchased a wreath and asked to be taken to the cemetery, where we located Steve Biko's grave. There was nothing special about it; there were no distinctive grave markers and not enough to indicate the stature of the man. We laid the wreath, and unbeknownst to us, our photo was captured for the national evening news.

Later, the reporters asked me, as the originator of the Afrocentric Movement, what I thought about Biko. I said, "Biko is the bird who flew away to his own home long before the racists beat and cut life out of him. He is our consciousness, our strength, and we resolve to never let his name be forgotten."

Jimmy Seepe of Johannesburg's *City Press* cornered me and got me to agree to write a column in the spirit of Steve Biko, which I did for five years. I donated the small fee to Biko's wife as a token, as we can never repay her or her children's loss. Whatever else she becomes, she became, by her eternal sacrifice, one of the saints of liberation, and her husband's name will be remembered as long as there is a South Africa. Later in a dispute with management I would cease to write the column because the paper had ceased to give the fee to Ntsike Biko.

I was able to use my column to make a case for the South African government to accept President Jean-Bertrand Aristide when he was looking for a temporary home, and I was happy to hear later that the arguments I made helped many legislators to make up their minds to allow Aristide to stay. Unhappily for me, information about the diaspora does not flow as freely as it should in the African continent. This too will change in time.

Sadly, Jimmy Seepe, my great sponsor in South Africa, after returning from China, passed away in 2006, nearly three years to the day that he had asked me to write the column. His brother, Sipho Seepe, a scholar and intellectual, wrote to me and said how devoted Jimmy had been to our collective pursuit of advancing Steve Biko's dream of a risen African people. Like Mangaliso Sobukwe, Steve Biko had believed in the idea of one person and one vote. I had convinced Seepe that I wanted to resurrect the discourse on humanity that Sobukwe and Biko had initiated.

As one of the plenary speakers for the Symposium of African Intellectuals meeting in Dakar, July 27–30, 2009, I shared the platform with some of the most formidable thinkers from the African world. We represented fifty-five nations and numerous ethnic groups from every region of the world. We were united on one issue: Africa must unite and become one nation to survive in the twenty-first century. How to implement what had already been agreed to by at least half of the nations was our immediate goal.

On July 30, 2009, the night President Barack Obama met with Henry Louis Gates Jr. and Sergeant Crowley regarding the unfortunate arrest of Professor Gates in his own home, four hundred African intellectuals were ending the giant plenary on the United States of Africa. Those in the assembly hall heard and acted on our resolutions, plans of actions, and policies for implementation. There was an overwhelming feeling, with the voices and images of Nkrumah and Diop as well as their children, Samia Nkrumah and Cheikh M'backe Diop, in the audience, that the time had come for the United States of Africa. One was struck by the two incidents on either side of the ocean, however—one firmly embedded in the idea of black people in America seeking to be understood by the descendants of the former slave masters and the other in the idea that the great flow of history for the twenty-first century is in uniting the African peoples. These are not mutually exclusive goals, but one is eminently more fulfilling for me.

I would later encounter Henry Louis Gates Jr. as the cochair of the Search Committee for the Director of the Schomburg Center for Black

Research in Harlem. In July 2010 the announcement that a search committee headed by Gates would be responsible for selecting the next
director of the Schomburg agitated a large segment of the New York
black community. Gates had alienated the progressive wing of the
African American community by his aggressive interest in winning
white approval by bashing black people. Indeed, this is why many in
the African American community believed that his false arrest by the
police would be a wake-up call that racism was still quite active in
America. Nevertheless, Howard Dodson, who had held the post at the
Schomburg for more than two decades, was retiring. The community
meeting was held at the Schomburg and was attended by some of the
key intellectuals and activists in New York, including Omowale Clay,
James McIntosh, Camille Yarbrough, Councilman Charles Barron, New
York State Regent Adelaide Sanford, and others. They condemned the
attempt to minimize the Schomburg, the symbol of black research, to
make it a junior sister of the New York Public Library System by refusing to select an eminent scholar to run the institution.

Charles Barron gave a riveting speech at a public meeting suggesting
that Molefi Kete Asante should be the next director. Fortunately, I was
not in the meeting, but the next day Felicia Lee, a reporter for the *New
York Times,* left a message on my telephone asking me what I thought
about the situation. I was out of the country, but when I returned,
several members of the community in Harlem, including Omowale
Clay, Camille Yarbrough, Charles Barron, Adelaide Sanford, and James
McIntosh, called me to ask if I had any ideas about the next director. I
told them that I would urge them to consider the names of Dr. D. Zizwe
Poe of Lincoln University or Dr. Diane Turner of Temple University, two
extremely brilliant and well-qualified scholars with deep community
grounding. They said the Harlem leadership wanted to advance my
name and asked, "Would you be against us advancing your name?"

I was reluctant to advance my name given my history of independence, antiracist activism, and Pan-Africanism, but because of the
agency of the African American community and the fact that they
wanted me to allow them to put my name forward, as Dr. McIntosh
said, as the "top black scholar" at the head of the Schomburg, I relented
and said, "Okay, you can enter my name." My life in the academy had
always worked toward providing agency for African people, too long

outside of the arena of power. We knew when my name went forward that it would create chaos for the committee. As McIntosh said, "What would a committee headed by Henry Louis Gates Jr. do with an application by the most prolific African scholar alive?"

The process was long—several interviews, additional paperwork on strategic plans, and an informal dinner. Several people suggested that the committee was in a quandary trying to decide how to avoid my appointment. The committee even asked me to answer three questions about what I would do in the first ninety days in 250 words or less. I thought long and hard about the questions, and I interviewed friends such as Fred Bertley, Charles Fuller, Walter Lomax, and my cousin Bill Spivey. I then sent the search committee a document with these points in my answers.

> FIRST QUESTION: What is your plan for your first 90 days as director of the Schomburg Center?
>
> *A comprehensive asset mapping of the internal components of the Schomburg: This includes analysis of the scope of the 2D (books, documents) and 3D (carvings, objects) collections to fully understand the holdings. An informal audit will help me evaluate the financial condition for an intelligent strategy around future fundraising. To complement analysis of content, I will assess the human capital supporting the Center.*
>
> *A comprehensive asset mapping of the external components of the Schomburg: This includes meetings with stakeholders including but not limited to the President of the New York Public Library, Board members, Mellon and Ford Foundations, Apollo Theater, Abyssinian Baptist Church, Studio Museum, community and educational leaders.*
>
> SECOND QUESTION: What is your five-year strategic plan and how will it improve and/or broaden the Center's capacity in these areas?
>
> *There will be three objectives to such a plan: to digitize the entire Schomburg Collection as far as possible. The intent is to put Schomburg on a laptop. Anna Julia Cooper's first speech and Marcus Garvey's UNIA Bylaws should be available on desktop; to integrate the local, national, and international communities into the front view of the Schomburg staff and community; and to maintain the Schomburg at the center of*

Black Research as an active organizer of scholarship through forums, symposia, publications, and fellowships.

Third Question: Under your leadership, what will the Schomburg Center stand for in 10 years?
Under my leadership the Schomburg will stand for research excellence, accessibility to documentary materials, a highly efficient and technical staff, state-of-the-art protection and care of old and contemporary documents, and a Center of Black Research with a growing and enduring endowment.

Four months after the process started the search committee, headed by Henry Louis Gates Jr. and Gordon Davis Jr., selected a young, untenured scholar from Indiana University as the head of the Schomburg. The community's response was incredulity, and the decision caught the Harlem community by surprise. I was neither stunned nor disappointed because, as I wrote to the Coalition to Save the Schomburg, it was "one of the greatest honors" I had ever received to be nominated by the leaders of the New York community to this post because they thought it should go to the most published African American scholar. Earlier in 2010 the University of South Africa's Centre for African Renaissance had appointed me Professor Extraordinarius in the same spirit that the Coalition to Save the Schomburg had exhibited. One disappointed supporter wrote to the Schomburg and the community that the decision of Gates's committee showed "disrespect" to the black community. Gates, always the trickster, felt that the black community would accept the appointment as "an easy transition" because the new director was the great-grandson of Elijah Muhammad. Of course, Harlem is complex, and historical experiences constrain the narrative of Elijah Muhammad, particularly in relationship to Malcolm X in Harlem. Many people believed that it was Elijah's forces that conspired to murder Malcolm. Others were quite pointed in their observation that Gates, confronted with my work in African and African American Studies, could not make an objective judgment because of the subjectivity of his response to me since the 1980s when I began to criticize his portrayals of African people. I had no real opinion about Khalil Gibran Muhammad, the new director, and in fact, wrote him a congratulatory letter; after all, it was not Muhammad who made the decision but rather the search committee that decided that an untenured, young professor, with limited organic connections to the leadership of the Harlem community, could be more easily manipulated than a more mature scholar. One understands these to be political decisions, knowing all the time that that the decisions do not reflect the people's choice and the best credentials.

I was quite happy teaching at Temple and building the Molefi Kete Asante Institute for Advanced Afrocentric Studies and the Afrocentricity International in Philadelphia, but I would have gone to the Schomburg to help raise the stature of the venerable collection because the Harlem community had insisted on maintaining the institution as a leader of thought and progressive African scholarship. However, I have always leaned toward independent African American organizations, and creating an independent Think Tank, free of political or economic control had been my initial inclination. I was now ready to continue what I had started years earlier with the publication of *Afrocentricity*.

The real work of this century is not going to be about race, color, or Black Studies but rather about the deep quest for African identity, liberated from mental enslavement on the continent and in the Diaspora, and gaining a United Africa based on democratic power and founded on the realization of the dreams of Marcus Garvey, DuBois, Kwame Nkrumah, Muammar Gaddafi, and Cheikh Anta Diop. In seeking this grand flow of the African people I have come to count as friends Julius Garvey, Cheikh M'backe Diop, and Samia Nkrumah, children of my mentors who remain as committed to the goal of a United Africa as I am. This is the future, and Africa is squarely in the middle of it—and I am running as fast as I can toward this quest. Increasingly, I am not running alone.

INDEX

Abdul-Jabbar, Kareem, 3

abuse, 1, 29, 59, 71, 84, 100, 186–187, 221, 259, 263

Achebe, Chinua, 170, 196, 263

Adae people, 69. *See also* Ghana

Adams, Carolyn, 272

affirmative action, 144, 159, 278

Africa, 1, 6, 12, 27, 31, 45, 54, 56, 92, 107, 141, 144, 160–162, 166, 170, 173–176, 181, 186, 188, 194, 197, 200, 211, 217, 219, 221, 223–224, 226, 228, 231–234, 239–240, 242, 250, 258, 261–265, 267–268, 273, 279, 283–284, 287, 294, 305–306.

African American(s): 1, 3–4, 21–22, 27, 29–30, 33–37, 43–44, 65, 70, 87–88, 90, 93, 97, 105, 113, 120–121, 130, 136, 139, 140–144, 150, 155–159, 161–162, 166, 171, 174, 180, 186, 189, 191–192, 194, 198, 202, 204–205, 221–223, 227, 231, 233, 236, 239, 247–249, 251–252, 257, 268–272, 275–276, 278–281, 283, 294–295, 304, 307, 309–310

African American military divisions: 183rd Combat Engineers, 9; 24th Infantry, 9; 761st Tank Battalion, 5; 92nd Division, 5; 99th Squadron of the Tuskegee Flyers, 9

African American Studies, 19, 157–158, 270–273, 275, 280–281, 309

African National Congress (ANC), 142, 245–247, 305

Africanity, 2, 165-166, 240, 286

Africanus, Shakur, 212

Afrocentricity, 12, 144, 156, 159–160, 199–200, 241–242, 251, 256, 262, 265, 274–279, 302, 304–305, 310

agency, 6, 144, 156, 159, 267, 272, 275, 279, 299, 304, 307

Ajayi, Jacob Ade, 171

Akan people, 103–104, 107, 109, 143, 146, 178, 243, 283–297

Akyem: people, a nation of the Akan, 283–286, 289–294, 296, 298; and the Kyebihene, 285–286, 290, 293; and the Okyame, 284–285, 288, 290, 293, 297; and the Okyehene, 285–286, 289–290, 292–293

Alabama; state in general 30, 32–33, 71, 162; Birmingham church bombings, 167; Montgomery Bus Boycott, 59, 71–72, 215; Talladega, 32; Tallusahatchee, 32; Tohopeka, 33

alcohol, 37, 54, 78, 100, 160–162,

Ali, Muhammad, 3, 158

alienation, 21, 94, 132, 161, 166, 307

ABOUT THE AUTHOR

Author of seventy-two books and more than 500 articles, Molefi Kete Asante has appeared on *Sixty Minutes, Nightline, BET,* and numerous other local and international television shows. A founder of the Afro-centric movement, Asante continues to speak throughout the world.